# STUDIES IN
# BRITISH GOVERNMENT

### N. H. BRASHER, M.A.
*Senior History Master, Bexley Grammar School*

SECOND EDITION

MACMILLAN

First Edition 1965
Reprinted 1968
Second Edition 1971

*Published by*
THE MACMILLAN PRESS LTD
*London and Basingstoke*
*Associated companies in New York Toronto*
*Dublin Melbourne Johannesburg and Madras*

SBN 333 04023 6 (hard cover)

*Printed in Great Britain by*
WESTERN PRINTING SERVICES LTD
*Bristol*

STUDIES IN BRITISH GOVERNMENT

# Preface to the First Edition

IN subject matter this book ranges over several issues of current constitutional interest. It follows broadly the syllabuses set by examining boards for pupils studying government. The growing emphasis on general studies for both the Arts and Science student should lead to a closer study of the workings of government by the non-specialist also, and it is hoped that the book may be of value for this purpose. Whatever else students may become they will certainly be citizens, and knowledge of the present-day institutions of government is still not a universal characteristic in schools.

The emphasis in the book, however, is on ideas, changing habits of government, and possible reforms, rather than on the provision of a mass of factual information. It is intended to be an accompaniment, or sequel, to the textbooks, a bridge between them and the study of specialist books. Much of it is directed towards the stimulation of discussion which forms such a large part of advanced work in particular. An outline and theme are given at the beginning of each chapter so that its pattern may be quickly grasped. Many of the issues discussed are controversial. While it would have been possible to prepare a cautious and uncommitted assessment of present-day tendencies in government, I felt that this would blunt the critical approach which the book is designed to foster. I have thought it best to put forward my own views positively, not only in the expectation, but even a little in the hope, that the views of readers may frequently differ sharply from my own. I hope, too, that the ideas put forward will rouse sufficient thought to lead students to make constructive use of the specialist books in order to support or reconsider their own views. If this happens a worthwhile purpose will have been achieved. To help this process I have added a book-list with comments. My own debt to many of the authors mentioned there will be very plain.

A short book of this kind, dealing with a variety of important topics, will inevitably have many omissions. There are also several issues, potentially rich in controversy, to which it has only been possible to make a fleeting reference, though this may sometimes be a sufficient starting point for argument. The emphasis in the book is on modern governmental practice rather than on its historical roots. What has concerned me, however, is less the pursuit of topicality for its own sake than the examination of recent trends in government which seem to be of permanent importance. In this respect the book may also be of interest to the general reader. Readers will discover a strong emphasis, for instance, on the growth of central direction by modern governments. The fact that this is a familiar theme makes it no less important. The formal barriers to the authority of the Government in Britain are negligible; it is all the more important, therefore, where public opinion is the only ultimate restraint on Government action, to know which of the traditional rights are expendable, and which are not. Making the distinction is difficult, especially in the changing conditions and emergencies of modern times, but there can be few matters of greater importance. It would be one of the sadder ironies of our history if the freedoms which have been so vigorously won and defended should wither away through cynicism and ignorance of their worth. Fortunately Britain has nothing worse to fear at the moment than the benevolent despotism of the Cabinet or the involuntary dictatorship imposed largely by the pressure of outside events. Yet it would be as well to remember that this is not the full extent of the risk to be faced in a country whose traditional flexibility of constitutional habits is not an unmitigated advantage, especially when there are pressures on the central Government to tighten its control. Considerable attention has been given in the book, therefore, to matters which are symptomatic of the more authoritarian approach of modern governments.

Those who are familiar with the workings of government will not, however, expect a consistent pattern to emerge. In the early chapters, in particular, there are frequent references to the greater centralisation of modern times. Yet in the chapter on local government it is apparent that, except in the unlikely event of the Government having intentions of the most Machiavellian subtlety, local authorities have been given, or will be given, greater freedom than they had before. Beyond this, the movement towards self-government of the new Commonwealth countries could, in a different way, be regarded as an outstanding example of decentralisation. It has not proved to be possible, therefore, to find a single theme which can be said to characterise all aspects of the work of a modern

British Government. In a country where government is based largely on empirical methods the absence of a consistent approach is the less surprising.

Adequate acknowledgment to those who have helped in different ways in the preparation of this book would be impossible. I must, however, give particular thanks to Dr. D. G. Southgate, lecturer in Modern History at the University of St. Andrews, and to Mr. P. D. Whitting, G.M., B.A., who, until his retirement, was senior history master at St. Paul's School. Their judicious blending of encouragement and criticism has been of the greatest assistance to me. Imperfections which remain are my own, but I am well aware how many more there would have been without the help of these two advisers. I have also received very generous information from the Electoral Reform Society and from the research department of the Labour Party, although, as it happens, on the specific issues concerned I differed from their views. Mr. Malcolm Shaw, the Director of Studies and Information of the Hansard Society for Parliamentary Government and subsequently Lecturer in Politics at Exeter University, the staffs of Her Majesty's Stationery Office, and of the Orpington and Bromley Libraries have been most helpful in the verification of references. My publishers have been admirably patient; so, too, have been my wife and family, who have contrived to give me the peace without which the book could not have been written at all.

N. H. B.

## Preface to the Second Edition

THERE were few institutions of government which remained untouched by actual or prospective reform in the 1960s. The monarchy has continued to fulfil its traditional role, its basic functions unaffected by minor, and possibly unnecessary, attempts to popularise itself, nor has the power of successive Prime Ministers varied significantly. In the mid-1960s it was the fashion amongst academics to say that Cabinet government had been superseded by Prime Ministerial government. Now it is apparent that the limitations on the powers of Prime Ministers are at least as strong as they were a decade ago. Yet though the powers of the titular and the actual heads of government thus remain much the same as they have

always been in the post-war years, in other directions the reforming pressures of the 1960s have partly succeeded in modifying
the British system of government and the assumptions upon which
it was based. Super-Ministers have been appointed, new Government Departments have been created, the Fulton Report has begun
to modify the training of Civil Servants, a Parliamentary Commissioner has been appointed, the financial procedure of the House
of Commons has been changed, a determined, though unsuccess-
ful, attempt has been made to reform the House of Lords, the
Redcliffe-Maud Report has proposed radical changes in the structure of local government, the Allen Committee has sharply criticised the rating system, and the age-old requirement of jury
unanimity has been abandoned; all these are major indications of
the reforming pressures at work. Less tangibly, but discernibly, the
relationship within the Commonwealth has altered. Then, too, the
behavioural approach to political studies has emphasised the importance of pressure-group activity in the British system of government. Linked with this, the question of the proper limits of
Executive power in a modern democracy remains as prominent as
before, and the difficulty of answering it is increased by the rapidity
of change. All these developments have necessitated substantial
additions of material in this second edition. I have also taken the
opportunity of introducing a fairly lengthy analysis in the last
chapter of the American and French systems of government. This
has not been done merely to provide information but to show by
contrast with the American and French systems the strengths and
weaknesses of the structure of government in Britain. Examination
of the governmental systems of two fellow democracies shows how
they are dealing with comparable problems and puts our own
attempts in better perspective.

I owe a debt of gratitude to the Prime Minister, the Rt. Hon.
Edward Heath, M.B.E., M.P., who generously found time to give
me some factual guidance on the negotiations preceding the abolition of Resale Price Maintenance. I hasten to add that this has been
his only connection with the book; the views on this and the many
other issues discussed are merely the product of my own thought
and reading. I am again indebted to my wife for the typing of the
lengthy additions to the first edition.

# Contents

# 1

## The Monarchy

Decline of monarchies. The flexibility of the British monarchy illustrated from its historical development. Its powers and limitations, with examples from nineteenth- and twentieth-century history. The monarchy does not need to be justified simply by its practical political duties. Value of the monarch's social duties. Relationship to the Commonwealth countries.

THEME: The powers of the British monarch are neither dangerous nor superfluous.

In a world where social upheavals have become commonplace the power of the British monarchy to survive makes it of special interest. Its existence, rooted deeply in the past, is based on the concept of a definite hierarchy in society of which it is the apex. It might seem, therefore, to represent a view of society which is anathema to the social reformer. Criticism of it is to be expected and involves no novelty in itself, for the institution of monarchy has been subjected to the most violent attacks for over three hundred years. The events of the seventeenth century culminating in the Bill of Rights of 1689 marked the fiercest phase of the conflict, but ripples of the controversy continued to be felt until the end of the nineteenth century. By the beginning of the twentieth century, however, the Crown had tacitly accepted the position that for almost all practical purposes personal intervention by the monarch in politics was undesirable. This largely removed the long-standing grievance against despotic or arbitrary actions by the monarch, but has led to criticisms of a different kind, that, as the political powers of the monarch have dwindled away almost to vanishing point, the retention of a non-functional institution is merely a social pretence out of keeping with the modern world, like medieval battlements on a New York skyscraper.

This criticism that the monarchy has become redundant in

modern times attracts a certain measure of support. It is true that it is no longer possible to defend the institution of monarchy with the mystical arguments used in the time of James I, when the theory of the Divine Rights of Kings to govern made criticism on a par with impiety. That theory was violently discredited when, on January 30th, 1649, in Whitehall, the head of Charles I was displayed to the crowd attending the execution. A more significant stage still was reached on January 21st, 1793, when the guillotine severed the neck of Louis XVI amid cries of 'Vive la nation!', for to the French Revolutionary leaders the movement against the monarchy had become an idealistic campaign. The Parliamentarians in England were waging a struggle against a monarch: the early French Revolutionaries wanted to wage an international struggle against monarchy, and their influence was correspondingly greater. The precedent, once set, was swiftly imitated. Monarchs were no longer sacrosanct, and revolution continued to find new victims. In France, revolutions in 1830 and 1848 disposed first of Charles X, then of Louis Philippe. In 1848 there was a brief experience of Republican government before the monarchical principle was revived under Napoleon III, but in 1870, following the Prussian defeat of France at the battle of Sedan, the monarchy was finally discredited and Republican government has been adopted ever since. Spain, having witnessed the deposition of Queen Isabella in 1868, reverted to a monarchy only to dispense with it in 1931 when King Alfonso XIII was deposed. In July, 1918, the Tsar of Russia, who had governed with the kind of despotism reminiscent of the Bourbons before 1789, was murdered at Ekaterinburg in central Russia, as a result of the 1917 Russian Revolution. A few months later his recent enemy the Kaiser was in exile in Holland, with theatrical demands being made by some of his opponents that he should be hanged. Along with the Kaiser there had disappeared the Austrian Emperor and the whole penumbra of minor German kings. In modern Italy the monarchy after years of humiliating subordination in the Fascist state was replaced by a republic in 1946. Altogether the Royal casualty list makes impressive reading. Apart from Britain no major European power has retained a monarchical system, and though some of the smaller powers have done so, the hostility of many nations to such a system is only too clear.

Critics who point out, therefore, that Britain, in retaining a monarchy, lags behind many of its Continental contemporaries in constitutional development, have substantial evidence at their disposal. The argument based on comparison with Continental practice deserves consideration, for imitation is an accepted feature in constitutional practice, and the constitutional habits of our neighbours are not necessarily bad ones because we failed to invent them ourselves. There are, however, other factors to consider. Historically, the British monarchy, at least since the Civil War, can be compared with advantage with the European monarchies. It has greater continuity than imperialism or monarchy in France or Germany; it is stronger than the Italian monarchy of Mussolini's time; it rules over a more united country than Imperial Austria, or Spain in the inter-war years; it is free of the vices of absolutism of Tsarist Russia. All these kingships contained the seeds of their own destruction. If the British monarchy revealed failings similar to those which led to the abolition of these monarchies in Europe then the argument by comparison would be more powerful. As it is, this has not been suggested, and to propose to abolish the monarchy simply because many of our neighbours have done so would be patently absurd.

The essential advantage which the British monarchy possesses over these Continental monarchies lies in its flexibility. Opposition to the principle of monarchy, or to particular aspects of its working, has led in the past to revolution, and to reduction of the monarch's powers. Yet the monarchy, apart from the brief interlude of 1649–60, has survived. Its authority no longer rests on Divine Right. It has become a constitutional monarchy dependent on Parliament for its powers, and even for its existence. There is now little danger of any abuse of power by the monarch. To understand why this is so it is necessary to trace the changing relationship between Parliament and the monarchy from the late seventeenth century onwards. In doing so, two facts of equal importance will emerge. One is the obvious point that Parliament has increasingly been able to establish its supremacy over the Crown; the second, complementary to this but less obvious, is that only a monarchy of a most flexible nature could have adapted itself to these changes. Moreover, this flexibility is not only significant in understanding the historical development of the monarchy; it could clearly have some bearing on its future development too. It is worth noting also that the changed relationship between Parliament and the monarchy has been brought about without a recurrence of the violence of the seventeenth century, yet also without such a complete suppression of the rights of the monarchy as to make it a nullity.

The terms imposed by Parliament in the Bill of Rights, following the abdication of James II, hedged the monarchy with restrictions which William III was bound to accept if he wished to establish his personal right to be a co-monarch with the lawful successor, his wife Mary, and to ensure Parliamentary support for his war with Louis XIV. These restrictions were based on the experiences of the century. They mark a vital change in that they assure the constitutional supremacy of Parliament in some spheres of government. Parliamentary sanction was required for the collection of taxes. The monarch was not to be a Roman Catholic, nor could he marry a Roman Catholic. The power which James II had exercised in favour of the Catholics to exempt them from the normal working of the laws, such as the Test Act of 1673, which had required acceptance of the fundamental doctrines of the Church of England by judges, mayors, and officers, was removed. Furthermore, the King was not to have a standing army in peace-time, a restriction imposed no doubt because of the Parliamentarians' recent memory of James II's menacing Irish levies stationed at Hounslow within comfortable distance of London. Parliamentary control of the army was shortly reinforced by the Mutiny Acts of 1689 and 1717 providing for the discipline of the army. The clauses of these Acts, particularly when coupled with Parliamentary control of the pay of men through the Army Estimates, made it impossible for the armed forces to continue in being without Parliamentary sanction. The Bill of Rights also secured freedom of speech and of debates on proceedings in Parliament. Again, recent events, such as the disagreements with Charles II and James II, played their part in the insertion of this clause. These restrictions, therefore, were devised as solutions to immediate problems, but they have remained as permanent features of the constitution. By means of these restrictions Parliament had already by 1689 partly removed the possibility of royal supremacy in the constitution. There were frequent references in the Bill of Rights to the fact that its provisions could not be altered 'save by Act of Parliament'. In 1701 a further decisive stage was reached when the Act of Settlement made it clear that as well as primogeniture (the right of the first-born to succeed) Parliamentary approval was also necessary to ensure legal succession to the throne. This had already been evident in practice in 1660 at the restoration of Charles II, and in 1688 with the choice of William and Mary as co-monarchs. Now, in making arrangements for the succession after the death of William, Parliament was giving statutory form to the principle that the royal title rests on Parliamentary approval, a background factor which was clearly of importance in recent times when Edward VIII decided to abdicate in 1936. The Act of Settlement also made it impossible for the King to remove judges from office. They held office 'quamdiu se bene gesserint', that is, so long as they fulfilled their functions with probity, and they could only be removed by a joint petition from the two Houses of Parliament.

The constitutional importance of these changes of the 1689–1701 period lies in the fact that the long-voiced claims of Parliament to play a continuous role in the process of government were now given a much more effective basis. This, in itself, was at least a potential limitation of royal influence, and as time went on it proved to be much more. Historians are rightly cautious about ascribing undue importance to single dates in history, but there are reasonable grounds for regarding 1689 as an exception. The Revolutionary Settlement clearly opened the way for the development of many of the features of the Parliamentary system which we now take for granted. Once regularity of meeting was assured then, very slowly, the need for party support, for a good working relationship between ministers and Parliament, and for collective responsibility for Ministerial actions was made clearer by sheer pressure of circumstances rather than by preconceived constitutional theories. The effect, in practice, of these changes was to reduce still further the extent of royal influence. They are, it may be noticed, concerned with matters of conventional usage rather than statutory limitations on the powers of the monarch, yet it could be held that it was the statutes of 1689 which gave the strongest impetus to the development of the modern constitutional relationship between Parliament and the monarchy. That the devisers of the Settlement themselves would have been astonished by its later consequences is one of the commonplaces of history.

Attention has been drawn to the slowness of constitutional change in Britain since 1689. This in itself has been an asset to the monarchy, since the strain on its adaptability has been less intense than in some of its Continental counterparts, for instance the French monarchy of the eighteenth century. Royal influence remained strong long after 1689, nor was this generally regarded as undesirable, still less unconstitutional. William III, in spite of the statutory limitations on his power, was still the active commander of the nation's forces in the field. He could still wage an unpopular war. He could still preside at meetings of ministers, and these indications of continuing royal power remained in force for many years to come. George II led British and Hanoverian troops into action at Dettingen in 1743. His zealous interest in Hanover led him at times to take a direct part in foreign policy, particularly during the war of the Austrian Succession. At home Carteret's dependence on royal support between 1742 and 1744, and George's exclusion of Pitt from the 1744 ministry on personal grounds, provide well-known instances of the extent of royal power at the time. Nor were these actions in the least unusual. George III's strongly formed views on measures and men are well known. His determination to subdue the American colonists, his decisive part in securing the defeat of the Fox-North coalition in 1783, and his action in choosing the Younger Pitt as chief minister, though the latter could not for a time command a majority in the House of Commons, are outstanding examples of the crucial importance still of the Crown influence. Patronage played a part in bolstering up the strength of the Crown, but this would not have been sufficient had there not been also a strong feeling among the many independently minded M.P.s that Crown activity, so long as it did not infringe the limits imposed by the Revolution Settlement, was entirely legitimate.[1]

Yet, alongside this view, based on well-established traditions, a newer one was growing up of greater significance for the future. This was the slow emergence of the idea of government by a Cabinet with some sense of collective responsibility. To be completely effective it needed the backing of the fully organised party support which is clearly lacking in the eighteenth century in spite of the efforts of the Treasury managers, the great landowners, and the extensive use of jobbery. In fact the most effective support, that given to the Younger Pitt, sprang not from self-interest nor from party policies, an anachronism anyway in the eighteenth century, but from admiration of his personal qualities. Whatever

[1] For a defence of George's actions see J. Steven Watson, *The Reign of George III, 1760–1815* (Oxford—Clarendon Press, 1960).

the basis of collective responsibility, however, as soon as there is evidence of its existence, no matter how tenuous, at that point it can be said that the exercise of royal power in the manner which had been customary up to the end of the eighteenth century is under immediate threat. Students of constitutional history will know better than to expect any change to be rapid, simple, or, in detail, continuous. George III was able to bring about the resignation of Pitt in 1801, for instance, over the question of Catholic Emancipation, and colleagues of Pitt continued to serve in the succeeding Addington ministry. There are later instances, too, of this negative control by the Crown on particular issues which roused strong feeling, such as George III's dispute with his ministers over Catholic Emancipation in 1807, and the dissolution of the Melbourne ministry in 1834, stemming partly from the personal antipathy of William IV for Lord John Russell, whom Lord Melbourne wished to make Leader of the House. Yet there is abundant evidence to show that as Cabinet Government gathered strength and Crown patronage declined, so the positive direction of policy passed almost entirely from the hands of the Crown. It is this long process which constitutes the Glorious Revolution rather than the so-called Glorious Revolution itself.

The change in atmosphere becomes clearly discernible in the reign of Queen Victoria. Much is made at times of the forcible views expressed by the Queen on matters of personality and policy. Her horror of radicals, her dislike for Gladstone and her attempts to oust him from party leadership, her antipathy to the Russians at the time of their war against Turkey; these and many other of her political foibles are well known. Nor was her influence by any means confined to the expression of opinion. As late as 1892, for instance, she was able on personal grounds to refuse to accept Sir Charles Dilke and Mr. Labouchere for any office, an action recalling the constitutional habits of the eighteenth century. On policy decisions too, she did not hesitate to state her opinions strongly, but it is open to argument that she was more active than influential especially after 1868. Joseph Chamberlain, for instance, whose radical views were as unpopular with the Queen as those of Fox had been with George III, was able to develop his distinguished career unmoved by royal displeasure. Gladstone, in the face of strong royal hostility, was able to be Prime Minister for a total period of over thirteen years, and to carry through policies which were anathema to the imperialist Queen. But it would be unjust to represent the Queen merely as a reactionary fractiously struggling against the accumulating pressure of constitutional custom. It is characteristic of the self-denying principle we have grown to expect from modern British monarchy that the reduction in royal influence after 1837 was caused not merely by the pressure of external events but also by voluntary withdrawal. N. Gash in *Politics in the Age of Peel* has drawn attention to the crucial importance of the Windsor by-election in 1845. Queen Victoria, supported and probably advised by Prince Albert, made it clear to Peel, then Prime Minister, that the practice by which the Crown had virtually secured the right of nomination to one of the Windsor seats would be discontinued. Writing after the interview to Sir William Fremantle, Peel said, 'The Queen does not wish to interfere in Elections and there is no separating in this matter the Court from the Sovereign.'[1] Admittedly the extension of the franchise and the growing strength of the collective responsibility doctrine would in themselves have involved a considerable reduction in the opportunities for royal intervention in politics. Yet it was a good omen for the future sound relations between the monarchy and the government of the day that there had been this willingness on the part of the Crown to surrender some measure of its former influence. It is of incidental interest, perhaps, on this subject that while the opinionated views of Queen Victoria have been strongly assailed, by a curious reversal of attitude there have been occasional suggestions that it would be of value to the country if the monarch were less reticent in matters of opinion. It is arguable (though difficult to maintain) that, since the balance of the constitution has been upset in this century by the predominance of the Executive, there might be some advantage in the monarch advancing opinions which would gain in strength through her independence of party connection. These opinions would be the more valuable if they were based on the experience of a long reign.

It is evident that since 1689 the monarchy, through statute and custom, has been deprived of any effective means of exercising arbitrary power. Although this process owes more to usage than to law, it is usage based on strong sanctions. A monarch who challenged the authority of Parliament would find that the machinery of government would come to a standstill, that the Armed Forces

---

[1] N. Gash, *op. cit.*, p. 382 (Longmans, 1953).

could not continue in being, and that no revenue and no Civil List allowance would be forthcoming. In practice, long before any of these stages had been reached a recalcitrant monarch would have been removed and replaced by someone more amenable: this removal would be made the more certain by knowledge of the ultimate sanctions which Parliament has in reserve. Criticism of the present-day monarchy is based, therefore, less on the charge that it is dangerous than on the charge that it is useless. An examination of the functions of the Crown will show how much truth there is in this allegation.

It is true that the Queen, who is in name the Head of all the major functions of government, exercises for the most part purely nominal powers. Her connection with Parliament is primarily confined to the State Opening at the beginning of a session, and the granting of Royal Assent to Bills. No monarch since Queen Anne in 1708 has withheld this assent, and even then she was acting on the advice of her ministers. The danger of royal opposition is negligible. In addition, the extension of the franchise has removed the possibility for the Crown of intervening in Parliamentary affairs on behalf of the mass of the people against the class interests of representatives elected on a limited franchise, and often corruptly, for this was the state of affairs before the nineteenth-century Reform Bills. Now this reason, which might become merely a pretext, no longer applies. Furthermore, the long struggle for financial dominance between Crown and Parliament was decisively settled in favour of Parliament by the Bill of Rights in 1689. The grant of a Civil List has increased the Crown's dependence on Parliament. Direct participation in the affairs of Parliament of the kind practised regularly by George III, and occasionally by Queen Victoria, can be excluded. In this respect the monarch has become a spectator rather than a participant. She merely receives information about Parliamentary proceedings from the daily reports of the Vice-Chamberlain of the Household, and from the frequent visits by the Prime Minister.

Yet this passive role in Parliamentary affairs does not exhaust all the possibilities. The powers of the monarch in political affairs are severely circumscribed but they are not extinct. Bagehot's assessment of the nineteenth-century situation was that the monarch had three rights—'the right to be consulted, the right to encourage, and the right to warn, and a King of great sense and sagacity would want no others'.[1] In fact, as has been seen, Queen Victoria was not content with this subordinate role. Vigorous partisanship of this kind no longer applies in the twentieth century; it would be neither necessary nor welcome so long as circumstances are normal; but everlasting normality is too much to expect in the fluid world of politics where personal strains and the speedy onset of crises in modern times may at any time present novel or peculiar constitutional difficulties.

Even in the twentieth century, when monarchs have willingly abandoned the political influence freely used by Queen Victoria, there have been occasions when royal initiative in politics has become desirable. One instance was the crisis of 1910 over the Parliament Bill. George V was confronted on this occasion with a situation where his prerogative powers needed to be used with the greatest care. He had to decide whether to promise the Liberal Government to create sufficient peers to ensure that the Parliament Bill would pass through the House of Lords against the opposition of the Conservative Lords. In addition, he had to decide on the propriety of a dissolution. There had already been one dissolution in 1910 to allow public opinion to be expressed on the deadlock between Lords and Commons over the 1909 Budget. These decisions were far from nominal, and the personal attitude of the King was a strong factor in the situation. In fact, King George V agreed both to dissolve Parliament and to create enough peers to ensure the passage of the bill if the Liberals won the election. Both decisions were wise, but the essential point is that in the intense pressures to which the monarch was subjected during this violent controversy other decisions were possible without infringing constitutional usage. The Leader of the Conservative Opposition, Mr. Balfour, had suggested, for instance, before King Edward VII's death, that the monarch should refuse to give a dissolution and should ask the Opposition to form a Government. In short, there was enough uncertainty in the situation to make the element of personal decision by the monarch a reality. George V's personal influence was again experienced in 1931. After consultation with the party leaders, made necessary by the financial crisis and the instability of the Labour Government, he was advised to propose the formation of a National Government with ministers drawn from the main parties and led by Ramsay MacDonald. This sug-

[1] *The English Constitution*, p. 111 (Fontana Library Edition, 1963).

gestion was accepted by the King, and MacDonald, though many of his Labour colleagues left him, accordingly formed a new coalition government. This is an important instance, since it illustrates one of the fundamental duties of the monarch, often overlooked, namely the vitally important function of ensuring continuity of government. With the Labour Government divided over the measures necessary to recover from the financial crisis, the first consideration of the monarch had to be the establishment of a more stable ministry. King George may not have initiated the idea of a coalition government but his decision to accept or reject the idea was clearly of some consequence. Lord Morrison in *Government and Parliament* is critical of the decision which was taken,[1] but he accepts the fact that there was no breach of constitutional propriety in the King's action. It is true that the decision was damaging to the Labour Party, which found itself seriously divided, but it was essential in the financial crisis of 1931 to secure a Government which could maintain majority support in the House of Commons, and a National Government was able to do this. The electorate's support for this view was amply demonstrated at the General Election held shortly afterwards. Although monarchs have given advice on political matters since then, the 1931 crisis was the last occasion on which the monarch has had a major role in the formation of a Government. The recurrence of a similar situation remains possible however.

The monarch's duty to ensure continuity of government is thus demonstrably of some significance still, though the possibility of the monarch being able to exercise real personal influence in the choice of a Prime Minister has now been virtually eliminated. The adoption by the Conservatives in 1965 of a clear-cut electoral procedure for choosing their leader reinforces this view. Previously their practice had been to groom a successor for the leadership in order to avoid the suggestion of divided opinion which an elective system necessarily implies. The danger of this practice was illustrated in 1957 and 1963, though it is significant that the danger lay rather in the creation of political uncertainty than in the risk that the monarch would be able to influence the choice of a Conservative leader. Sir Anthony Eden (later Lord Avon) resigned the Premiership in 1957 owing to ill-health accentuated by the strain of the brief campaign against Egypt over the Suez Canal

[1] *Ibid.*, pp. 77–80.

dispute. Events had moved too swiftly for the Conservative Party; instead of one certain successor there were two possible ones, Mr. Macmillan and Mr. Butler. In a situation of this kind it could be argued that the monarchy with its reputation for impartiality was well suited for the role of arbitrator. Queen Elizabeth, however, had then reigned for only five years. It is clear that in exercising her prerogative right of choosing a Prime Minister she relied upon the advice given to her by senior Conservative statesmen, notably Sir Winston Churchill and Lord Salisbury, and on soundings of Cabinet opinion. Normally the advice of the outgoing Prime Minister would also be an important factor in choosing a successor, but this does not appear to have been so in 1957. Whether a monarch who had reigned for many years would have been able to exercise more personal influence in the choice is a matter of conjecture. When the consultations had been completed Mr. Macmillan became Prime Minister. He, in his turn, was obliged to resign in 1963 as a result of ill-health, and again the succession was uncertain. Acting on the advice of members of the Cabinet and of Conservative Party officials, the Queen invited Lord Home to form a Government. Had he been unable to do so—and this was a real risk—and had the other Conservative contenders for leadership been unable to do so, the Queen could quite properly have turned to the Leader of the Opposition, Mr. Wilson, and asked him to form a Government. A recurrence of such a situation seems unlikely now that the Conservatives elect their leader. On the other hand, the monarch's personal influence might still be of some significance if, after a General Election, the Liberals, though incapable of forming a Government themselves, had sufficient seats to place in power whichever of the other two main parties they wished. This could produce a political deadlock which an experienced monarch might well provide a means of resolving.

The examples given show that there are still some situations demanding a degree of initiative and personal decision by the monarch in political matters. Nor do these examples by any means exhaust the possibilities of royal intervention. Sir Ivor Jennings points out in *The Queen's Government* that if a defeated Prime Minister refused to resign, in spite of a vote of no confidence, the Queen would resolve the deadlock by commissioning the Leader of the Opposition to form a new Government.[1] Acceptance of the

[1] *Ibid.*, pp. 41-3.

conventions makes this situation unlikely, but it is desirable to have the constitutional mechanism available to deal with any emergency of this kind; this function the monarchy fulfils admirably. There is, furthermore, the special power vested in the monarch in relation to the dissolution of Parliament. Dissolution is normally ordered by the Sovereign on the advice of a Prime Minister, but it would be quite wrong to infer that the personal opinion of the monarch is never of any account in matters affecting the dissolution of Parliament. In his biography of George VI[1] Sir John Wheeler-Bennett has described very clearly the attitude of the King during the 1950–1 Labour administration when stability of government was severely hampered by the precarious majority held by the Labour Party. During this time the King's rights both to press for a dissolution, and, in certain circumstances, to refuse one were far from being merely academic matters. The King was about to undertake a tour to Australia and New Zealand, and was characteristically anxious as a conscientious monarch that a political crisis should not develop in his absence. This was a strong possibility, since the Labour majority was only six. It was of some relevance, too, that the King was aware of his own failing health and was anxious that his daughter should not be confronted with a political crisis immediately on her accession. King George VI, therefore, wrote to Mr. (later Lord) Attlee, sounding him on his intention to ask for a dissolution, and making it plain from the tone of the letter that there was urgent need to secure greater political stability than obtained at the time. Lord Attlee later denied (in an article for the *Observer* of August 23rd, 1959) that he was pushed into asking for a dissolution by some pressure from the King. 'There is no substance in this, but the position of the King was one which I personally had to take into account.' In a situation of this kind royal advice is clearly not decisive. Lord Attlee speaking on B.B.C. television in February, 1963, stated that the strain on the health of Labour members helping to maintain the Government's slender majority was his predominant motive in seeking a dissolution. He was no doubt also influenced by the desire to secure the most politically opportune moment for the election. Yet if royal wishes were not decisive in 1951 neither were they negligible. Implicit in Lord Attlee's attitude is an acceptance of the fact that the monarch still

[1] Sir John Wheeler-Bennett, *King George VI: his Life and Reign*, pp. 791–6.

retains a measure of responsibility for the maintenance of political stability. This is the fact which justifies King George's approach to Lord Attlee. It is also a reminder that the monarchy should not be regarded as if it were of no political consequence whatsoever.

Another aspect of the right of dissolution was also closely scrutinised in the 1950-1 period This was the right of the monarch to refuse to grant a dissolution. The essence of the matter is contained in a letter written to *The Times* on May 2nd, 1950, by Sir Alan Lascelles, the Private Secretary to King George VI. This letter is quoted in the official biography of King George VI.[1] It states that no wise Sovereign would refuse to grant a dissolution 'unless he were satisfied that: (1) the existing Parliament was still vital, viable, and capable of doing its job; (2) a General Election would be detrimental to the national economy; (3) he could rely on finding another Prime Minister who could carry on his Government for a reasonable period with a working majority in the House of Commons'. Refusal by a monarch to grant a dissolution is clearly unlikely, more so in practice than the Lascelles letter suggests, but it is not impossible.[2] It is desirable for a monarch to seek advice on a matter of such importance, as King George VI did from Sir John Anderson in particular during the period described. Yet his own opinion may well be a factor in the final decision in the unusual, but not unique circumstances of the kind which prevailed in 1950-1. One further development which might have materialised, but which did not, is that the 1951 election might again have returned a Government without a working majority. King George VI and his advisers were ready for this eventuality, as is evident again in the official biography. The solution would have been a recommendation by the King for the formation of a National Government. The likely reactions of the leading politicians to this possibility had been assessed before the 1951 election took place, and had that election produced an indefinite result royal intervention with the object of securing a stable government by means of a coalition might well have taken place.

It is evident then that, constitutionally, the monarch is not merely a figure-head—the Crown is too closely concerned with

---

[1] Sir John Wheeler-Bennett, *op. cit.*, p. 775.
[2] Cf. Lord Asquith's speech at the National Liberal Club, 1923 (Le May, *British Government 1914-53*, p. 155) for a justification of the monarch's right to refuse to accept a dissolution of Parliament.

the management of the steering-wheel for that comparison to be apt. Nevertheless, its powers of real decision would be reserved for quite exceptional situations, and there have been occasions in this century when royal wishes have been respectfully heard but ultimately overruled. As a legal concept the supreme authority in the country is the Crown-in-Parliament but, in general, it is the will of the elected Assembly which must prevail, and the pre-eminence of the Commons in practice has been accepted both by the monarch and the House of Lords in modern times. Queen Victoria's wish to avoid having Gladstone as Prime Minister was circumvented by the refusal of the other Liberals to accept the office. More recently it is clear from the private papers of King George VI, quoted in his biography by Sir John Wheeler-Bennett, that the King had strong opinions over certain appointments. In 1940, King George made it very evident to Neville Chamberlain, at the period of his resignation, that he was strongly in favour of Lord Halifax succeeding as Prime Minister.[1] Chamberlain advised him that Churchill would be a better choice: this the King accepted, though with some reluctance. Again, although it has been asserted that royal influence was brought to bear over the appointment of Mr. Bevin rather than Sir Hugh Dalton to the post of Foreign Secretary in 1945,[2] this is denied by Lord Attlee who said in the *Observer* of August 23rd, 1959, that, although he naturally took into account the King's view which was very sound, 'it was not a decisive factor in my arrival at my decision.' Lord Morrison stated in *Government and Parliament* that on two occasions he formed a different opinion from the King on the subject of reprieves for condemned persons.[3] In theory the grant of a reprieve is part of the Royal prerogative powers. In practice Lord Morrison, having listened respectfully to the King's views, decided that he could not agree, and it was Morrison's views which prevailed. The scope for royal initiative in policy is therefore narrowly circumscribed but not negligible. Furthermore, there is not the least risk of royal intervention, except on easily justifiable grounds, since the House of Commons by its control of finance, including the annual grants to the Royal Family from the Civil List, could easily bring government to a standstill in the highly improbable event of being confronted by dictatorial intervention by the monarch.

[1] Sir John Wheeler-Bennett, *op. cit.*, pp. 443–4.    [2] *Ibid.*, p. 638.
[3] Lord Morrison, *Government and Parliament*, p. 81.

The remaining prerogative powers of the Crown have largely
lost significance with the passage of time and the development of
the doctrine of Ministerial Responsibility. The making of peace
and war, the conduct of foreign affairs, the making of treaties, the
appointment of judges, the granting of charters of incorporation,
the award of the titles of honour, the headship of the Armed
Forces, and the appointment of high officials, these are all prerogative powers which sprang from what used to be the direct
personal authority of the monarch, but now these powers are delegated virtually in their entirety to the Ministers of the Crown. The
monarch's prerogative power to create peers has had more recent
significance. Until 1911 the Lords' power of absolute veto gave
them, in a sense, constitutional supremacy. The monarch's power
to create peers could therefore be of some political value, as it was
in the 1910–11 disputes when King George V agreed to create
sufficient peers to ensure the passage of the Parliament Act
through the House of Lords. Once this Act was passed constitutional dominance passed to the Commons, and their position was
further strengthened by the Parliament Act of 1949 reducing the
Lords' power of veto to one year. Thus the necessity for royal
intervention as it occurred in 1911 has largely passed away, and
this aspect of the prerogative has also virtually lost any element of
political significance.

If the justification of the monarchy rested merely on the occasional exercise of the prerogative powers it would still be an adequate defence of the institution. Political and constitutional crises
do arise, as the earlier examples quoted show, and a monarch is
better fitted to deal with them than a President, whose actions
would inevitably be more vulnerable to the criticism that his
decisions were influenced by his political associations. In fact, there
are other aspects of the monarch's service to the nation which are
of almost equal benefit to the community, though less dramatic
than participation in constitutional crises. One aspect of this work
is the frequent appearance of the Queen among her subjects
visiting hospitals, schools, exhibitions, factories, scientific estab-
lishments, the Armed Forces, and the great occasions of sport.
This has double value. It suggests a complete fusion of interest
between the Queen and those who are working in a great variety of
occupations. Secondly, in spite of the superficial cynicism which
many affect, it is a stimulus towards high achievement for any

group of people to discover that their activities are sufficiently valuable to the nation to justify a visit from the monarch. It is true that this function could also be performed by a President, but the continuity of the British monarchy makes it unique among the nations of Europe, and earns for it a special respect; immunity from invasion and from destructive revolution has made it easier and more attractive to preserve in Britain our contacts with the past; the monarchy is an outstanding example. It would be a radical break with the past to replace monarchy with a Presidential system of government. Moreover, while it is true that a President could perform the social duties of the monarch with almost equal effectiveness, and without the suggestion of the existence of a social hierarchy implicit in the British concept of monarchy, the political impartiality of the monarchy gives that institution a clear advantage over a Presidential system, both in the occasional exercise of the prerogative powers and, in addition, in the unique role which the monarch holds in relation to the Commonwealth.

The acceptance of the Crown as the symbolic focal point of the Commonwealth is still of some importance. Loyalty to an abstract conception of Commonwealth unity is remotely feasible, but the ability of the Queen by her visits to personify the conception is a far more effective and satisfying reminder of the links between member countries than any other solution which could be devised. A President has party associations as well as being the representative of the nation. He will represent much to which party politicians and other members of the Commonwealth communities will have the strongest objections. Against the Queen, remote from political controversy, similar objections could not be raised. Yet because in recent times so many of the Afro-Asian members of the Commonwealth have become Republics, it may be thought that their links with the monarchy are totally insignificant. For them the monarch is not personally a ruler in the sense that she is Queen of Canada or Queen of Australia. Self-absorbed in the problems of their newly-won independence, and at times bitterly critical of British policy, the Afro-Asian members seem to have moved so far from the simple concept of Commonwealth unity that it may appear a ridiculous sham to pretend that the monarchy still retains some symbolic significance for them. This is a mistaken view. Admittedly, self-interest is more important than sentiment in maintaining Commonwealth unity, but so long as there is a Commonwealth—

and, like Charles II, it may be 'a longer time a-dying' than its critics hope—the unique capacity of the monarchy to personify the Commonwealth concept ought not to be treated as if it were of no account. The Queen's visits to Commonwealth countries show that they accept and welcome the role which she performs. What possible advantage would there be in seeking to destroy the popular enthusiasm which these visits create? On the contrary, the monarch commands a respect and affection which no President could match, and which add to the prestige not only of the monarchy but also of Britain and of the Commonwealth itself.

'The state of the monarchy is the supremest thing upon earth' said James I. His confidence looks strangely archaic now. Yet, shorn of most of its powers, the British monarchy has enough of its ancient vigour left to make it of some value still. Moreover, its essential flexibility has enabled it to adapt itself to the present background of modern democracy without any incongruity, and to change from the direct personal rule of the old Empire to the unique symbolic leadership of the Commonwealth. When the constitutional functions of the monarchy are fully understood, the arguments that the monarchy is an anachronism carry little conviction. Many of the functions performed by the monarchy are useful; some of them are essential, and are far better performed by a non-partisan monarch than by a politician. If, for instance, the monarchy were to be abolished, and the monarch replaced as Head of State by a politician, the political impartiality, which is one of the strongest assets of monarchy in governmental crises, would disappear with that institution itself. Nor would it be at all easy to preserve that dexterous division between power and prestige, which, on the whole, is maintained at the moment. The social influence of the monarchy is variable according to the personality of the ruler, and there may be variations for better or worse in this respect accordingly. What is far more important is the special constitutional position the monarchy has acquired in this country by a mixture of historical accident and good sense; to abolish it would be an act of constitutional nihilism.

## FURTHER READING

Sir Charles Petrie, *The Modern British Monarchy* (Eyre & Spottiswoode, 1961).

D. Morrah, *The Work of the Queen* (Kimber, 1958).

H. Nicolson, *King George V* (Constable, 1952).

Sir John Wheeler-Bennett, *King George VI* (Macmillan, 1958).

W. Bagehot, *The English Constitution* (Fontana, 1963).

See also Comments on Further Reading, p. 211.

# 2

# The Supremacy of the Cabinet

The dominant position of the Cabinet. The need for close scrutiny of the term 'Cabinet'. Cabinet functions. Comparative stability of British Governments. Party discipline. Collective responsibility. Supremacy of Act of Parliament. Factors leading to greater centralisation. The degree of Cabinet freedom over policy-making. Public opinion. The Press. Back-benchers. Pressure-groups. The Opposition. The influence of conventional attitudes on political behaviour.

THEME: Cabinet authority has been greatly extended. Formal limitations to its power are negligible, and, in practice, custom provides the best protection.

The supremacy of the Cabinet in the constitution is now generally accepted. The theory of Parliamentary sovereignty might have been tenable at times in the nineteenth century, when it was possible for Bagehot to regard the Cabinet as merely a committee of Parliament, but it is not held to have much relevance to present-day conditions. In *The British Constitution* Sir Ivor Jennings writes 'No change or development of policy of any importance would be carried out without Cabinet sanction'; and earlier in the same book he writes 'The Cabinet can always have the last word'.[1] Other commentators have come to the same conclusion that it is the Cabinet, not Parliament, which is the driving force behind the machinery of government. That this should be so is one more example of the paradoxes of the British constitution, for the Cabinet, in spite of its importance, is scarcely mentioned at all in statutes. Yet the Cabinet does not possess unbridled power. L. S. Amery in *Thoughts on the Constitution* writes 'In no other country is there such a concentration of power, and such a capacity for decisive action as that possessed by a British Cabinet', but he

[1] *Ibid.*, p. 153.

goes on to say 'provided always that it enjoys the support of a majority in the House of Commons'.[1] If this were so it might be arguable that Parliamentary sovereignty is not so moribund an idea as it is sometimes thought to be. In fact, as will be seen later, the influence of the House of Commons over the Cabinet falls far short of sovereignty, though not to the level of being entirely negligible. The dominance of the Cabinet will emerge more clearly from a study of its functions, but it may be of value at the outset to point out that the degree of Cabinet supremacy is apt to elude even the most expert analysis. The supremacy of the Cabinet is not that of an Augustus, nor a Robespierre. It is far more subtle; it relies on co-operation, not coercion, and is itself subject to pressure both from within its own ranks and from outside.

To isolate and describe all the influences which lead to policy decisions is a task which has not been fully attempted yet, nor is it likely that such an analysis will ever be successful when it is made by those whose knowledge is theoretical. The secrecy of Cabinet proceedings establishes a barrier which can be penetrated here and there by intelligent speculation, based on constitutional knowledge, but the man with authoritative knowledge of the influences which shape Cabinet decisions is the Prime Minister. Nor is it likely that these influences will be constant. Prime Ministers and their Cabinets will take more or less account of special interest groups —trade unions, business interests, party groups, and the rest— and of personal and professional advisers according to personal outlook. These matters are apt to be assumed without being explicitly stated in speaking of the constitutional position of the Cabinet. This begins as a matter of convenience since it is easier for frequent reference to speak of 'the Cabinet' than of the variously composed specialist groups whose influence on policy-making is probably greater than that of the Cabinet as a whole. Yet there is a danger in using the term 'Cabinet' indiscriminately if it creates the impression of policy decisions being evolved by the Cabinet of some twenty ministers acting as a single unit. This point has been clearly made in *The British Cabinet* by J. P. Mackintosh. He shows that most of the functions which are normally described as being performed by the Cabinet are in practice performed by smaller groups of powerful Ministers and professional advisers under the central direction of the Prime Minister. This is necessary

[1] *Ibid.*, p. 70.

partly because of the unwieldy size of the Cabinet, and partly because of the highly specialised knowledge which is required if discussions are to have any value. It may well be desirable, for instance, to include a Minister for Employment in any modern Cabinet, but it would be surprising if he had any original contribution to make on matters outside his immediate sphere, such as colonial affairs or trade agreements. Mackintosh goes so far as to say that the formation of policy is not primarily a matter for the Cabinet at all. 'Decisions are made in the departments, in Cabinet Committees, in private talks between the Prime Minister and the Ministers mainly concerned, and the differences that remain are settled in the Cabinet itself.' He goes on to say that 'The main task of the Cabinet is to co-ordinate the work of the various departments and committees, and thus ensure that the activity of the government has a certain coherence'.[1] This view is valuable in removing the ambiguity resulting from the use of the term 'Cabinet' as if it performed the functions of government as a single entity. This does not mean, however, that the Cabinet is merely a channel through which policy decisions flow. While it is true that most of the Cabinet Ministers will be specialists in relatively narrow sectors of policy, all of them are politicians. They are fully entitled, therefore, to oppose a decision because of its possible political repercussions; and, in this respect, the fact that they lack the expert knowledge to formulate the policy or to criticise it in detail is of no consequence whatsoever.

Even on this basis alone, therefore, the Cabinet as a single unit is still in a position of outstanding importance in the constitution; and if one uses the word 'Cabinet' as an umbrella term to comprise the activities of the policy-making groups previously described, the statements made about the dominance of the Cabinet are fully justified, as is evident from any formal statement of its functions. Using the term 'Cabinet' in the sense just described it can be said that the Cabinet initiates most legislation, controls the timing of its entry into Parliament through the advice of its Legislation Committee, and safeguards its passage through its Parliamentary stages by the exercise, when necessary, of the powers of party discipline. The Queen's Speech at the beginning of each Parliamentary session is, in fact, a statement of the programme of the Government, and is prepared by the leading Ministers of the Cabinet. The

[1] J. P. Mackintosh, *The British Cabinet*, p. 382.

Cabinet controls all executive activities of central Government. It reorganises Departments, as when the Colonial and Commonwealth offices were merged in 1966; it sets up new Ministries, such as the Department of the Environment; it settles disputes between Departments; it secures co-ordination by ensuring that Government Departments work towards a common purpose, such as reduction in expenditure, or by mutual consultation and the circulation of information, so that no one Department takes action prejudicial to another simply through a failure of liaison. The Cabinet examines all major issues of foreign and domestic policy: political crises, our policy at the United Nations, the European Common Market, the attainment of Commonwealth statehood by dependent territories, economic policy, safeguarding oil supplies, emergency arrangements in the event of transport strikes, these and a host of other matters are not merely subjects for discussion, but also at times for urgent decision. The only exception of any real consequence to this constant review of matters of high policy is the Budget, since it is desirable that the detailed terms should be known to as few as possible before its 'opening' in the House of Commons.

In addition, the Cabinet through its various committees is responsible for the specialised examination and planning of major aspects of Government work. Details of these Cabinet Committees are not disclosed until after the lifetime of the Government concerned. This is the standard practice with both parties and is due not to any reprehensible obsession with secrecy, but to the wish to leave chairmen of Committees and members free from the influence of public and political pressure groups while the necessary researches and negotiations are put into effect. This does not by-pass criticism since ultimately the work of the Committees must be submitted to the Cabinet, and then, if approved, to Parliament. This valuable preliminary planning cannot be carried out in an atmosphere of heated controversy, though the Government will have to face this later when the proposals are scrutinised in Parliament in the form of legislation or policy. There is, therefore, nothing sinister in the secrecy associated with Cabinet Committee proceedings. It is true, nevertheless, that planning the development of the main aspects of government, which is the direct responsibility of the Cabinet, is a far-reaching power, even though it does not involve in Britain conscription and direction of labour, as it does, and has done, elsewhere. Although details of the committees of the present Government are not available, Lord Morrison in *Government and Parliament* described very fully the committees used by the 1945–51 Labour Governments.[1] A few of these, such as the Reconstruction Committee, will have lost their relevance now, but many of the others were dealing with recurrent issues and are likely to have survived in the organisation of later Governments. The names alone of the most important committees, and there are thirty in all mentioned by Lord Morrison as being in existence at different times in this post-war period, give some insight into the range of subjects examined by Cabinet Committees, and from this their extensive influence can be deduced. Because of their extreme importance there must be a Defence Committee and an Economic Policy Committee. Because of post-war developments and the nature of the issues involved, a Cabinet Committee on Commonwealth Affairs would be as appropriate now as it was in Mr. Attlee's Government, when he himself presided over it. The frequency with which the Prime Minister appeared as chairman of Cabinet Committees—he was chairman of seven in the 1945–51 Labour Governments—is in itself some indication of their importance. There will naturally be a Legislation Committee to assist in working out the priority of the various legislative proposals to be brought before Parliament. Amongst many other committees Lord Morrison also mentioned committees for specific areas, such as the Far East and Middle East Committees, committees on economic matters, such as committees for Production, and for Distribution and Marketing, and committees for social services, such as Housing and the National Health Service.

This examination of the functions of the Cabinet gives some indication of its dominance. Apart from the work it does, however, there are political and constitutional factors which give it a stability not enjoyed, for instance, by French Cabinets in recent years. The expectation, based on history, that British Governments of the twentieth century are far more likely than not to last for a period of four or five years is a factor in this stability. At the end of the five years an election becomes statutory, and only the occurrence of war or some other great emergency would render this inoperative. Sometimes a Prime Minister will seek a dissolution after four years of power, as Mr. Macmillan did in 1959, not because a dissolution

[1] *Ibid.*, pp. 16–27.

was forced upon him by the weakness of his Government, but because the moment seemed opportune. This is a perfectly legitimate political device towards the end of a Government's period of power. Dissolutions after a shorter period of power would in normal circumstances be regarded with some suspicion, so that it is a fair assumption that a party with a sound working majority will stay in power for four or five years, with all the advantages involved of continuity of policy over that period. Where there have been exceptions in this century they have been due mostly to situations created by election results unlikely to occur very commonly. The Labour Governments of 1924 and 1929–31, for instance, had no absolute majority, and were therefore dependent on Liberal support, a weakening factor. The 1950–1 Labour Government had such a slender majority that Mr. Attlee, to avoid the physical and mental strain involved for his supporters in the constant need to use the votes of every Labour M.P. on every major occasion, asked for a dissolution; similarly Mr. Wilson obtained an early dissolution of Parliament in 1966, after gaining an overall majority of four in the 1964 General Election. The Conservatives, too, have experienced brief sessions of power, as when Mr. Baldwin in 1923, after a few months, appealed to the voters for their views on Protection.

These incidents, however, involved rather special circumstances, and there is no intrinsic reason why a Government with a working majority should expect anything less than four years of power. The basis of that power is the will of the electors expressed through their votes. After that initial stage has been reached, and the victorious party has formed a Government, party discipline adds to its power. Party discipline is not enforced with mechanical rigidity. It is obvious that not all M.P.s in the Government party will have identical views on all issues. The post-war Parliaments alone give ample evidence of these differences of opinion within the parties. Peter Richards, analysing these incidents in *Honourable Members*, points out that there were nine major Labour 'rebellions' during the 1945–51 Government; nor was the Conservative record very different.[1] 'Rebellion' may be a more dramatic word than the circumstances justify but it is clear that total obedience in all circumstances is fortunately still beyond the bounds of present possibility. It needs to be remembered also that if even a small

[1] *Ibid.*, pp. 148–53.

number of Government supporters vote against their party, or
abstain, the element of doubt created over the wisdom of Government policies is magnified out of all proportion to the numbers
involved, with consequent damage to electoral prospects. Admittedly this might be interpreted as an argument for greater coercion
of M.P.s by the Whips. In practice, uniformity of approach cannot
be secured by disciplinary measures alone in the parties as they are
constituted at present. The risk of losing the support of members
remains a deterrent against the adoption of controversial measures
in spite of the prevalence of the Gilbertian belief that M.P.s vote
'just as their leaders tell them to'. The opposition of back-benchers
to their leaders' policies is sufficiently commonplace to demonstrate the falsity of that idea. The Conservative leadership in 1954
was strongly challenged by the 'Suez Group' consisting of some
twenty-eight Conservatives opposing concessions to Nasser. The
Labour Government in 1967 had to face extensive criticism from
its back-benchers over the plan to apply for membership of the
E.E.C. It was even more strongly opposed over the controversial
Industrial Relations Bill of 1969 to curb unofficial strike activity by
direct Parliamentary control. Perhaps the most striking demonstration of the influence of back-benchers was the way in which
M.P.s from both sides of the House were so strongly opposed to
the bill of 1969 proposing the reform of the House of Lords that it
had to be dropped, although the leaders of the major parties had
accepted in principle the idea of a reforming bill. Persistent
opposition to party policies may mean that the recalcitrant back-
bencher will have the party whip withdrawn, yet, even in the
Labour Party, which is more likely to use this sanction, the rarity
of such an event makes it a remote deterrent. For the Conservative
Party, if any penalty at all is incurred it is more likely to be the
penalty of not being re-adopted for the next election rather than
expulsion from the Parliamentary party. These facts lend some
support to the belief that party discipline is neither so rigid nor so
intolerant of individual differences as is sometimes alleged. Even
when the Chief Whip interviews M.P.s hostile to some aspect of
Government policy his primary purpose is persuasion rather than
coercion.

Any assessment of the leader-member relationship within the
parties should take into account the existence of the Parliamentary
Labour Party, and also of the 1922 Committee for the Conservative

Party. These private party meetings of M.P.s give an excellent opportunity for the thrashing out of differences without the restraints imposed when the parties are engaged in the widely publicised activities of the House of Commons. There are differences in their organisation. The Conservative leader and his ministers, for instance, do not normally attend meetings of the 1922 Committee, but the leader is kept informed of the views of members. Contact between the Labour leader and the Parliamentary Labour Party is closer, especially when the Labour Party forms the Opposition. Differences between the two organisations matter less, however, than their similarities. The central purpose for each organisation is to ensure that liaison is maintained between the leadership and members so that all are well informed on the mood and objectives of their respective parties. This gives opportunities for the removal of causes of discord before the issues are brought to public attention. It is a further advantage in securing genuine unity of feeling within the party that ministers have themselves been back-benchers, and may become so again. The precariousness of political office is thus, in itself, an incentive towards good relations between the leadership and members.

When all these necessary reservations have been made it is still true that party discipline is a support for the power of the Cabinet. When there is a sufficient margin of support for the Government to ensure that there is no danger of its defeat it is reasonable for Government M.P.s to make their protest against legislation they dislike, in the hope that this action will bring forcibly to the Government's notice the need for some modification of the bill. There is a consoling factor for British Governments in that, while Government supporters may voice their protests against particular features of Government policy, their dislike for these measures falls far short of their dislike for the policy of the Opposition. The convention by which if a Government is defeated on a major issue of policy it then resigns is a great source of strength to the Cabinet. Most back-benchers would be content to stomach certain unpalatable features of Government policy rather than bring about the downfall of their own leadership. For some it may be a personal factor which influences their outlook. A dissolution of Parliament means a new General Election and the attendant risk of losing one's seat in the House of Commons for a period of four to five years. For the ambitious politician, and for the man who has no satisfactory alternative to a political career, fighting a General Election is not always a hazard which he would willingly bring upon himself before he is obliged to do so. For others the ability of their party to continue as the Government for the full term of office is, ultimately, of more importance than differences over individual acts of policy. Thus it may come about that a member is hostile to a Government measure, but will still vote for it rather than run the risk of shattering party unity. It would be wrong to infer that strong individual feelings are always repressed when party unity is at stake; there are matters of principle involved in individual governmental acts where it may be impossible for an M.P. to continue to give support to the Government. Conservative policy towards Nasser's Egypt illustrated this point, and in pre-war days there was a powerful section of the Conservative Party which opposed the Government policy of self-government for India. But these situations are exceptional. The great bulk of Government legislation and policy receives support which can be counted on with complete assurance, especially if there is the slightest risk of a Government defeat. Obviously this is a source of great confidence to the Cabinet. The stability of government which results is, in general, desirable, but there has been increasing disquiet in postwar years over Cabinet dominance of the party system. Whenever allegations are made that the Executive has become over-powerful in the modern constitution the influence of party discipline will almost certainly be a central point of the argument. How strong that influence is can, perhaps, be assessed from the foregoing remarks.

Just as the maintenance of party unity involves the exercise of some degree of party discipline, so, too, Cabinet unity is maintained by the doctrine of collective responsibility. Individual criticisms of Government policy will be made in the privacy of Cabinet meetings, but everyone concerned is thoroughly aware of the dangers of exposing differences within the Cabinet during Parliamentary debates. A Cabinet split will almost inevitably lead to a party split, and a divided party cannot govern. The rift in the Balfour Government of 1902–5 over the question of the adoption of Protection is a clear illustration of this. Decisions made by the Cabinet require the support of all the Ministers. Individual Cabinet Ministers who have doubts about the wisdom of particular actions have the choice of overcoming their objections or of resigning. On matters of strongly held principle the latter course is the only one. Thus Lord Snowden and Sir Herbert Samuel resigned in 1932 from the National Government because of differences over the economic policy of the Cabinet, and Mr. Mayhew resigned from the Labour Government in 1966 through disagreement over defence policy. These were fundamental issues where it would have been impossible for these Ministers to give even passive acquiescence to the policies proposed. Objections on less fundamental differences can be endured by Ministers who value party unity highly, and the working of this doctrine is a further source of strength in Cabinet Government. Both this doctrine and the sanction of party discipline have gained in force in this century from the realisation that in Britain there has almost always been a numerous Opposition party, ready instantly to take the place of a wavering Government.

Cabinet dominance is further encouraged by the omnipotence in Britain of Acts of Parliament which can do everything 'but make a man into a woman and a woman into a man'.[1] The Judiciary has no power to refuse to put into operation any law which has been approved by Parliament, however repugnant the measure may seem to a judge's concept of justice. Nor is there a written constitution in Britain, as there is in the United States and elsewhere, laying down fundamental principles which the Executive and Legislature may not infringe. Constitutionally, there are no permanent guarantees of individual freedoms. Magna Carta, Habeas Corpus, the Ballot and Representation of the People Acts could be swept out of existence by Act of Parliament. The abolition of Habeas Corpus followed by the arrest of members of the Opposition would not be constitutionally impossible. The absurdity of the idea suggests that there are other restraints, and these will be considered later, but the fact that Acts of Parliament are now, in practice, an expression of the policy of the Cabinet does mean that there is no formal, impassable barrier to the establishment of an autocratic authority in Britain. Many reasons make such an action wildly improbable, but the knowledge of this potentially ultimate authority does strengthen the position of the Cabinet in putting into practice authoritarian policies of a milder nature. The controls imposed by the Labour Government of 1945–51 give some indication of the stringency of direction possible even in peacetime.

[1] Though, legally, there is no bar to this either!

The tendency towards authoritarian policies is reinforced by the emergence of new political concepts in modern times. The extension of the franchise in the nineteenth century meant that the main parties acquired a direct interest in the welfare of the working class, and from that time 'laissez-faire' became an outmoded doctrine. The growth of State welfare schemes, of the concept of equality of opportunity, and the increasing need for planned development of the means of transport, and of public services, such as electricity, have meant that it has become commonplace nowadays to accept directions from the Executive over issues which simply did not arise in Victorian times. This not only gives the Cabinet more influence over the individual citizen through legislation closely scrutinised in the Houses of Parliament, but also, because of the pressure of time and the complexity of the issues, leads to the increasing influence of instruments of the Executive not directly controlled by Parliament. Special interest groups and expert opinion will often need to be consulted before legislation reaches Parliament, where the increasing volume of legislation makes detailed examination of all issues impossible. Once the Act is passed, the Statutory Instruments—the regulations necessary to make the Act sufficiently detailed to work in practice—are devised by Civil Servants in the Government Departments. Provision is made in Parliamentary procedure for the examination of these regulations to some extent by the whole House of Commons, and also by Select Committees of the Lords and Commons. The sheer volume of regulations makes it physically impossible to scrutinise in detail every Statutory Instrument. In effect, the power of regulation-making has to be delegated to the Civil Servants in the Government Departments, though under general Parliamentary control. It does mean, however, that the normal process by which the Legislature can cushion the general public against unwise decisions by the Executive is not so fully applicable to this kind of legislation. The scope of this legislation is, of course, limited, since the regulations cannot exceed the powers given by the original statute, but it is not always possible to anticipate the full effects of the statutory regulations from the form of the original Statute itself. This is, therefore, another instance of the way the power of the Executive has increased in modern times.

Pressure of time has also meant the development in Parliament of various devices for shortening debate. There is the 'Closure' motion 'that the question be now put'; if a hundred members support it, this has the effect of bringing the debate to an end. There is also the 'Guillotine' procedure, by which the Government can allocate definite times for the completion of the necessary stages of Parliamentary bills, and the 'Kangaroo' procedure which is used in committees, so that the chairman of a Standing Committee can choose the most important amendments for discussion and omit the others. Shortening of debate and of the examination of bills involves obvious dangers since these devices could be exploited by a Government with autocratic tendencies. They are, however, a necessary feature of the political scene when shortage of time handicaps Government legislation; moreover, the Opposition can make so much political capital out of any attempt to evade Parliamentary discussion that the situation rarely occurs.

There is strong evidence to show, therefore, that changing political circumstances in modern Britain have made it more likely that a strong Executive will emerge. So far as this has happened, however, it is due to a change in circumstances and not to any intrinsic change in the outlook of the members of the Cabinet itself. Additional powers are now required, but they are used, in general, with discretion, and with the realisation that the Cabinet is answerable to Parliament, and ultimately, to the electorate itself. Considering the rapid changes there have been on the Continent in this century, with the emergence of totalitarian governments and of Executives of very great power, and considering also the comparative decline of Legislatures—for Parliamentary Government in the nineteenth century used to be looked on as the apex of political achievement—it is a notable fact that the Cabinet is still believed to be more akin to a representative institution than would be possible in a dictatorship. If it seems at times to be autocratic in its behaviour, it is an autocracy not welcomed, but an involuntary 'dictatorship' forced on the Cabinet by pressure of time and circumstance. It is always possible for critics to infer more sinister motives, but the limits which all Governments must impose on the absolute freedom of citizens if they are to govern at all are more elastic in Britain than those which exist in the governmental systems of many other major powers.

There is no doubt, however, that, even in Britain, individual and group freedoms are less solidly based than they used to be. In view of this increasing challenge to what have generally been regarded as fundamental rights, it would be of interest to examine the limitations on the power of the Cabinet. If the final test of authority in the State lies in the power of dismissal of other institutions of government, who possesses this ultimate authority in Britain? It is clearly no longer the monarch. Edward VIII's abdication showed that if there was a divergence of opinion between the monarch and a Government, acting in the name of a duly elected House of Commons, it must be the monarch who gives way. The Cabinet has claims to supreme authority in that it can dismiss Parliament if the Prime Minister asks for a dissolution. It is also true that Parliament can dismiss the Cabinet by passing a vote of no confidence. Whichever takes place the matter does not end there. In dismissing Parliament the Cabinet is dismissing itself and a General Election becomes necessary. If, on the other hand, Parliament dismisses the Government by giving majority support to a vote of no confidence, that does not involve an immediate election since a Government can be formed from the victorious party. It has been the practice, however, except when wartime exigencies make it impossible, to follow up a Government defeat of this kind with an election very shortly afterwards. Government resignations in 1905 and 1922, for instance, were followed very rapidly by General Elections. This suggests that the final authority in the constitution resides not in Parliament, nor in the Cabinet, but in the electorate itself. Yet this opinion needs to be scrutinised more closely before it is accepted.

It is undoubtedly true that the British live in a sufficiently free society to be able to make the Government fully aware of the state of opinion in a variety of ways. What is much less certain is the degree to which Governments are influenced by public opinion. Newspapers are sometimes considered to be representative of public opinion though in fact the opinions they express may simply be those of their editors and proprietors and are not necessarily representative even of their own particular readers. Their influence on policy-making is normally negligible. Where they can be valuable is in their exposure of any obvious abuse of power by politicians or civil servants. Respect for the individual freedoms is still well established in Britain, though less so in modern times. It is still easy for the Press to rouse public sympathy for hardship imposed by intolerant treatment of individuals. This is a different matter from the forming of policy, however, and in policy-making it appears that the influence of the Press and of public opinion is of little account. As an example, Governments which were entirely responsive to public opinion would be far more hesitant than they have been in their intention to take Britain into the European Common Market. Governments are expected to provide leadership. This they can hardly do by consulting newspapers and public opinion polls before they act. Public reaction to policies after they are formed may, on the other hand, be a matter of close interest to Governments since unfavourable reactions can obviously mar a party's electoral prospects. Even in this respect Governments can afford to remain unmoved in their policies for much of the time since the modern public is apt to lose all critical sense in the volume of news with which it is deluged, and its memory is notoriously short. The Conservative Party was able to re-establish itself sufficiently to win the 1959 election in spite of the vehement criticism of the Suez Canal expedition in 1956. In the last months of office the Government will be anxious to make a favourable impression upon voters, but there is no reason to suppose that the influence of the general public is of great consequence otherwise.

It could perhaps be claimed that the back-benchers represent another way of bringing pressure to bear on Cabinet policies on behalf of the general public. The extent to which back-bencher opinion is influenced by opinion in constituencies is one of the many imponderables in politics. It is clear, however, that Cabinet policies cannot be put into effect without reference to the opinion of Government back-benchers, conveyed to the Party leaders by means of private meetings or by the Party Whips. The views of functional committees of Government back-benchers, for instance, deserve particular respect. The support of the party's back-benchers must obviously be retained if a Government is to survive. This is not generally difficult since both the Cabinet and the back-benchers are strongly bound together by the belief that, whatever their differences in detail, their own continuance in office is of greater importance still. Governmental splits have broken up ministries, but there have been no post-war instances of this situation, so that the threat of the withdrawal of back-bencher support is not likely to be felt acutely by Cabinets. The chief value of back-bencher opinion is that it acts as a pressure-gauge of party feeling. This opinion does not influence the activity of the Cabinet very much so long as the reading is normal, but is a valuable instrument for indicating when an explosion is about to take place.

Special interest groups such as Trade Unions, employers' organisations, and City interests, are in a stronger position for modifying the formation of Cabinet policy, partly because their specialist knowledge places them upon a nearer equality with the expert advisers who formulate policy under the direction of the Prime Minister, and to some extent of the whole Cabinet. Apart from that, the powerful interests represented by these pressure-groups make their co-operation desirable. Yet it is absurd to visualise government being carried on as a kind of conspiracy against the nation with the Prime Minister and Cabinet giving a frontage of constitutional respectability to the machinations of shadowy figures representative of Big Business, Trade Unions, or some other favourite aversion. Pressure-groups represent special interests; as a result their view of politics is both narrow and vulnerable. The Prime Minister and his chief ministers, with their wider view of politics, can sometimes, for instance, rely on opposing influences to cancel each other out, as the left wing of the Labour Party and the Trade Union leaders are apt to do. Sometimes a Government can show that in the interests of wider national progress the special interests of a pressure-group may have to be overridden. This is a critical test of the extent of Government authority over the powerful special interest groups. An example of this situation occurred in 1962 in the negotiations between the railwaymen's unions and the British Transport Commission over the latter's decision to reduce railway staffs in the interests of economy. Even though the large Trade Unions are extremely powerful, there was no indication in this episode, and little indication in previous ones, that Governments could be coerced into modifying an unpopular policy. The Government usually has the advantage in dealing with these pressure-groups that it can legitimately claim that the whole is more important than the parts, that national interests matter more than sectional interests, and that even the most powerful of the pressure-groups only represents a minority of voters. Nevertheless, if a Government lacks whole-hearted party support it is vulnerable to a strong pressure-group, as was evident in the way in which Trade Union criticism compelled the Labour Government to abandon its Industrial Relations Bill in 1969.

A further restraint to be considered on the dominance of the

Cabinet is the existence of an Opposition capable of forming an alternative Government. Far from Opposition being regarded as iniquitous, or even treasonable, as it has been elsewhere, the leader is given the title of Leader of Her Majesty's Opposition, and is paid a salary of £4,500 a year to emphasise the importance attached to criticism of Government policy. A strong Opposition can, when thoroughly organised, bring intensive scrutiny to bear on Government policy. Its criticisms receive a very wide circulation through the Press, television, and radio, and this helps to produce an atmosphere of opinion to which the Government cannot be entirely indifferent. But, as previously indicated, it is unwise to stress very strongly the influences of public opinion upon Government policies. It is fair to point out also that considering the pressure of Parliamentary business the Opposition is quite well served in the time allotted to it. Apart from the twenty-nine Supply Days the Opposition has further opportunities for criticism in the debate on the Queen's Speech, in the debate on the adjournment, in committees, and in motions[1] and questions. It may even happen, as it did with the Labour Governments of 1945–51 on the issue of nationalised industries, that the Government will itself allocate additional time to the Opposition for debates. Yet, in practice, there is very little relationship between the volume of criticism made and the amount of change effected. A Government with a safe majority can afford to ignore the advice of political opponents. It is in the meetings of the Standing Committees to examine the details of legislation rather than in the more spectacular setting of the House of Commons debates that the Opposition can most effectively bring some influence to bear on Government policy.

The view that the authority of the Cabinet can be tempered by public opinion is broadly true in that there are many ways in which the opinions of the general public and of particular sections of it can be expressed. But it should be clear from the foregoing remarks that the Cabinet is not under any irresistible pressure from any quarter in its policy-making. A determined Government can override the objections of even the strongest pressure-group so long as it can count on the support of its own party. It may even pursue a policy to which a minority of the party has strong objections provided again that an essential nucleus of support remains. Sections

[1] An official Opposition motion of censure must be debated, by Parliamentary convention, within a few days of its appearance on the paper.

of the Labour Party opposed Mr. Attlee's defence policy; similarly, the Suez crisis of 1956 and the financial policy of the late 1950s roused disquiet among some Conservative M.P.s; Mr. Wilson's Government was exposed to strongly expressed criticisms from its own back-benchers on different aspects of its defence and economic policies. Yet the Governments mentioned gained a sufficient momentum of general support within the party to make it possible to continue in power. It may seem, therefore, that a Cabinet differs very little from more specifically authoritarian Governments. Yet it should be remembered that there are restraints on the Cabinet less tangible than those so far described, but more effective. These are the restraints which spring from the habitual attitudes of governors and governed, from convention, from tacit assumptions on what constitutes a reasonable degree of Government control over the activities of the people it rules. These are the real limitations on Cabinet authority. Their effectiveness will last as long as public opinion is sufficiently educated to recognise them. It is obvious, however, that limitations of this type lack the precision of legal definition. The Cabinet, using that term to comprise the various informed groups who devise policy, has sufficiently wide powers over a great range of activities to justify the claim that it is supreme in the constitution.

FURTHER READING

J. P. Mackintosh, *The British Cabinet* (Stevens, 1962).
Sir Ivor Jennings, *Cabinet Government* (C.U.P., 3rd Edition, 1959).
Lord Morrison, *Government and Parliament* (O.U.P., 3rd Edition, 1964).
Lord Campion (Ed.), *British Government Since 1918* (Allen & Unwin, 1950).
Lord Campion (Ed.), *Parliament—A Survey* (Allen & Unwin, 1963).
J. D. Stewart, *British Pressure Groups* (O.U.P., 1958).
R. T. McKenzie, *British Political Parties* (Heinemann, 2nd Edition, 1963).
S. A. Walkland, *The Legislative Process in Great Britain* (Allen & Unwin, 1968).
Patrick Gordon Walker, *The Cabinet* (Cape, 1970).
G. Marshall and G. C. Moodie, *Some Problems of the Constitution* (Hutchinson, 1961).
    See also Comments on Further Reading, p. 211.

# 3

## Prime Minister and Cabinet

---

Membership of the Cabinet. The responsibilities of the Prime Minister. The choice of Ministers. Organisation of duties. The relationship of the Prime Minister to the Cabinet, the Crown, Parliament, his party, the Civil Service, and to the community. The burden of Ministerial work. The idea of a small Cabinet.

THEME: The pressure of governmental work in modern times; its influence on the Prime Minister's position and on Cabinet organisation.

---

The number of Ministerial posts has risen remarkably since the First World War. Including the Ministers of State, Under-Secretaries, Parliamentary Secretaries, and other lesser posts the total is little short of one hundred. The holders of these offices are nominated by the Prime Minister, who also nominates the Cabinet. There will normally be some twenty members in the Cabinet, though in war-time urgency of decision makes necessary a smaller number. Winston Churchill's war Cabinet consisted of a maximum number of nine members, for instance. In peace-time the size of the Cabinet has usually varied little during the century. Lord Salisbury's Government at the beginning of the century had a Cabinet of twenty as did Mr. Attlee's Government at first in 1945. This tendency for most Prime Ministers to appoint Cabinets of virtually the same size suggests that there are certain basic considerations to be observed irrespective of the differing qualities of individual Prime Ministers.

From closer examination of the membership of the Cabinet it is apparent that certain Ministers will inevitably be included because of the importance of their office. The Foreign Secretary, Home Secretary, the Chancellor of the Exchequer, and the Lord Chancellor are all, almost *ex officio*, members of the Cabinet. Some Ministers will be members because of their representative capacity. The Secretaries of State for Scotland, Wales, and Commonwealth

Relations, come into this category, which can almost be defined as geographical representation.[1] A few members, the Lord President of the Council, the Lord Privy Seal and, often, the Chancellor of the Duchy of Lancaster, will be included, not because of the importance of their formal duties in connection with these posts, for they are almost nominal, but to allow some flexibility in the performance of new functions. Mr. Macleod, in the Macmillan Government, combined the office of Chancellor of the Duchy of Lancaster with that of Leader of the House. These 'spare' Ministers are also useful for their ability to act as chairmen of Cabinet Committees. The Lord President of the Council was chairman of the Cabinet Committee examining the plans for the nationalisation of industries in the first post-war Labour Government, and led several other Cabinet Committees too. The additional freedom of the non-departmental Ministers also enables them to lead important delegations. Mr. Heath, then Lord Privy Seal, fulfilled this role in respect of the 1962 European Common Market negotiations. The remaining places in the Cabinet are filled partly by reference to the function performed; thus the Secretaries of State for Defence, for the Environment, for Social Services, for Trade and Industry, and for Employment, have been included in Mr. Heath's Cabinet. Other leading Ministers are less assured of Cabinet rank. The Minister of Education, for instance, was excluded in 1951. But, in addition, the Prime Minister will choose members for personal reasons. The doctrine of collective responsibility means that there must be a strong sense of unity among Cabinet members, and some readiness to compromise is a desirable qualification. The Prime Minister must be guided in his choice, therefore, by his assessment of the willingness, or otherwise, of colleagues to recognise that extremes of individualism are as undesirable as extremes of loyalty.

Amongst all the Ministers of the Crown the Prime Minister, as his title suggests, is pre-eminent. He has been described as 'the first among equals' to stress the democratic nature of his position, but an examination of his responsibilities suggests that this is an underestimate, and that his powers between elections are very great indeed, stronger, for instance, than those of a President of the United States. One of his duties is already plain from a study of the

[1] In October, 1968, the Foreign and Commonwealth offices were combined.

way in which the Cabinet is composed. The choice of Ministers is essentially his own. There may be pressure for the inclusion of certain outstanding personalities amongst his colleagues, and he may yield to this pressure, but only if he is satisfied that his action will in no way weaken his own leadership or endanger Cabinet unity. These are the primary considerations which will influence his choice, and the popularity of possible Cabinet Ministers is only one factor in his decision. It may even be that he will offer a Cabinet post to someone who is not a Minister, or even an M.P. In forming his Cabinet in 1964, for instance, Mr. Wilson included Mr. Cousins as Minister of Technology, though the latter was not an M.P. In practice, however, a Minister chosen in this way becomes an M.P. as quickly as possible, either by means of a by-election or a life peerage. This practice illustrates the freedom of choice of the Prime Minister in a vital function of government.

Having chosen the Cabinet the Prime Minister must allocate the duties according to his judgment of the special abilities of the members. He must decide what Cabinet Committees there will be, appoint the Chairmen, preside over some Committees himself— Mr. Attlee was chairman of Committees for Commonwealth Affairs, Far Eastern Affairs, Economic Policy, Housing, National Health Service, Food and Fuel, and Indian Affairs, during his two Ministries, 1945–51—and keep in touch with the work of the other Cabinet Committees, where he does not preside himself. The importance of the guidance and co-ordination he supplies can be deduced from the vast range of topics discussed at Cabinet Committee meetings. The Prime Minister's central position admirably fits him to give advice to the chairmen of these Committees, and to individual Ministers. He can do so the more effectively since modern British leaders are likely to have acquired lengthy and varied political experience both as M.P.s and as Ministers before they become Prime Ministers. We are never again likely to have a twenty-four-year-old Prime Minister like Pitt, George III's nominee in 1783.

The Prime Minister organises the agenda of Cabinet meetings. He has been greatly helped in recent times by the work of the Cabinet Office. This organisation is valuable not only for its routine office activities and research findings from its statistical and planning sections, but also for the assistance which it can give to the Prime Minister in co-ordinating the activities of the Cabinet,

Cabinet Committees, and sub-committees. These are tasks which would be beyond the power of one man, but which nevertheless need central direction. The Cabinet Office is almost becoming a Prime Minister's Department on its own. In 1962 the post of Secretary to the Cabinet, which had been combined with the function of Head of the Civil Service, became a separate appointment. The salary has been fixed at an amount larger than that paid to the heads of Government Departments, an indication of its great and growing importance. The decision by Mr. Heath in October 1970 to create a central policy review staff to give an objective expert appraisal of the merits and consequences of Government policies will further strengthen Cabinet Office organisation; this will reduce the risk of departmental expertise becoming unduly influential.

The Prime Minister's task of acting as chairman of Cabinet meetings is of crucial importance. He has a heavy responsibility, for it is at these meetings that Government policy must be hammered into shape before it is transmitted to Parliament. The burden becomes additionally great if there are differences of opinion between Ministers at the meeting. The duty of reconciling these differences belongs directly to the Prime Minister; if he fails, he may shatter the Government and the party and leave his leadership self-condemned, as Balfour's was by 1905, though Balfour was working against difficulties which, objectively, invite sympathy. Differences within the Cabinet do not always have this spectacular effect, but the ultimate threat of an overthrow of the Government must always be present as a latent factor in any division of opinion. Prime Ministers, no doubt, are often successful in patching up differences, but the general public hears nothing of disputes successfully settled. Sometimes the dissentient at a Cabinet meeting gains little or no support from his colleagues, and then, if he persists in opposition, the only recourse open to him is resignation. This is less serious from the point of view of maintaining the Government in power, but it will still not be a cause of satisfaction to the Prime Minister who must be conscious at all times of the paramount need to maintain unity of outlook. No one has responsibilities akin to his in this vital respect. He is undoubtedly helped by the convention that votes are not taken at Cabinet meetings; instead, the Prime Minister declares the sense of the meeting, thus giving him more room for manoeuvre.

One of the most significant features which emerges from an analysis of the functions of the Prime Minister is that his personal influence is dominant in so many different phases of Government activity. The Queen's prerogative powers, for instance, are now harnessed with rare exceptions to Government policy; conventional constitutional usage and the close relationship which springs up between a monarch and the Prime Minister from their frequent contacts give the Prime Minister considerable influence over the remaining powers of the monarchy. He has the duty of keeping the monarch informed of political developments, and Lord Rosebery, for instance, when he was Prime Minister in 1894, was severely taken to task by Queen Victoria for failing to give her prior notice of the sharp criticisms he made of the House of Lords. The Prime Minister also advises the Crown on the use of the prerogative power of dissolution, and, except in unusual circumstances, this will be his personal decision (see Chapter 1). The prerogative powers of appointment are also exercised on the advice of the Prime Minister. Governmental posts, numbering over a hundred, are filled by his choice. He chooses the Governors of colonies, and can influence strongly the compilation of the Honours List, particularly in the creation of peers. He also appoints bishops, though the advice of the Archbishop of Canterbury should weigh heavily with him here; there is, too, a growing feeling that these episcopal appointments should be made exclusively by the Church itself without reference to lay opinion however distinguished. Apart from the formal relationship to the Crown in the exercise of the various prerogative powers, the Prime Minister will also act as a personal adviser to the monarch, particularly on matters such as the desirability of visits to Commonwealth and foreign countries. The consultations between the Queen and Mr. Macmillan which preceded the royal visit to Ghana in 1961, when there seemed to be an element of personal danger involved for the monarch, are an example.

Towards Parliament in general, and towards his own supporters there in particular, the Prime Minister has special responsibilities. The extension of the franchise and the reductions in the powers of the House of Lords have made it virtually certain that nowadays the Prime Minister will be a member of the House of Commons. The last Prime Minister in the House of Lords was Lord Salisbury who resigned in 1902. The extensive duties of the Prime Minister make it unlikely that he will hold the formal office of Leader of the House of Commons, but there will be many occasions during the life of his Ministry when he must be the official spokesman and defender of Government policy. He may have to defend one of his colleagues in difficulty, he may need to rally wavering elements in the party, he may need to take the lead over some vital national issue. These are great responsibilities and failure to inspire confidence in Government policies can only lead to defeat and resignation. Balfour's failure to unite the Conservatives over the Protectionist issue, and Chamberlain's failure to inspire confidence over the Government's measures to meet the German offensives of 1940 are instances. Effective leadership must be based on close contact with party opinion. The aloofness and reserve of Ramsay MacDonald and of Neville Chamberlain, and the indifference of Lloyd George to the need to secure maximum party support, all militated against sound leadership. Ideally the Prime Minister should have a personality which earns him not only the loyalty of his own party but also a measure of grudging respect from the Opposition. If, unlike MacDonald for instance, he takes some pleasure in the hurly-burly of debate, and has a combative nature, his duties in the House of Commons will run the more closely with his inclinations. Apart from these more stirring duties, it is also the responsibility of the Prime Minister to plan Parliamentary business with the Government Chief Whip, whose offices at 12, Downing Street are conveniently close.

Since the Civil Service, in its Administrative Grade particularly, provides the mechanism by which the decisions of the Government in Parliament can be put into effect, the Prime Minister has the ultimate authority for appointments to senior administrative posts. A change in Government means that a new set of personal relationships has to be established between the newly appointed Minister and the leading Civil Servants, such as the Permanent Secretary of his particular Department. The tradition of loyalty to the Minister, and concentration on the means of making a policy workable, irrespective of the worth of the policy itself, makes it improbable that Civil Servants will become at cross-purposes with their Ministers. If this does happen, however, it is undoubtedly the duty of the Prime Minister to resolve the crisis, and he can transfer a Permanent Secretary from one Department to another if he wishes. He will be reluctant to do this since, if it happened very often, it could destroy the goodwill that exists between the Civil Service and the Government. He will also be consulted about all new appointments and has the general responsibility for seeing that Government policy is being put into effect in an efficient and co-ordinated way by the many different Government Departments.

An account of the Prime Minister's duties lends some substance to the allegation that, between elections, his powers differ little from those of a dictator, not perhaps the ideological dictator of modern times, but the 'benevolent despot' of eighteenth-century history with his all-pervasive influence in society. Moreover, the holding of Summit conferences has added to the power of the position. There is, however, a fundamental difference as compared with dictators past and present, and that is in the Prime Minister's relationship to the general public. He must give them guidance and leadership, as Winston Churchill did during the war, or, in a rather different context, as Lord Attlee did in 1948, when he made his successful appeal to the London dockers to end their strike; to that extent there is some kinship between the direct personal impact on the nation exercised by a dictator and that exercised by a Prime Minister: this aspect of his work is, after all, a necessary adjunct of any leadership. The essential difference lies in the idea of account-ability to the nation. Now that television, in particular, has made possible more immediate contact between the Prime Minister and the people, explanation of Government policy through the tele-vising of party political talks, interviews, and great occasions, has become a familiar phenomenon. Consciousness of the need to pro-ject a favourable party image to increase prospects of success in any General Election, coupled with realisation of the value of securing popular support for any major issues of Governmental policy, have combined to make the nation much more conscious of the outlook and policies of the Prime Minister than ever before. In a sense, this has led increasingly to 'the cult of the individual', of which the Communists have been so critical in respect of their own past Governments, but the whole approach and manner of these public appearances in Britain make it plain that the Prime Minister is conscious of his accountability both to his party and to the nation.

It would take too long to analyse the functions of the many other Ministers of the Crown as fully as this. The Prime Minister's duties have merited special attention because of their paramount im-portance, and because of the argument that his powers have become dangerously extensive. His duties certainly require tremendous physical and mental resilience, and the briefest examination of the work of the chief Ministers of the Crown leads to the same conclusion, that the responsibilities of government have become so great that a fundamental reorganisation of duties may well become necessary. Lord Morrison's description in *Government and Parliament* of his daily duties during his extensive experience of Ministerial office gives a good insight into the obligations imposed.[1] The reading of official papers, attendance at the House of Commons, possibly to take a decisive part in proceedings there, directions to departmental officials, conferences, deputations, attendance at official functions, Cabinet meetings, and preparation for the next day's business, make heavy demands on the Minister's energy. Moreover, the weight of work is increased by knowledge of its importance and the far-reaching effects of any wrong decision. Nor is the strain greatly relieved at week-ends since the Minister will often need to attend functions and to deal with constituency problems. Speech-making has become more requisite now with the development of an educated and critical electorate, more avid for news and information than ever before. This burden of work applies to all Ministers but the consensus of opinion is that the duties of the Foreign Secretary, the Chancellor of the Exchequer, the Home Secretary, and of the ministers responsible for housing, local government, the social services, and employment, are particularly onerous; so too are those of the Lord President of the Council if he has the co-ordinating duties which Lord Morrison had in the Labour Government. The Ministers for Transport and Employment may find their duties suddenly extended by the onset of some special emergency such as strike action. There is little doubt that the strain of Ministerial life has shortened the political careers, and even the lives, of some of our post-war leaders. The particular strains of direction of foreign policy, involving the vital issues of war and peace, took their toll on Mr. Ernest Bevin, and later on Sir Anthony Eden (now Lord Avon), and the direction of the nation's economic policy, hampered by the many post-war difficulties, placed great strain on Sir Stafford Cripps in the post-war Labour Government.

Pressure of Ministerial business has led to an examination of possible remedies. The prospects are not very encouraging. The

[1] *Ibid.*, pp. 60–3.

essential consideration is whether there can be any delegation or division of duties. It is difficult to see that there is any possibility of a formal limitation of the functions of the Prime Minister. It is essential that he should be able to intervene, at times, to influence decisions of his Ministers, if only because the nature of his office gives him a deeper sense of national needs than anyone else. He may, therefore, have to overrule a partisan departmental policy from the wider knowledge which he has. His extensive functions prepare him admirably for this essential duty of co-ordination in the national interest. The strain is bound to be great, but he can safeguard himself, as Lord Attlee did, by some measure of delegation. Ministers of strong character, in charge of foreign affairs and economic affairs, for instance, can do much to ease the burden on the Prime Minister, and 'spare' Ministers such as the Lord President of the Council can be useful in that they can be made responsible for important sectors of government, possibly involving supervision of two or three individual Ministries. Thus, by wise selection of Ministers and by careful organisation, the Prime Minister can reduce his duties without losing effective control. The increased importance of the Prime Minister's position in this century has made it unlikely that Premiers will combine with their office that of any other Ministry, as MacDonald was Foreign Secretary, for instance, as well as Prime Minister in the first Labour Government, and as Sir Winston Churchill was Minister of Defence in his 1951 Government.

The idea of a division of duties has led to suggestions for a reorganisation of the Cabinet into two sections, an inner 'planning' Cabinet, and an outer ring of Ministers concerned with day-to-day management of Government Departments. There are several variants of the scheme but the best known is probably that put forward by Mr. Amery in *Thoughts on the Constitution*. He suggested that there should be a Cabinet of some half dozen members.[1] These Ministers would be freed of departmental duties. They would deal with current administrative problems by summoning the appropriate departmental Ministers to their meetings, but they would, in addition, have regular meetings to discuss future policy. Both administration and planning would be facilitated by the use of committees. These committees, dealing with matters of immediate urgency, would be presided over by one or other of the

[1] *Ibid.*, pp. 86–94.

super-Ministers. The committees concerned with future policy would be assisted by a research and planning staff. Government policy would be divided into broad groupings such as External Affairs, Economic Policy, and Social Welfare. Over each of these committees a super-Minister would preside unless, as might often happen, the Prime Minister himself attended. The Policy Committees would be responsible for the most effective use of national resources by means of long-term planning.

The plan has much to commend it. One of the main difficulties of Ministers is that it is very easy for them to get so heavily involved in the day-to-day running of their Departments that this factor, coupled with their Parliamentary duties, cramps their outlook, and as one problem presses hard on the heels of another, so it becomes less and less probable that they will be able to take the wider view of policies which would lead to effective long-term planning. Mr. Amery's scheme appears to remove this difficulty, and there would be the added advantage that, with smaller numbers to consult, decisions would be easier. Critics of the scheme are doubtful whether Mr. Amery's claim that there would be no divorce between policy and administration is justified. They feel that the creation of super-Ministers will accentuate a tendency already apparent, to concentrate effective power in the hands of fewer and fewer men. It is feared that these planners, increasingly remote from the realities of personal contact with the problems of day-to-day administration in the Departments, will busy themselves with the production of theoretical reforms of little practical value. Their position of supremacy would lead to a loss of contact with the general state of opinion both in their party and in the country. These criticisms are not entirely convincing. They are based on the assumption, probably false, that these Cabinet Ministers would devise their policies without reference to political realities. There is really no very strong evidence to believe that this is probable. They would be men with practical experience of the Government Departments they were supervising; even if their experience had been of other Government Departments — and this is unlikely — departmental problems have much in common, so that experience of one gives some guidance as to what may happen in another. Moreover, the Prime Minister at the moment performs very much the same functions as these co-ordinating Ministers and this role is not yet regarded as too exacting for one man to perform. The Cabinet Ministers would still be members of Parliament, they would still represent particular constituencies, and they would still depend for their continuance in office on party support, so that the criticisms made would not appear to have much substance. A criticism with rather more point to it is that the doctrine of accountability of Ministers is harder to apply when there is a supervising Minister as well as an individual Minister in charge of a Government Department. The inconvenience is increased when the supervising Minister is in the House of Lords, and this was a difficulty experienced in Sir Winston Churchill's 1951 Government. There was a small-scale experiment then with the idea of 'overlord' Ministers when Lord Woolton was given control of the Ministries of Agriculture and Food, then separate. Lord Leathers became responsible for the Ministries of Transport, Fuel and Power, and Sir Winston Churchill himself was Minister of Defence as well as Prime Minister. The fact that two of these Ministers were in the House of Lords necessarily made it difficult to allocate responsibility for policy decisions in a way acceptable to the House of Commons, but it is a defect which need not always apply.

Although there are objections to the scheme for a smaller Cabinet, they are not insuperable. It may be that the Cabinet suggested by Mr. Amery is too small in number, but a reduction in numbers along similar lines with some distinction between planning Ministers and those concerned with everyday policy would seem to be worthwhile. There are already signs that changes in this direction are taking place. It has been pointed out previously that the Cabinet is not ideally composed either in numbers or specialised knowledge for detailed policy-making (see Chapter 2). In practice, policy is formulated by consultation between the Prime Minister and a few leading Ministers, supplemented by the advice of Cabinet Committees, and of men with specialist knowledge of the problems involved. Mr. Amery's idea of relieving the 'policy' Ministers of the pressure of departmental business has also been partly realised by the appointment of Ministers of State to assist the Ministers in charge of large Government Departments. Ministers of State have been appointed, for instance, as deputies to the Foreign Secretary. It is in the major Departments especially that their ability to share the duties of the Minister is of the greatest value in enabling him to stand back a little from the furore of routine business. This is hardly the same as the more thorough-going suggestion for reorganisation put forward by Mr. Amery. It would be characteristic of the British approach, though, if re-organisation of the duties of Ministers took place in this piecemeal way rather than in the adoption comprehensively of some new scheme.

The tendency to group together ministries under a supervising Minister has another advantage in that it gives these super-Ministers the opportunity of dealing with the Prime Minister on a footing of great equality; their co-ordinating responsibilities add to their authority within the Cabinet. This is particularly significant in modern times when the political influences at work have accen-tuated the power of Prime Ministers to an extent where commen-tators are apt to speak of Prime Ministerial sovereignty as the hub of political action rather than Cabinet sovereignty.[1] They may be overstating their case. There are limitations on Prime Ministerial power both inside and outside Parliament, as has been shown. The overused phrase about Prime Ministers needing to be 'good butchers' of their fellow Ministers has sometimes led to the mis-taken belief that Prime Ministers can lay low Ministers with the berserk destructiveness of the Red Queen. No Prime Minister who did so would survive for long. Management of able and ambitious colleagues, and of party and public opinion, is far too subtle an art to be contrived by crude dictatorial methods of this kind. The 'butcher' analogy is plainly false. Are butchers ever con-fronted with resurrected cows indignant at their harsh treatment? The real danger is not that Prime Ministerial government will become tyrannical but that it will become inefficient through an undue pressure of responsibility upon the Prime Minister himself. The virtue of the Amery scheme is that it gives the Prime Minister valuable assistance in the heavy responsibility of co-ordinating administrative and legislative policy by a realistic degree of delega-tion of authority to the 'overlords'. Mr. Wilson's adoption of an Inner Cabinet, Mr. Heath's belief that modern Cabinets have tended to be unwieldy in size, and the frequent mergers of

[1] A useful argumentative analysis of this theme is provided in two contrasting accounts in *Parliamentary Affairs*, 'The Prime Minister's Power' by G. W. Jones (vol. XVIII, no. 2, Spring 1965), and 'The Prime Minister and the Cabinet' by J. P. Mackintosh (vol. XXI, no. 1, Winter 1967–8).

Government Departments in recent years[1] all provide evidence that the kind of Cabinet organisation which Amery envisaged may eventually emerge. The problem of adapting governmental structure to fit modern needs is obviously not confined to Britain alone. Even in authoritarian Russia, so long accustomed to one-man rule, the need for collective rather than individual leadership has been increasingly realised in the post-Stalinist era.

[1] In 1964 the three Service ministries were merged with the Ministry of Defence. In 1968 the Commonwealth Office, having previously absorbed the Colonial Office, was itself merged with the Foreign Office. At the same time the Ministry of Health and the Ministry of Social Security were merged. Under Mr. Heath the process has been more widely extended. The Ministry of Technology and the Board of Trade were merged to form the Department of Trade and Industry in October 1970. Simultaneously the Ministries of Housing and Local Government, Transport, and Public Building and Works, were grouped together under the aegis of a Secretary of State for the Environment.

FURTHER READING

B. E. Carter, *The Office of Prime Minister* (Faber, 1956).
Sir Ivor Jennings, *Cabinet Government* (C.U.P., 3rd Edition, 1959).
Rt. Hon. L. S. Amery, *Thoughts on the Constitution* (O.U.P., 1953).
Lord Campion (Ed.), *Parliament—A Survey* (Allen & Unwin, 1963).
Anthony King (Ed.), *The British Prime Minister* (Macmillan, 1969).
Patrick Gordon Walker, *The Cabinet* (Cape, 1970).
See also Comments on Further Reading, p. 211.

# 4

## Ministers and Civil Servants

An assessment of the authority of Civil Servants based on their influence over Parliamentary legislation, their contacts with official organisations, and their influence over administrative decisions. Administrative tribunals. The doctrine of Ministerial Responsibility and its importance. The Fulton Report, 1968.

THEME: Civil Service powers are increasing, but the doctrine of Ministerial Responsibility gives reasonable safeguards for the individual citizen.

In the intellectual ability of senior Civil Servants, in the closeness of their association with Ministers, in the extensive and important duties of the Civil Service, and in its permanence (for Governments change, but the Civil Service remains the same), there would seem to be strong reasons for believing that the influence of the Civil Service may be a powerful factor in the formation of Government policy. That Civil Servants are sheltered by anonymity does not make the situation any more reassuring. Nor does the fact that their numbers have increased by over half since pre-war days, partly because of the expansion of work of existing Government Departments, partly because of the creation of new Government Departments. The Ministries of Social Security, Technology, Employment and Productivity, Post and Telecommunications, and the Department of the Environment, for instance, have all been set up since 1914. In the distant period of the eighteenth century it was considered sufficient at one period to have only two Secretaries of State. Now Government activity has developed so much that it is doubtful whether even the present large number of Government Departments is enough, and from time to time suggestions are made for new Ministries; Ministers for Coastal Protection (against oil pollution), and for Justice, are possibilities.

Pressure of governmental work has led to an increase not only in the number of Civil Servants, but also in their power, since a certain measure of delegation of functions by Parliament to the Civil Service has become essential. Lord Acton's maxim that power tends to corrupt, and its exemplification in the corruption of the Civil Servants in France and Russia in the period preceding their Revolutions in 1789 and 1917, are disquieting reminders of the influence of an over-powerful Civil Service. They are restrained neither from below, since unlike politicians they have no constituents, and have no need to win elections, nor, in the instances quoted, were they restrained from above since the central Governments were little concerned with the implications of their policies in local matters. In more recent times, the German Government in the pre-Nazi period, and the French Government during the Third Republic, had to contend with some measure of opposition from the Civil Service, which obviously involved considerable obstruction in the application of policy. The dangers of a powerful Civil Service are only too apparent. Suggestions that the Civil Service has become too strong in Britain have been made. Lord Hewart's book *The New Despotism* is often quoted as an example of this criticism, and this was published as long ago as 1929. More recently, Civil Service influence on legislation, in the form of Statutory Instruments, and on administrative decisions, in episodes such as the Crichel Down inquiry of 1954, has led to renewed criticisms. It is appropriate, therefore, to examine what opportunities Civil Servants have for influencing governmental policy in Britain.

Legislative activity is primarily a matter for the Government and Parliament, but there are several stages in the process by which a bill becomes an Act where Civil Service influence is felt. There are some types of legislation, concerned with administrative neatness rather than with the initiation of some completely new service, where the senior Civil Servants may quite possibly have a fuller grasp of the requirements than the Minister himself. From their long experience of one particular Department they will have become aware of anomalies in legislation which necessitate the rewording of previous Parliamentary Acts. It may well come about that senior Civil Servants will be the initiators of legislation of this type by suggesting to their Minister the idea of amending legislation. The Minister will become conversant with the range and limits of the changes proposed, but the details of adjustment will largely be left to the Civil Servants themselves. Legislation of this 'tidying-up' kind involves no real risk of abuse of power, and it will have to clear the necessary procedural hurdles in the Houses of Parliament before it is accepted as an Act of Parliament.

A more interesting consideration is the degree of Civil Service influence in general legislation. At whatever level suggestions are put forward involving new legislation on major issues a preliminary committee will have to be appointed with clear terms of reference. Suppose, for instance, that it was suggested that there should be compulsory Civil Defence training for all fit persons between the ages of eighteen and twenty. Since Civil Defence is a Home Office responsibility the Minister would appoint the necessary committee, and, with the help of his senior advisers, would devise specific questions for them to answer. The members of the committee would be drawn largely, possibly exclusively, from his own Department. Detailed plans would involve consultation with a number of Government Departments, the Treasury and the Ministry for Employment being obvious examples in this instance, and the various research and statistical groups would be approached for information on the numbers of people involved in specific areas of the country. Local government authorities would have to be consulted on matters such as the availability of buildings for training centres. The results of the investigations of the committee would then be submitted to the Minister. If he is satisfied with the information given he is then in a position to make a report to the Cabinet, which itself is likely to have been the initiator of an idea as important as this. Up to this stage the work of the Civil Servants, though of value, has clearly been of secondary importance compared with the responsibilities of the Minister and of the Cabinet. The terms of reference for the Committee, and the decision on whether the information given provides a sound basis for legislation are matters which are decided by the politicians. This relationship, with the Civil Service concerned with the provision of information, and the politicians with the responsibility of decision, applies throughout most of the subsequent stages of the bill.

Once the Cabinet has approved the bill in principle, and the Legislation Committee of the Cabinet has decided when the bill is to be fitted into the Parliamentary time-table, the Minister, the departmental Civil Servants, and a Parliamentary counsel, will then spend some considerable time in devising the wording. After several drafts and meetings the bill is then ready for Parliament.

The early stages do not make heavy demands on the Civil Servants. The First Reading is a formality, and before the Second Reading a complete text of the bill must be made available to M.P.s. The Second Reading, the debate on the principles of the bill, can be an exhaustive test of the Minister's grasp of its implications. It would be difficult for a Minister who had allowed his Civil Servants to become dominant to disguise that fact. The exacting barrage of criticism from the Opposition, on major bills at least, leaves little hope of concealing ignorance. The Civil Servants provide the explanatory memoranda for the Minister's use to clarify difficult passages in the bill, but that is the limit of their influence. The crucial question of whether the bill will pass its Second Reading stage is decided not by the clarity of its wording, but by factors involving party loyalty and party policy over which Civil Servants have no influence at all. The Committee stage with its detailed analysis of each clause of the bill gives more opportunity for Civil Service influence. Civil Servants do not intervene directly in proceedings, but are present in the Committee room, and the Minister will often choose to consult them on the practical wisdom of accepting proposed amendments. This advice they are well-qualified to give from their long experience of assessing the probable administrative difficulties involved in making Parliamentary legislation work in practice. It is the Minister who decides, however, whether to accept their advice and it is the M.P.s serving on the Committee who decide by their votes what alterations shall be made at the Committee stage; these alterations are concerned with wording, not with the general import and principles of the bill. The Report and Third Reading stages are briefer. M.P.s may introduce additional amendments at the Report stage and this could lead to further consultations between the Minister and Civil Servant advisers, who are present in the House of Commons behind the Speaker's Chair, but in general these last stages of the bill are considerably less important than the Second Reading and Committee stages.

Assuming that the bill is introduced in the House of Commons, it then has to go through the same stages in the House of Lords. Since most Ministers are in the House of Commons it will often be necessary to nominate a Peer to pilot the bill through its various stages in the House of Lords. The growth of the practice of using Ministers of State as official deputies to the fully-fledged Ministers has made it easier to find in both Houses members with detailed knowledge of departmental work. This, in turn, makes it easier to ensure a smooth passage through the second House, since, if the Peer in charge of the bill is imperfectly acquainted with departmental practice, or has little prior acquaintance with the bill, this increases the responsibility of the Civil Servants concerned. Their advice will become correspondingly important, but the general form of the bill will already have been decided in its passage through the Lower House; any amendments introduced in the Lords, and subsequently rejected by the Commons, become the subject of consultation between the two Houses, so that there is no opportunity for unilateral action by Civil Service advisers.

Once the bill has gained Royal Assent, and the Minister has appointed the day when it will come into force, the Statutory Instruments, that is, the detailed regulations necessary to make the Act work, have to be issued, and the responsibility for devising them rests very largely on the Civil Service. It would be inappropriate and time-devouring for Parliament to concern itself with detail of this kind. Even in the nineteenth century, when political life was more leisurely and Statutory Instruments less numerous, matters of administrative detail were not normally considered by Parliament. There are a host of matters nowadays, such as insurance contributions and exceptions, national assistance, and health regulations, where either the complexity of the issue or the need for speedy action makes it expedient to rely on the specialist knowledge of Civil Servants. Their decisions are limited, however, by the fact that they cannot act beyond the scope of the powers conferred by the parent Act.

In addition, there are Parliamentary Committees specifically required to scrutinise Statutory Instruments. The House of Lords has had a Special Orders Committee since 1925. More important is the Statutory Instruments Committee set up by the House of Commons in 1944. This Committee is required according to its terms of reference, 'to consider every Statutory Instrument laid or laid in draft before the House . . . with a view to determining whether the special attention of the House should be drawn to it on any of the following grounds . . .', and these grounds, comprising broadly any irregular or unusual feature in the Instrument, are then stated. The findings of the Committee may lead to the moving of a prayer in the House of Commons to annul an unsatisfactory order. As a matter of Parliamentary convention members of the Committee itself are not expected to move these prayers, since their function is conceived simply in terms of the provision of information upon which other members may act. Otherwise criticism of a Minister by members of the Committee might be interpreted as part of a deliberately conceived campaign. Considering that there have been many thousands of Statutory Instruments since 1945, the numbers reported by the Committee for the attention of the House are very few, frequently less than ten a year. But the work of the Committee should not be under-rated. Apart from the possibility of causing action to be taken in the House of Commons over a particular order, the Committee has the power to issue statements on general principles relating to the issue of Statutory Instruments. These principles based on detailed observations of the form of the Instruments are valuable for the guidance of Civil Servants, as well as being, in effect, a means of circumscribing their authority in their subsequent attempts to devise the wording of Instruments satisfactorily. Civil Servants are keenly aware of the need to avoid actions likely to be criticised in Parliamentary Committees, and possibly in Parliament itself subsequently. This state of mind is produced not only by the fear that such criticism may jeopardise their careers, but also by the realisation apt to be felt in any historic organisation that actions are conditioned by tradition. In Britain the weight of tradition is heavily in favour of Civil Service dependence on Parliamentary authority. It is true, however, that Civil Servants have great powers of initiation of these Instruments within the terms of the parent Act. The extent to which Statutory Instruments can be made to work fairly depends, in the first place, on the approach of Civil Servants to their responsibilities, and on well-informed supervision by the Minister of the work of his Department.

There are some risks, therefore, that Civil Service influence on the making of Statutory Instruments may be imperfectly controlled, but in the devising of the parent Act the Government and the Minister must clearly have the dominant role. This does not accurately describe the situation where financial bills are involved since, in this respect, Treasury influence is very great indeed; its views are an important consideration also in deciding the fate of other bills which involve the spending of public money. The question of the relationship of the Treasury to Parliament is of extreme importance, and merits more detailed examination than is possible within the space of this chapter (see Chapter 6). The complexity and importance of decision-making in national financial policies have accentuated governmental dependence on Treasury expertise.

Apart from its work in connection with legislation the Civil Service has several other general administrative duties to perform. These duties give scope for decisions which may be resented, and it is in this sphere of activity that concern for individual rights has been most strongly felt in recent years. Surrounded by able and well-informed Civil Service advisers the Minister will feel amply justified in delegating to them important responsibilities. Senior Civil Servants will meet representatives of industry and local government for an exchange of views on the implications in practice of departmental policy. The Civil Servants may well have to give some guidance to those they meet, and, at the same time, discussions with the men and women who are experiencing the effects of Government decisions will give the Civil Servants an opportunity at first hand to assess the merits of that policy. The outcome of the meeting will be a report to the Minister and, if he feels it necessary, further meetings at which he himself may preside. There is a chance that a Minister, lacking in zeal or in time, may increasingly delegate this liaison work to Civil Servants so that his supervision becomes purely nominal. They will then, in effect, be discharging his powers, and, confident in the knowledge gained from their meetings with the various outside organisations, will have a rapidly diminishing respect for the ability of their Minister to give sound decisions. This is the situation which can come about through inadequate Ministerial supervision. It is not that the Civil Servants are consciously seeking power, but simply that the vacuum created by inadequate leadership will be filled by the expansion of the powers of the Civil Service, so that the processes of government may continue effectively. Nor is it at all certain that the Civil Servants would perform their additional responsibilities with any less wisdom and fairness than the Minister. It is certain, however, that the Civil Servants, sheltered by their anonymity and comparative immunity from the risk of dismissal, are much less vulnerable, and therefore much less sensitive, to public opinion

than their politician Minister. Since our constitutional system is
based on the ultimate accountability of the Government to the
people it is undesirable that Civil Servants should have much
freedom of decision in administration. While it is unfair to describe
them as 'paper workers', seeing little company except their own
kind, it is true that those whom they meet are the more able,
influential, and persuasive members of the community: sensitivity
to the feelings of the masses, essential for the politician, is not a
necessity for the Civil Servant. This is why it can be dangerous for
a Minister to delegate too extensively to his Civil Servants powers
of policy decision and interpretation. There are checks which can
be imposed, as will be seen later, but these will generally operate
after, and because some damage has already been done.

The danger of Civil Service influence becoming unduly assertive
in the co-ordination meetings with group organisations is only one
of the factors producing concern. These meetings, after all, are
only to implement and interpret policies which have already been
approved: even so they should be closely supervised by the
Minister. A more dangerous situation is produced when the Civil
Servants are in a position when they virtually initiate decisions.
Private Bill procedure, which can be expensive and slow, has been
partly superseded in recent years by the growing use of Provisional
Orders, which are subject to Parliamentary approval later. A local
authority may apply for a Provisional Order, or a Government
Department itself may by means of a draft order secure powers to
make possible some project, such as a large-scale road-building
scheme envisaged by the Ministry of Transport. The effective
power of decision rests with the Minister, but Civil Service influence can play a greater or lesser part in the decision according to
the relationship of the Minister and his advisers. Parliament must
give its attention predominantly to national matters, and the
intensity of scrutiny it can bring to bear on these decisions in local
matters is not very great, until after some complaint has already
arisen. There are means of making public objection to orders of
this kind, but these means are often only imperfectly understood,
and the individual citizen is apt to be out of his element in disputes
with the experts. A road-building scheme, in particular, will almost
certainly involve acquisition of land by means of Compulsory
Purchase Orders and these, too, have frequently been a subject of
complaint, partly because of their infringement of individual

freedom, partly because the compensation given to the owner has
fallen short of the price to be obtained from a normal private sale
on the open market.

The powers of compulsion vested in Government Departments
have grown in recent years with the increasing centralisation of
administration, and the tacit acceptance of the fact that administrative efficiency may make necessary further reductions of individual liberties. It has led to the ejection of farmers on the grounds
that they are incapable of performing their work effectively, and it
has led twice in recent years to serious Parliamentary concern over
departmental powers for the compulsory acquisition of land. The
first occasion concerned some seven hundred acres of land at
Crichel Down which had originally been acquired by the Air
Ministry in 1937 by compulsory purchase. After the war the land
was handed over to the Ministry of Agriculture. It was decided by
this Ministry to let the land, which was a perfectly reasonable
decision, although many people, including a Lieutenant-Commander Marten, were hoping for an outright sale. Marten's
father-in-law had owned some of the original acreage acquired by
the Air Ministry in 1937. A tenant was then found, recommended
by the estate agents acting on behalf of the Permanent Commis-
sioners of Crown Lands. The Civil Servants at the Ministry of
Agriculture failed to inform the prospective purchasers, as they
should have done, of their proposed action, and these people felt
that the omission to do so was irregular and high-handed. Marten,
in particular, was given active support by several M.P.s in pressing
the matter in the House of Commons, where, following unsatisfactory answers at Question-time, a full debate took place. Pressure in
the House of Commons by supporters of Lieutenant-Commander
Marten led to the appointment of a judicial inquiry. When the
report was published, criticism of the Minister and of senior Civil
Servants was so pointed that Sir Thomas Dugdale, then Minister
of Agriculture, felt obliged to resign. The case roused considerable
concern and led to the issue of a warning to Civil Servants by the
Permanent Secretary to the Treasury of the dangers involved in
any abuse of their powers. Furthermore, one of the Civil Servants
involved was transferred to other duties. The situation was the
more disquieting in that the actions of the Ministry might not have
been effectively challenged at all had it not been for the energetic
persistence of Lieutenant-Commander Marten.

It was felt for some years after 1954 that the Crichel Down episode was an isolated one, and that the stir it created had virtually removed fears of a repetition. In 1970, however, the Compton Bassett case roused fresh fears that administrative decisions could ride roughshod over the claims of individual citizens. The Air Ministry, in 1942, acquired 37 acres of land in Compton Bassett from a Mr. Henly at a price of £41 an acre. The land was subsequently found to contain industrial sand and was sold by the Defence Ministry to a major sand-producing firm as part of a 100-acre plot for £500 an acre. The Henly family would have been prepared to make a realistic bid for the original 37 acres, but the disposal of the land as a single 100-acre plot placed it beyond their means. They felt that they should have been given first refusal rights for the original acreage: a statement by Sir Thomas Dugdale in 1954 had recognised that the former owners of compulsorily acquired agricultural land should be given a special opportunity to repurchase this land when it was no longer required by the Government. The Defence Ministry's view was that the land had ceased to be predominantly agricultural since planning permission for sand extraction had been obtained. Furthermore Sir Thomas Dugdale's statement had also asserted the right of the Government to judge each case on its own merits; then, too, it was the duty of the Government to protect public interest by securing the best bargain possible for the land; 'administrative clarifications' in 1957, 1958, and 1966, had buttressed the legality of the Government's actions even more firmly: the Parliamentary Commissioner, to whom appeal was made, supported the view that no maladministration had taken place. Nevertheless the case led to strong protests in both Houses of Parliament. There was grave doubt over the extent to which the administrative revisions since 1954 had been adequately publicised and considered: beyond this was the frustrating feeling that natural justice seemed to stand little chance against administrative fiat.

In order to deal with objections by citizens against policies which may be injurious to them, several Departments make use of administrative tribunals. They have been used since the war for matters such as appeals for deferment of national service, for hearing objections to development plans, and for problems involving pensions and national insurance. These tribunals are recognised to be necessary. The probable alternative would be to make

use of the law-courts, but this would lead to an undesirable con-
gestion of business there, and would be fundamentally inappropriate since decisions at these tribunals are not judicial in the fullest
sense; they have to be based at times on expediency, and for their
settlement require the detailed expert knowledge of the departmental officials. Moreover, the flexibility and informality of
administrative tribunal procedure may well be advantageous to the
citizen whose interests are affected. The boundaries of a judge's
authority are limited by statutes and Common Law, but tribunal
members have greater scope for avoiding a mechanical interpretation of the laws. This greater discretion, however, carries with it
greater risks, and emphasises the need for close Ministerial and
Parliamentary supervision. The safeguards which are so scrupu-
lously provided in a court of law were very imperfectly applied
until the Government implemented the main recommendations
embodied in the report made by the Franks Committee in 1957.
Previously the citizen, lacking legal representation and adequate
knowledge of the issues involved, was often unable to state his case
properly, and an imperfect appeal system, which gave the Minister appellate powers in matters concerning his own Department,
meant that the danger of unfair decisions was greatly magnified.

Those recommendations of the Franks Report acceptable to the
Government were embodied in the Tribunals and Inquiries Act of
1958, and the Town and Country Planning Act of 1959. By the
former act a Council on Tribunals for England, Wales, and Scotland was set up, appointed jointly by the Lord Chancellor and by
the Secretary of State for Scotland; its purpose is to exercise
general oversight over the composition and procedure of tribunals.
The Franks Committee had advocated that tribunal proceedings
should be based on the three principles of openness, fairness, and
impartiality. The detailed application of these principles in practice
could obviously not be defined by statute alone, but Ministries
have brought these principles specifically to the notice of officials
involved in tribunal work. The Act also effected an improvement
in that members of the public concerned now receive much fuller
information than before about the reasons for Compulsory Purchase Orders, and the reasons for refusal of planning permission.
In connection with the latter there is, under the Town and Country
Planning Act of 1959, a right of appeal to the courts when planning
permission is refused.

This recent legislation has strengthened the position of the citizen in relation to Government Department decisions, but defects still remain. One of these springs from the fact that the Franks Committee was limited in its terms of reference to considering defects evident in quasi-judicial procedure. Many administrative decisions involve no such formal mechanism and as Mr. Utley has pointed out, 'it cannot be made too clear that the Committee did not consider such circumstances as those of Crichel Down within its terms of reference'.[1] Another possible weakness in the present situation concerns appeal procedure. Appeals to courts of law, or to superior tribunals, are not absolutely debarred. There are difficulties to be considered, however. Appeals to the courts may only be on a point of law, and tribunal decisions may well produce a strong sense of grievance without infringement of the law. Appeals to superior tribunals are only possible when there exists a definite hierarchy of tribunals. It may happen, for example, that a tribunal of first instance is very strongly composed in its membership, and in that event there may not be a superior tribunal. It should be added, in fairness, that unlimited freedom of appeal would be very time-wasting, and that the courts of law are by their nature far better fitted to deal with the legal matters which are rarely in dispute than they are with the discretionary judgments which are much more frequently controversial. A further protection for the citizen exists in the fact that appeals are now more likely to go to an appellate tribunal rather than to the Minister himself, though this is not invariable. Furthermore the Council on Tribunals is empowered to propose new rules for the conduct of tribunal proceedings, thus giving further scope for improving the situation.

Striking a balance between the rights of the citizen and administrative convenience is far from easy however. The report of the Council on Tribunals (March, 1962) on the Essex 'chalk-pit case' has given some insight into the problems which can still arise. A company, known as Heath and Son, Ltd., was refused permission by the Saffron Walden Council to work chalk on land in Essex on the grounds that the chalk-dust would be detrimental to pigs and ponies on the adjacent land. An inspector's inquiry supported the Council's view. The company appealed against this decision and, after a ten months' delay, the Minister of Housing and Local

[1] T. E. Utley, *Occasion for Ombudsman*, p. 27.

Government allowed the appeal, following consultation with the Minister of Agriculture. One of the objectors to the chalk-pit working, a Major Buxton, appealed to the High Court against the Ministry decision, but the High Court could find no legal basis for action. To the objectors the disturbing feature about the case was the way in which further advice was taken by the Minister of Housing and Local Government, namely from the Minister of Agriculture. It was felt that this fresh advice should either have been obtained earlier so that it might have been made known at the inspector's inquiry, or that a fresh inquiry should have been started so that the parties concerned might state their views on this advice from the Ministry of Agriculture. The essence of the matter was the old maxim that justice should not only be done but that it should be seen to be done. This was apparently the view of the Council on Tribunals. Following the case it proposed that when the Minister intends to disagree with his inspector's recommendation he will notify the parties concerned so that they can protest before a decision is made. Furthermore if fresh evidence becomes available after an inquiry any of the parties can ask for a re-opening of the inquiry.

It is evident from the practices considered in this chapter that the Executive has considerable latitude in making decisions. It is the more important, therefore, that the relationship of the Minister to his Civil Servants should be closely defined so that responsibility for actions can be fairly assigned. This does not remove the possibility of maladministration but makes it less likely. This was more fully realised after the Crichel Down case, and Sir David Maxwell Fyfe, then Home Secretary, made a statement defining Ministerial Responsibility in this connection.[1] From this it became clear that if a Civil Servant is merely carrying out an order given by the Minister the latter must obviously bear full responsibility. This responsibility is hardly, if at all, diminished if the Civil Servant's action is in accordance with the known policy of the Minister. The Civil Servant has to use some degree of initiative in decisions, and if he acts in good faith, as he believes the Minister would wish him to do, it would be unsatisfactory for the Minister to shield himself by disowning responsibility for the action. On the other hand, there are occasions in large and busy Government Departments when Civil Servants exceed their authority and act in a way of which the

[1] House of Commons Debate, July 20th, 1954, cols. 1285 ff.

Minister would certainly disapprove. It may be a relatively minor fault which is exposed, as, for instance, when the stationery of one Government Department was used by an employee a few years ago for distributing party propaganda. The Minister cannot be held responsible for every peccadillo committed by the thousands employed in his Ministry. He must, however, explain the position to Parliament and take the necessary corrective action. The same principle applies if a major fault in the working of a Government Department is exposed. If it is sufficiently serious the Minister may feel obliged to resign, as Sir Thomas Dugdale did after the Crichel Down episode. On the other hand, the defection of Burgess and Maclean to Russia, though obviously of serious importance, could not reasonably be made the occasion for censure of the Minister or Civil Servants, since the Fuchs case and other comparable examples since the war have shown how easy it is for individuals to conceal their political allegiance from those with whom they work.

The doctrine of Ministerial Responsibility, therefore, has to be applied with some discrimination, but there is no doubt that it is taken seriously. This is a factor of considerable importance in assessing the relationship of the Minister to his Civil Servants and is buttressed by the fact that the Minister, in conjunction with the Treasury, has effective powers of discipline over his Department. It is important to realise also that Ministerial Responsibility does not only apply when some aspect of maladministration is publicly revealed. It is a factor which must influence the whole day-to-day management of the Department. Lord Morrison in *Government and Parliament* made it plain that Civil Servants prefer to have a vigilant and energetic Minister,[1] and a Minister with these qualities, from his wide experience of the practical effects of policy decisions, will often be able to give valuable guidance to Civil Servants, thus removing by anticipation any undesirable features from administrative decisions. This is the best form of Ministerial Responsibility.

If Civil Servants are to perform their tasks competently, then plainly the quality of the personnel and of their training is of paramount importance. The internal development of the Civil Service was broadly conditioned for over a hundred years by the recommendations made in the Northcote–Trevelyan Report of 1854.

[1] *Ibid.*, Ch. XIV.

This might be construed as a criticism and in some ways it is. The gifted amateur, better equipped by his education to solve the administrative problems of Ancient Greece or Rome than of modern Britain, may seem an anachronism only possible in a country where respect for tradition has disastrously parted company with common sense. Yet, judged by pragmatic standards, the Victorian reforms of the Civil Service were remarkably successful in producing Civil Servants whose intelligence, industriousness, and integrity are virtually universally accepted. Nevertheless, the growing complexity of modern governmental problems and knowledge of the different approaches adopted in France and North America, particularly, towards the problems of the organisation and training of the Civil Service led in 1966 to the appointment of the Committee on the Civil Service under Lord Fulton. In its Report, published in 1968, the basic criticism made of the Civil Service was that it was 'still essentially based on the philosophy of the amateur'. As a consequence there were deficiencies, particularly in the key Administrative Grade, of specialist and managerial skills and a lack of contact between Civil Servants and the rest of the community. An unnecessarily elaborate division of the Civil Service into many grades and classes hampered mobility for the able man eager to advance his career rapidly.

The major recommendations made by the Committee were as follows. A Civil Service Department with a Minister of its own, who would also be a member of the Cabinet, should be set up; the Permanent Secretary of this Department should be designated Head of the Home Civil Service. This was more clear-cut than the previous arrangement by which the Treasury was responsible for Civil Service pay and management. The new Department was also to absorb the Civil Service Commission, formerly responsible for recruitment. There was little doubt that the creation of this new Department would give the Civil Service the valuable advantage of unified control, and the Labour Government brought it into being in November, 1968. The Government also accepted the recommendation for the abolition of classes within the Service, which can similarly be regarded as an important step towards unification. The Committee made several recommendations designed to strengthen the Service in its professional and managerial skills. It advocated, for instance, that a Civil Service College should be established to provide training courses in administration and management. This, too, was accepted by the Government. The concept of providing courses of this kind was by no means new. Courses, extending for twenty weeks, at the School of Administrative Studies had been in existence before this, and though very brief compared to the two and a half years spent by French Civil Servants in rigorous and specific training for their work, were a useful adjunct to the experience acquired daily in departmental administrative work. The formal establishment of a College, however, should lead to a great expansion in the numbers of courses and in the numbers of Civil Servants receiving specialist training.

Other recommendations by the Committee, though superficially desirable, took too little account of the human factors which, fortunately, prevent institutions from being manipulated as if they were computers. Specialists, it was suggested, should be trained in administration; administrators should be trained in specialisation. Promotion procedures should be rationalised so that all have the opportunity to progress as far and as fast as possible. There should be greater mobility between the Civil Service and other employments; whether this can be achieved in practice remains uncertain, and it is not self-evident that it is even desirable as a principle. The creation of management units in each major department was also proposed, no doubt with an eye to business efficiency, though the terms are not necessarily compatible. Each major Department should, the Committee suggested, have a planning unit responsible for long-term policy planning and headed by a senior policy adviser working closely with the Minister. This official would be additional to the Permanent Secretary, who would retain his overall responsibility, under the Minister, for the Department.

There is a streak of unrealistic idealism about several of these proposals which makes it unlikely that all, or even many, of them will have great influence on the running of the Civil Service. In its own unspectacular way the Civil Service had been moving towards greater flexibility in recruitment, training, and promotion procedures. 'The cult of the amateur' so roundly condemned in the Report scarcely tallies with the favourable comments on the professionalism and industriousness of Civil Servants made by post-war politicians of both major parties. Even if this criticism were fair, and this is at least doubtful, it is not immediately obvious that the cult of the specialist is an improvement. Professional advisers, from outside the Civil Service if necessary, can be, and are, consulted as required. The senior Civil Servant has to advise the Minister on general policy issues in which specialist knowledge is one factor but not the only one. The adviser therefore needs to have the quality of mind which can give specialist knowledge its due proportion of attention but no more. Is it likely that a specialist adviser would be capable of the same restraint? Nevertheless, those recommendations of the Committee, mentioned earlier, which have been accepted by the Government, unquestionably mark an advance in the organisation of the Civil Service. Civil Servants, particularly those in senior departmental positions, have a crucial role in modern government and it is clearly undesirable that their effectiveness should be reduced by organisational weaknesses.

In this chapter the main purpose has been to examine the relationship of the Minister to his Civil Servants. The influence of the latter over non-financial bills is normally slight; in this respect, they have a useful but subordinate role. They have wide powers in the devising of Statutory Instruments, and it is difficult for Parliament to supervise all the details involved in this form of delegated legislation. Over financial matters their power is very great, as will be seen later. In matters of policy decision the situation has dangers too, since basically it rests on the variable factor of the relationship between the Civil Servant and his Minister. It is some protection that the Civil Service itself has a tradition of impartial administration, and that the Permanent Secretary to the Civil Service Department has disciplinary powers over Civil Servants, as the Ministers have also. These internal factors may modify policy decisions in favour of the citizen, but are insufficient in themselves as absolute guarantees of individual rights. Whether such guarantees exist for the citizen in his relationship both with the Departments and with the Government remains to be seen in the next chapter.

FURTHER READING

Lord Morrison, *Government and Parliament* (O.U.P., 3rd Edition, 1964).
T. A. Critchley, *The Civil Service Today* (Gollancz, 1951).
G. A. Campbell, *The Civil Service in Britain* (Pelican Books, 1955).
T. E. Utley, *Occasion for Ombudsman* (Johnson, 1961).
Lord Bridges, *The Treasury* (Allen & Unwin, 1963).
B. Chapman, *British Government Observed* (Allen & Unwin, 1963).
W. J. M. Mackenzie and J. W. Grove, *Central Administration in Britain* (Longmans, 1957).
Lord Fulton, *Report of the Committee on the Civil Service* (H.M.S.O., 1968).

See also Comments on Further Reading, p. 211.

# 5

# The Redress of Grievances

Historical basis for the redress of grievances. Methods of expressing grievances and an assessment of their worth: letters, lobbying, Parliamentary Questions, petitions, pressure-groups. The possibility of legislative action. The historic freedoms and their present-day relevance. Additional protection needed for the citizen in modern conditions. The Parliamentary Commissioner.

THEME: The traditional guarantees of citizens' freedoms are losing their effectiveness and new forms of protection are required.

The increasing power of the Executive in modern times is only too apparent; yet in Britain law, strongly reinforced by custom, secures essential freedoms for the citizen. Moreover, the long struggle for supremacy between the monarchy and Parliament in the seventeenth century was based in the first place on the principle that there should be 'redress of grievances before supply'. In defending its own constitutional rights so zealously Parliament was also fighting the war on behalf of the individual citizen. It is obvious that Parliament was not a fully representative institution in the seventeenth century, and was not to be so until universal franchise was achieved in 1928, yet some of the principles secured during the struggle with the Stuart Kings, such as freedom of speech in Parliament, the abolition of prerogative courts, and the removal of royal authority to levy taxes, concerned the citizen as much as they concerned the position of Parliament in the constitution. In demanding that redress of grievances should precede supply the Parliamentarians were thinking of their own position in relation to the monarchy; the benefit to the mass of the citizens was incidental but no less real. In modern times there has been a change of outlook. Parliament still has the duty of acting as a check on any abuse of authority by the Executive, that is, the

Government and its various subordinate instruments of power, but in this capacity nowadays M.P.s are less conscious of constitutional rivalry with the Executive and more aware of the need to give the fullest ventilation to the grievances of citizens. The extension of the vote has obviously had some influence in this respect. It would appear, therefore, that there are strong historical, legal, and practical grounds for expecting that a citizen with a grievance against the Government would command vigorous support in the House of Commons.

Assuming then that a citizen has a grievance against any manifestation of Government activity he will probably seek a remedy first by writing to the Government Department concerned. Sometimes, if there are local offices of the relevant Ministry, the citizen may call there to discuss his grievance. Should these procedures fail to give him satisfaction he may then have recourse to a number of other methods. If his grievance is shared by many others, as it might be, for instance, when pits are closed down by the National Coal Board, then deputations of miners to the Coal Board, and to lobby M.P.s at Westminster are possible. Lobbying has become a familiar routine in recent years; it has been used by miners, teachers, and car-workers amongst others. There is no decisive evidence to indicate that it is a successful method of remedying complaints. It gives them a brief publicity, soon submerged in the flood of world news which pours out every day from radio, television and the Press. In a sense it can be argued that lobbying is almost an admission of defeat, a desperate expedient devised to stimulate M.P.s into more vigorous action than they would be likely to undertake in the ordinary way. Very often lobbying simply underlines the obvious, that a certain group of the community is discontented with some aspect of Government policy. M.P.s will know this already, and, as lobbying is generally employed over matters where a firm Government decision has recently been made, neither Government supporters nor the Opposition can do very much about it. Lobbying, therefore, seems an empty form of protest so far as securing a remedy is concerned, though it may make some M.P.s more vividly aware of the nature of the grievance than they were before.

It is also possible for groups or for individuals to write or to visit their M.P. privately in the hope that he will act as an intermediary for their complaint. He may either write to the Minister concerned, or, if this fails to produce satisfaction, he may ask a question in the House of Commons. It was in this latter way, for instance, that the Crichel Down case, mentioned in the last chapter, was first forced upon the attention of the House of Commons. Grievances are not always so spectacular, but they may be equally important for the individuals concerned. A refusal by a Service unit to grant compassionate leave, for instance, will only affect a very small number of people, but it could well be the subject of a Parliamentary question. There are occasions when a question in the House is an effective way of dealing with a complaint. This is particularly so when it can be demonstrated that the complaint stems from high-handed actions by the Executive. To demonstrate this is far from easy, however, for the administrators are likely to have a more detailed knowledge of their powers than the individual has of his rights. Moreover, as a Parliamentary question is sometimes a last resort following a long period of correspondence, concessions by the Minister answering the questions are by no means certain. By means of supplementary questions, allowed at the discretion of the Speaker, the questioner may be able to put the Minister at such a disadvantage that he can successfully press for the matter to be raised again in the Debate on the Adjournment. Factors other than the merits of the issue, however, such as the availability of Parliamentary time and the power of a well-prepared Ministerial answer to avoid controversy, have a bearing on whether the matter is likely to be discussed again. At one extreme, therefore, the Parliamentary question can be a very damp squib in which an M.P. raises the issue, the Minister gives a smooth but not very revealing answer, the M.P. follows with an ironic or critical supplementary question, and there the matter rests. At the other extreme a question may touch on a matter so fundamental that the Government may appoint a Committee of Inquiry and its report may well lead to new legislation. The setting-up of the Franks Committee on Administrative Tribunals and the resulting legislation provide an example of this process. In general, however, it would be unduly complacent to believe that Question-time in the House provides a universal remedy for all grievances.

It is possible that a Parliamentary question which does not receive a satisfactory answer may become the subject of the Debate on the Adjournment. As the Whyatt Report[1] points out, the pro-

[1] *The Citizen and the Administration*—a report by Justice, pp. 38–44.

cedural apparatus both for the Parliamentary question and the Debate on the Adjournment is imperfectly adjusted for the redress of grievances springing from a dispute between a Government Department and a citizen. The essential weakness is embodied in the Report's comment that 'the proceedings which began as an investigation have turned into a contest in which the spokesman on each side identifies himself with his cause and consequently it is rare for either side to give any ground; moreover it is often an uneven contest in the sense that the Minister has access to documents and information which are denied to his opponent'.[1] The most conspicuous criticism of a Parliamentary tug-of-war of this kind is that the procedure is simply not appropriate to the problem raised. There is admittedly the further expedient of an *ad hoc* inquiry ordered by the Government on matters considered sufficiently important. Yet this is too monumental a process to be used very often and is clearly of remote value to the citizen suffering from hardship of individual but not national importance.

The other means of securing Parliamentary redress of grievances are more circuitous, and some of them probably of negligible value. Petitions have a lengthy ancestry. In the early history of Parliament, in the fourteenth century, petitions were the normal method of drawing attention to grievances. Later on they reached their most spectacular form in the bulky petitions presented by the Chartists to the House of Commons in 1839 and 1842. The frivolous forgery of signatures and the theatrical method of presentation brought petitions into disrepute. In modern times the details of the form and presentation of petitions have been rigidly prescribed. They are occasionally used still. Some citizens of Orpington, for instance, sent a petition to Parliament in February, 1962, praying for an early by-election, on the grounds that they had had no M.P. since the resignation of their previous representative some months before. Petitions are not a very convincing form of argument however. The motives for signing them may be very mixed and they are accordingly liable to be received with some cynicism by the House. In an educated and politically informed society the mere accumulation of signatures does not significantly add to the force of the arguments used, and the petition procedure seems almost archaic.

Special interest groups—the 'pressure-groups'—are more effective

[1] *Ibid.*, p. 41.

in the removal of specific grievances, though, as has been seen (Chapter 2), their influence on policy-making is much less certain. They vary enormously in size. There are the Trade Unions which sponsor approximately 100 Labour M.P.s, the Co-operative Societies, which are also an integral part of Labour Party organisation, professional associations such as the National Union of Teachers and the National and Local Government Officers' Association, which are not committed to any one political party, groups such as the Federation of British Industries, which protects the interests of industrial management, and a large number of small societies such as the Lord's Day Observance Society and the Anti-Vivisection League which are concerned with narrower objectives. The term 'pressure-group' is sometimes used with a rather sinister connotation, as if M.P.s were no more than ventriloquists' dummies, the uncritical mouthpieces of shadowy groups whose activities are none too clearly discerned. 'Pressure-group' is, however, simply a new name for a very old form of activity. The Church, the barons, and landowners have all belonged to pressure-groups in the past and provided a greater threat to social progress than the pressure-groups of the present day. Sometimes these groups have been the source of valuable reforms. The emancipation of women, for instance, came about through the persistent advocacy and action of groups such as the National Society for Women's Suffrage founded in 1867, and the Women's Social and Political Union founded in 1903. The tactics of the extreme suffragettes may have been faulty, but the existence of these organisations undoubtedly hastened the movement towards greater equality of the sexes.

The great advantage which these groups have over the individual is that Governments are much more likely to take account of their influence in modifying legislation. The possibility of an individual being able to influence Government legislation can be almost discounted. If his grievance is such that it needs new legislation to remove it, his prospects of success are slight. He may be able to induce some appropriate authority to introduce a Private Bill, but because of the expense involved in employing counsel and summoning witnesses at the Committee stage if the bill is opposed this is not a very popular form of action. It is conceivable, but highly improbable, that an M.P. would see in the grievance of a constituent a general defect in the national system which could be righted by a Private Member's Bill; but he would have to be lucky in the ballot for the right to introduce such a bill, and he would have to be luckier still to manage the difficult process of getting the bill through all its stages in Parliament. So far as a citizen has any personal initiative in righting a grievance it is plain that his best chance, by far, will be to join a group or society to press his claims. Otherwise, in the procedures available to the individual citizen there are elements of chance which make it uncertain whether satisfaction can always be given.

Pressure-groups are far better fitted than individual citizens to protect rights and interests against undue encroachment by Governments. The solitary heroism of a John Hampden battling against Executive authority may occasionally find a modern counterpart, but this grows less and less likely. Most pressure-groups have the funds, experience, organisation, and contacts to wage a continuous campaign to secure and maintain what they regard as essential rights, and they can do so much more effectively than any private citizen. This is by no means intended to suggest that pressure-groups have a very high degree of success in achieving their aims. Governments are chosen by popular mandate; their strength is buttressed by firm party discipline and by the specialist knowledge of departmental officials; they are responsible for the whole ambit of policy. Against this formidable array of power it is not easy for a pressure-group to establish that its own sectional interests should have priority over everything else.

In assessing the influence of pressure-groups it should be remembered too that there are some variables to be taken into account. There is plainly a relationship, for instance, between size and influence in a country where Governments are chosen by regular free elections. The Trade Union movement, with some ten million members, is patently a force which Governments must take into account in their legislative plans, as the fate of the 1969 Industrial Relations Bill conspicuously demonstrated. When the unions can speak with one voice, as they can on the general principles to be observed in wage negotiations, then their power is particularly great; organisationally, they are assisted by the fact that the Trades Union Congress can speak collectively for a very large number of the individual unions. This identity of interest does not operate in all circumstances; individual unions, however powerful, have achieved only moderate success in persuading Governments of the justice of their claims. The Miners' Union, for instance, experienced one set-back after another in the inter-war years. Since the war sectional interests in the mining industry have clearly been subordinated to national interests; the number of coal-mines was reduced by almost a third and the number of miners by about a sixth between 1949 and 1960. This process has continued subsequently. Since there were twenty-seven sponsored Members of the 1966 House of Commons representing mine-workers, and since coal-mining is still not of negligible importance in the economy, it might have been expected that mining, as a pressure-group, would have been able to mount strong resistance to change. In practice this was not so. 'The Trade Unions', said Sir Walter Citrine in 1946, 'have passed from the era of propaganda to that of responsibility.' The prevalent impression that the British Trade Unions use the strike weapon heedlessly was, until recently perhaps, hardly justified. Even the unofficial 'wild-cat' strikes have been relatively rare. By international standards post-war Britain has been one of the most industrially peaceful nations, even though the temptation to use the strike weapon to resist redundancy in the mining and railway industries, for instance, must have been strong. The 'respectability' of modern British Trade Unions sets a boundary to the pressures which individual unions are prepared to exert. Consequently in dealing with pressure-group action of this kind, a resolute Government, with a convincing policy, can be reasonably certain that it will not be hampered in achieving its objectives by protracted irresponsible opposition. There is an important distinction to be made, however, between Trade Unions as pressure-groups and Trade Unionism as a pressure-group. The failure of the Labour Government to secure the acceptance of the Industrial Relations Bill was not only an obvious demonstration of the power of Trade Unionism, far greater than that of individual Trade Unions, but also a reminder that the potential power of a very large pressure-group could become alarmingly great. If, for instance, Trade Unionism were to become a kingdom within a kingdom, conducting its own negotiations with employers and producing in effect an economic policy of its own devising, then, in this vital sphere of affairs, the Government would become merely an irrelevance. Pressure-groups are undoubtedly an essential feature of democratic government, but whether the tail should be allowed to wag the dog is another matter.

Establishing a satisfactory relationship with pressure-groups presents difficulties for any Government. The degree of responsiveness cannot always be the same; relations are conducted against a shifting background of political and economic circumstances. From 1945, for instance, agriculture has been given substantial financial support by Governments. The need to give this country a degree of self-sufficiency in food production, partly for defence and partly to reduce food imports damaging to the balance of payments, predisposed Governments to give a very favourable hearing to representations made on behalf of the farming community by the National Farmers' Union, which includes about 90 per cent of British farmers. On the other hand, when the economic situation began to deteriorate in the early 1960s, reductions were made in the amount of aid given to agriculture. The fear of an individual union becoming so favoured a pressure-group that it could dictate policy to a Government Department appears too remote, therefore, to be alarming. There is more substance in the opposite idea that some unions, particularly the smaller ones or those which do not share the political outlook of the Government of the day, will be given less attention than they expect. It seems plain, for instance, that either as a result of governmental or ministerial policy in 1946 the British Medical Association was not effectively consulted over the National Health Service Act. The guiding influence was the Government's determination to put the Act into effect at the earliest possible moment. Detailed difficulties were removed by subsequent negotiations with the British Medical Association, a reversal of the normal sequence of events in governmental legislation.

It is an over-simplification of the complexities of politics to visualise the stock situation as one in which a single pressure-group is attempting, with more or less success, to persuade the Government to accept its ideas. Pressures produce counter-pressures. The Trade Unions are carefully organised individually and collectively to press their claims, but so are the employers. There are over two thousand employers' associations, mostly linked by a central association, the Confederation of British Industry, just as the separate unions are mostly linked by the Trades Union Congress. A similar balancing is evident among those pressure-groups whose support for a cause owes little if anything to financial motives. The National Campaign for the Abolition of Capital Punishment brought into existence a less well-organised but still vocal and active counter-group who wished to retain capital punishment. If the opposing groups are reasonably well balanced, naturally this enables Governments to press on more boldly with the legislation concerned; division of opinion at least ensures some support for Government action and adds to the likelihood that consensus opinion will not be alienated.

The abolition of Resale Price Maintenance in 1964 provides a very good example both of the diversity of pressures which may influence Government legislation, and of the methods which pressure-groups use. Resale Price Maintenance (henceforth referred to as R.P.M.) was a trading practice which enabled manufacturers to fix a price for the goods which they supplied to retailers. If this fixed price was ignored by the retailer, then the manufacturer could refuse to supply him with goods. Manufacturers were apt to take the view that the abolition of R.P.M. would cut profit margins, lead to cut-throat competition, and produce a decline in the quality of goods supplied as manufacturers tried to compensate themselves for lost profits. Small shopkeepers, fearful of being undercut by the supermarkets, were similarly opposed to the abolition. As a consequence of this disquiet the R.P.M. Co-ordinating Committee was formed, representing a very impressive array of wholesale and retail organisations. Leading figures in the tobacco, confectionery, electrical, motor, pharmaceutical, wine and spirit, and stationery industries worked hard to resist the bill. Intensive efforts were made to influence the opinion of M.P.s against the bill. They were lobbied at Westminster. Letters opposing the bill were written to every M.P.; many of them were invited to visit the business houses concerned for informal discussions. Interviews were secured with Mr. Heath, then President of the Board of Trade, the Minister in charge of the bill, and with senior departmental officials. In short, every method of swaying opinion in a democracy was used. Furthermore, the R.P.M. Co-ordinating Committee could draw encouragement from the fact that there was some division of opinion among Conservative M.P.s over the merits of the bill. Sympathy for the viewpoints of the manufacturers and of the small shopkeepers was quite strongly marked.

Opposition to the bill was thus powerful and well organised, but the Minister, too, could count on widespread support. Supermarkets have proliferated in Britain since the war; their size and trade turn-over made it possible for them to make price cuts from which a very large proportion of the population would benefit. The attraction of the idea to housewives trying to get the maximum value for their families from their housekeeping money is obvious. Popular support for the abolition of R.P.M. was strongly buttressed by official reports from many sources. Departmental policy at the Board of Trade had for some years been in favour of the abolition of R.P.M. The Cohen Commission in 1958, the Moloney Committee on Consumer Protection in 1960, the Monopolies Commission Consumer Council in 1963, and the National Economic Development Council in early 1964 had all made plain their objections to R.P.M. Political and personal influences likewise added to Mr. Heath's determination to secure that this bill should read the Statute Book. The bill was plainly overdue already. To have given way to the opponents of the bill would have suggested that the Conservative Party valued old shibboleths more than common sense. To those Conservatives who realised the importance of modernising the outlook of the Party, the need to secure the abolition of R.P.M. was patently self-evident. It might be thought that the knowledge that 1964 was an election year was another of the political circumstances which influenced the course of this legislation. This is too glib to be convincing. The benefits of the bill would scarcely be felt before the onset of the election; furthermore, the bill plainly involved the risk of creating division among the Conservative Party. A fairer assessment is the simpler view that the bill was seen to be necessary and was enacted in spite of a powerful flurry of opposition.

Some amendments to the bill were made at the Committee stage, but the main purpose of abolishing R.P.M. was achieved. The course of events illustrated that on those issues, and there are many, over which opinion is divided, a determined Minister has an excellent chance of imposing his will. The bill also illustrated another facet of pressure-group activity, namely that a pressure-group may have a transient *ad hoc* purpose only. Unlike the Trade Unions and the employers' associations, the R.P.M. Co-ordinating Committee was merely concerned with the fate of one particular bill. Having failed in its objective it lost its *raison d'être*; there was no point in organising a campaign for the restoration of R.P.M.

The 'cause'-groups such as the National Campaign for the

Abolition of Cruel Sports and the Campaign for Nuclear Disarmament are also *ad hoc* organisations, as their names indicate.
Unlike the R.P.M. pressure-groups they have no vested interest in
achieving their aims, and to some extent, therefore, find more
sympathetic support among M.P.s than do those groups whose
actions are largely dictated by self-interest. On the other hand
these cause-groups lack the funds and organisational strength
which the Trade Unions, for instance, enjoy. They lack, too, the
close contact with Ministers, M.P.s, and with departmental
officials which Trade Unions and employers' organisations have, as
a consequence of the vital role they perform in the economy. Cause-
groups have to give more attention to the necessarily slow process
of converting public opinion to support their beliefs before they can
hope for governmental support. The more influential pressure-
groups are not subject to the same limitation. The cause-groups
have achieved some notable successes, particularly for instance the
abolition of capital punishment in 1969. The Howard League for
Penal Reform has by cumulative pressure over a long period of
time influenced official thinking over prison conditions. Occasionally, as in the pressure which secured the passage of the Abortion
Act, a relatively short and vigorous campaign is successful, but this
is exceptional, and much depends on the personalities and political
circumstances of the time. 'Cause'-groups, whose aim is to prevent
legislation taking place, such as the Lord's Day Observance
Society, have a better chance of succeeding than those whose cause
can only be advanced by means of Parliamentary legislation, which
involves a host of attendant difficulties.

Enough has been said, perhaps, to dispose of the myth that
pressure-groups perform some sinister role in a democracy. If they
did not exist it would be necessary to invent them, as Governments
have done in fact in the creation of Consumer Councils. It would
be a mistake to suppose that pressure-groups, whether constructive
or obstructive, are merely a nuisance to Governments. Governing
is too important to be left to Governments. Pressure-groups have a
fund of practical day-to-day knowledge of their particular subjects,
which, in some respects, makes them better fitted to give advice to
a Minister planning legislation than the specialist Civil Servants in
his Department. This advice is particularly valuable in the pre-
Parliamentary stage of legislative activity, but it continues to be of
value when, after the enactment of the bill, the Minister has to

devise the detailed regulations which will make the Act administratively effective. The initially uneasy relationship between the Ministry of Health and the British Medical Association, for instance, made the National Health Service Act of 1946 less administratively sound than it might have been. Subsequent negotiations were more effective, however, and led to a series of new regulations, consolidated in the National Health Service (Amendment) Act of 1949. The City, representing the financial interests concentrated in London, though less formally organised than other pressure-groups, is another source of advice too valuable to be ignored by any Government; so, too, are the Trade Unions, and a wide spectrum of professional, industrial, and social organisations. Pressure-group activity is now so pervasive that one writer, Richard Rose,[1] uses the term 'composite government' to describe the British system. Another, S. H. Beer,[2] sees the system similarly as one dominated by pluralist politics. Much legislation is the culmination of negotiations and compromise between Governments and pressure-groups.

The term 'pressure-groups' creates a mental picture of an organisation carrying on a persistent harrying campaign against Governments and M.P.s in pursuance of their own sectional aims. This is not a completely accurate impression. Co-operation is more common than confrontation. Technical advice is given freely, partly for the sake of future good relations, partly because, even over a bill which the group dislikes, there is no point in worsening its effects by ill-informed regulations. On the other hand, if a pressure-group favours a bill, its acquiescence, or better still its approval, strengthens the Government's position by securing for it widespread support. Pressure-groups, it needs to be remembered, can exert pressure downwards upon their members, and, by propaganda, upon the general public, as well as upwards upon Governments.

Pressure-groups are useful, necessary, and inevitable in a democracy of the kind which exists in Britain. Nevertheless there are a few disquieting features about their existence and use. The proliferation of these groups in modern times is a natural reaction against the growing power of the State. Ideally, democratic government should achieve a balance between the needs of the

[1] *Politics in England* (Faber, 1965).
[2] *Modern British Politics* (Faber, 1965).

State and those of individual citizens. It is difficult to escape the belief that the balance which matters now is that between the State and the leaders of the more powerful pressure-groups in the country. Jean Blondel[1] sees a resemblance between pressure-groups and the medieval guild system, a disturbing comparison for those who believe in the overriding importance of the individual rather than of the group. Only at election time is it possible for citizens acting as individuals to feel that they can influence the course of events; the large numbers of those who abstain from voting suggest that many have doubts even about this. If those pressure-groups which represent the public, not as producers but as users of services, such as the Automobile Association, or Consumer Councils, or the local committees which press for improved train services, could be seen to be having a strong influence on Government policies, then the position would be more reassuring for the general public. The weakness of these consumer organisations is that, unlike producer groups, they have no bargaining power in dealing with a Government Department. They cannot offer higher productivity, nor technical advice. They cannot go on strike. They need essential goods and services more than the goods and services need them; in negotiations, therefore, their position is correspondingly vulnerable.

The other feature about pressure-group activity which causes some disquiet is that most of it takes place behind the scenes. M.P.s can, quite properly, belong to pressure-groups themselves; they may, for instance, retain business connections with firms for which they worked perhaps before entering Parliament. To abandon these connections in a career so precarious as politics would be quixotically absurd. Furthermore, Members are required to make 'a declaration of pecuniary interest' if contributing to a debate where that is relevant. The Select Committee on the Declaration of Members' Interests in 1969 recommended that this declaration should be given not only in Parliamentary debates but in all dealings with Ministers and Civil Servants. An apparently simpler remedy is to publish a register showing outside work from which Members receive payment or appointments. The Liberal Party publishes such a register showing the business connections of its M.P.s. The Committee, however, possibly anticipating a spate of sensational journalism about the business interests of Members,

---

[1] *Voters, Parties, and Leaders* (Pelican Books, 1966).

and also being unwilling to intrude into the private affairs of Members, did not accept the idea of a public register of business connections. Logically it would be necessary for Members to disclose their shareholding interests too. Possibly the Committee was too fastidious in defending the privacy of Members; there is something to be said in a democracy for justice 'being seen to be done', even if doubts on this score are few.

It is true, however, that the initiative in the removal of grievances does not always have to come from pressure-groups. It has been indicated already in the chapter on the Civil Service (Chapter 4) that by means of the doctrine of Ministerial Responsibility, and by means of the Statutory Instruments Committee, the Government and Parliament can protect the citizen against abuses by Executive officials. In addition, it is often asserted in admiration of the British constitution that, while there has been little attempt to define with legal precision the liberties of the subject, these liberties are more effectively secured by the atmosphere of public opinion than they could possibly be by Parliamentary statute. There are a few historic documents, such as the Habeas Corpus Act (1679), which have attempted to give documentary form to some of the essential liberties. Common law decisions also provide a point of reference in determining the liberties of the subject. It would be impossible, however, to give a satisfactory account of all the individual liberties by reference to statutes or common law decisions alone. Both statutes and law courts are subject to the authority of Parliament, and, to give one instance, the principle of fair judicial proceedings, which was one of the aims of the makers of Magna Carta (though only for their own class), was blatantly disregarded time and again in subsequent years. The links between past Acts of Parliament and the contemporary approach to individual liberties are apt to be somewhat tenuous. This has led to a flexibility in the interpretation of the rights of the individual citizen which is generally held to be greatly to his advantage. In theory, the absolute sovereignty of Parliament, now largely superseded by Cabinet dominance, could be indistinguishable from despotism between one election and another, and elections themselves could be made subject to governmental wishes; in practice, respect for individual rights is so ingrained that abuses of governmental power would appear as reprehensible to those who govern as to those who are governed.

If this were an entirely accurate assessment of the relationship between Government and the citizen there would be little cause for concern. Even if the various procedures for protection of the individual were imperfect in themselves, and there is some reason for believing that this is so, no serious harm could result since the long-established freedoms of the subject would be inviolable. To some extent this is true. Freedoms which no longer involve any challenge to Executive authority, such as freedom of religion, are firmly entrenched. It would be foolish to pretend, however, that in modern times all the traditional freedoms are secure from challenge. There are mounting pressures in world affairs, and in changing economic conditions, which make it expedient to strengthen the hand of the Executive, and this may increasingly involve infringements on the freedom of action of individuals. In Victorian times the extent of planning and control now accepted as natural by all the main parties would have been regarded as being out of character completely with the nature of the British constitution and, to that extent, abhorrent. However, opinion on the essential nature of the British constitution changes markedly, not only from century to century, but within much shorter intervals also. Since the last war there have been developments which clearly impinge on the liberties of the subject. These developments are not spectacular, but they are important.

The most conspicuous example of change is that the right to free possession of personal property is no longer regarded as sacrosanct. In former times, the English roads meandered on their course in deference to the sacred property rights of the English landowners, who preferred to keep the roads outside the boundaries of their estate. Railway stations in the nineteenth century were often sited inconveniently on the outskirts of cities in order to placate local hostility to these new mechanical horrors. Nowadays, Governments launching out on great road-schemes, or on the extension of the national grid system for the provision of electricity, are unlikely to be deterred by the obstinacy of a few freeholders. Compulsory Purchase Orders give the necessary sanction required. There is, admittedly, the possibility of a public inquiry attended by the Ministry Inspectors. The paramount need for an efficient road system, and for improved amenities, such as the supply of electricity, makes it unlikely that the objecting citizen will be able to press his claim with much hope of success. Diversions of proposed routes involve heavy additional expense, to be faced ultimately by the taxpayer, and it is highly probable that objections will be swallowed up by considerations of the general benefits of the proposed scheme for large sections of the community. All this is natural and understandable, but also much more frequent in recent years. It is fair to add that the Government has shown itself alive to the hardships which may be created by planned development. The Electricity Act of 1957, for instance, incorporated greater safeguards for those whose land was likely to be affected by extensions of the national grid system. This was brought about largely by the prolonged struggle between a Surrey farmer, Mr. Dudley Glanfield, and the Central Electricity Authority over the erection of a pylon line across his land.[1] It is disquieting that in this incident, as in others, legislation has followed a complaint, not removed it by anticipation. The power of the Ministry of Agriculture to evict inefficient farmers is another instance of the way in which the power of the Executive has intruded upon the full and free use of personal property; moreover, it is not a dormant power for it has been invoked, though rarely.

While it is generally conceded that governmental powers have extended in this way, it is often argued that the citizen in a modern community expects Government management of the economy and of social services, and is prepared in the interests of the community to accept the slight risk of some loss of personal rights. Besides he has other relevant privileges such as the right, since the 1947 Crown Proceedings Act, to sue a Government Department; the existence of an impartial judicial system is a further reassurance that soundly-based complaints will receive the consideration they deserve. Beyond these protections he has the privilege of free speech so that the attention of Parliament may be brought to the grievance of any citizen. In fact there are limitations to these privileges. The Courts are themselves subordinate to Parliament in the sense that they can only ensure that a Government Department has conducted its procedures in accordance with the terms laid down in the relevant statute. This may or may not be preferable to a system in which a wholly independent Judiciary could hamper the full application of Parliamentary statute by reference to principles of justice of its own devising. Whatever the opinion may be on this, it does not alter the fact that in the present system the principle of the equality of all

[1] T. E. Utley, *Occasion for Ombudsman*, pp. 68–77.

men before the law, which is ideally desirable, cannot be applicable when the dispute is between a citizen and a Government Department. The latter is inevitably placed in a position of superiority through having been associated itself, through its Minister, with the process of law-making. Furthermore, Government Departments may withhold evidence, if they wish, in the interests of State security, of which they must necessarily be the judges themselves.[1] The Government, too, has powers to strengthen its position against individual claims by further legislation. There may be sound reasons for all these advantages, but a dispute between a Governments Department and a citizen can hardly be conducted on the same level of equality as a dispute between citizens. It is true, however, that there is a further protection for the citizen, the privilege of free speech.

Freedom of speech is so basic a part of the British tradition that it has acquired a sentimental aura making perception of reality more difficult. Most people are familiar with the endearing story of the policeman silencing a heckler so that he may give undivided attention to the soap-box orator in Hyde Park furiously attacking the forces of law and order which the policeman himself represents. There is a sense of insular superiority about the policeman's amiable tolerance. From the incident one is expected to deduce the willingness of Government and of its officials to accept criticism without victimising the critics. It is possible to make a deduction of quite another kind from these facts, however, namely that the course and actions of the Government are unlikely to be altered one iota by self-appointed orators, and freedom of speech of this traditional kind is of negligible importance. It acts, as has been often said, as a safety-valve for society, but the real point of the comparison is that the steam which escapes through a safety-valve is simply wasted. Free speech, in the other sense, involving approach directly to Government Departments, or indirectly through Parliament by means of M.P.s acting on behalf of their constituents to remedy grievances, does not mean that a satisfactory solution can always be found. Parliament is overworked. It is largely for this reason that the devices for bringing a private or group grievance to public notice cannot be guaranteed to be effective.

[1] This power has been much more closely limited since the appeal judgement in the House of Lords on the *Conway* v. *Rimmer* case (1968) 2 W.L.R. 998.

There have been a number of incidents in recent years, many of which are very fully described in T. E. Utley's *Occasion for Ombudsman*, where Government Department decisions have involved hardship for citizens which might have been avoided. Human failings are inevitable in any great organisation where thousands are employed. The citizen is far more likely to acquire a sense of grievance against Civil Service decisions in the lower levels of Departments than he is on matters of sufficient importance to move Parliament strongly to action. Undoubtedly, too, he will often be deterred by the difficulties involved in remedying his grievance through the ordinary processes of Parliament. Lord Shawcross in his preface to the Whyatt Report uses the cogent phrase that 'the little farmer with four acres and a cow would never have attempted to force the battlements of Crichel Down'.[1] Obviously there have been many occasions when the existing procedure of letters to Departments, questions in the House, and so on have led to satisfactory remedies for the citizen; but increasing pressure on Parliamentary time, inadequacies of procedure, and the extension of Government administrative activity, often of great complexity, have combined to make Parliament a less effective watchdog of citizens' rights than it used to be.

Various remedies have been proposed. In France, the Conseil d'État,[2] which dates back to Napoleon's time, can act on behalf of a citizen with a grievance against an administrative decision. It is itself composed of Civil Servants, but its traditional concern for fair administration makes this no bar to the conscientious discharge of its duties. It has power to override Government Department decisions, which makes its position akin to that of a Supreme Court. Its powers over administrative decisions are wider, in fact, than those of the Supreme Court in the United States, since it makes its decisions not on the authority of constitutional statements but on the more flexible authority of natural justice. Mr. Utley convincingly points out that we could scarcely create the equivalent of a Conseil d'État in Britain since this would give too much untrammelled power to an unrepresentative group of officials.[3]

[1] *Ibid.*, p. xiii.
[2] *Conseil d'État*—supreme court of appeal for administrative matters.
[3] For this point, and for an assessment of the value of an Ombudsman in Britain, together with the possible alternatives, see T. E. Utley, *Occasion for Ombudsman*, particularly pp. 135–44.

British Governments and Parliaments have shown some reluctance to adopt any new constitutional machinery for the redress of grievances. In 1962, for instance, the Attorney-General, replying to a question in the House, defended the existing means of remedying grievances and pointed out that the appointment of a British Ombudsman, or Parliamentary Commissioner, would conflict with the concept of Ministerial Responsibility.[1] Parliament, too, has plainly felt reluctant to delegate any part of its crucial responsibility for defending the interests of the citizen. However, the pressures for change were too strong to be resisted. In the first place, the traditional means for securing redress of grievances could not be expected to be wholly adequate when the ambit of governmental activity has been so rapidly and widely extended. As one instance, the time allocated to questions now is exactly the same as it was when the procedure was last altered in 1906, though it would neither be possible, nor, perhaps, helpful, to extend the length of Question-time; hence, in part, the need for a Parliamentary Commissioner. Secondly, the vast improvements in modern communications have led to a much greater comparative interest in the constitutional methods of other countries, and to a breakdown of the insular prejudice which made imitation of those methods unthinkable. The Government White Paper (Cmnd. 2767) specifically states, for instance, that 'We have examined the arrangements made for the scrutiny of such individual grievances in Sweden, Finland, Denmark, Norway, and New Zealand'. There were national variations in the powers allocated to the Ombudsman in each of these countries, but if Sweden, the country from which the office originated in 1809, is taken as an example, his functions there are as follows. He not only investigates complaints against the Executive, with the necessary office staff, but can take action on his own initiative also. He has the power to prosecute, to visit institutions such as hospitals and prisons, to investigate complaints about local councils, and to see that there is no undue delay in judicial proceedings. His functions, in brief, are very wide-ranging indeed. Many of the complaints he investigates are unfounded, but the publicity given to his activities is a deterrent against arbitrary or irresponsible exercise of authority. Sweden since 1915 has also had a military Ombudsman to investigate complaints in the Armed Forces. Although study of the powers of the Ombudsman in other

[1] H.C. Debates, November 8th, 1962, cols. 1124–6.

countries was instructive, it was certain from the outset that Britain, with its greater population and its long tradition of Parliamentary government, would not be provided with an Ombudsman possessing the same degree of initiative as is found in Sweden and, to a lesser extent, in the other Scandinavian countries. It was the Whyatt Report, *The Citizen and the Administration*, published in 1961, which anticipated most closely the powers to be allocated to the British Ombudsman, or Parliamentary Commissioner as he is officially called. The Report, whose object was to advance suggestions for dealing with those acts of administration which fell outside the terms of reference of the Franks Committee, proposed that a Parliamentary Commissioner should be appointed to investigate conplaints of maladministration. He would receive complaints only from members of both Houses of Parliament, though later it might be possible to adapt the system so that members of the public could make their complaints directly to the Commissioner. He would be given reasonable access to departmental files. He would submit both annual and special reports to Parliament. There are, of course, many occasions where, although the administrative procedures have been correctly followed, thus nullifying any complaint of maladministration, the citizen may feel that a departmental decision offends against natural justice. The Whyatt Report drew attention to matters such as disputes between parents and the local education authority over the choice of schools for children, [1] and *ex gratia* payments by the War Office for damage caused to private property by blast or concussion of guns firing on War Department land, [2] where the citizen may feel strongly aggrieved by what is a discretionary decision by the authority concerned rather than an act of maladministration. The need for an impartial body to decide on matters of this kind could best be met, according to the Whyatt Report, by the creation of new tribunals or by the use of a General Tribunal to deal with appeals from miscellaneous discretionary decisions. The number of complaints of this kind will obviously be far too great to be handled by the Parliamentary Commissioner, assisted by a small staff. Up to the present the problem of dealing with unsatisfactory discretionary decisions has not been solved; it seems probable that the solution will be the creation of local Ombudsmen rather than the extension of tribunal organisation proposed in the Report.

[1] *Op. cit.*, paragraph 42.       [2] *Op. cit.*, paragraph 27.

The effect of these widespread investigations had been to produce an atmosphere favourable to the appointment of a Parliamentary Commissioner, and in 1967 the first Commissioner, Sir Edmund Compton, entered upon his duties. His functions were very closely akin to those suggested in the Whyatt Report. He investigates complaints of maladministration by central Government Departments, the complaints having been referred to him by members of the House of Commons acting on behalf of constituents. He makes annual and special reports to Parliament. Possibly more notable than the powers which he has been given are the powers which he has not been given. Local government activities, the National Health Service, the law-courts, nationalised industries, the police, personnel matters in the Armed Forces and the Civil Service, all fall outside his sphere of responsibility. Even in his rightful sphere, the investigation of complaints of maladministration by central Government Departments, his influence seems extremely slight. He has a small staff and a small budget. He has no executive authority. A Minister whose Department is criticised is entirely at liberty to rebut the criticism, and to ignore the recommendations of the Parliamentary Commissioner. In December, 1967, for instance, the Parliamentary Commissioner reported that there had been defects in administrative procedure in the Foreign Office over the question of paying compensation to British survivors from the Nazi concentration camp at Sachsenhausen. The Foreign Office had been unwilling to pay compensation. Mr. George Brown, then Foreign Secretary, announced in the House of Commons debate upon the Parliamentary Commissioner's Report that it had now been decided to pay compensation but that, at the same time, he disagreed with the Report's findings. He also expressed the fear that the introduction of a Parliamentary Commissioner would greatly weaken the doctrine of Ministerial Responsibility, since individual Civil Servants rather than the Minister himself would become identified with particular decisions, thus leading to a diffusion of responsibility. This view did not command universal support. There is undoubtedly a risk that the existence of the office of a Parliamentary Commissioner might diminish the overall responsibility of a Minister, but the appointment has been criticised far more on the grounds that the Commissioner has too little power than that he has too much. In the three years 1967–70 three thousand cases, many less than were expected, were referred to him. Half of these were rejected as being outside his sphere of responsibility, while of the remaining half only ten per cent revealed that there had been maladministration. It might be thought that this shows that administrative soundness is so deeply ingrained in Government Departments that complaints are rarely justified and that a Parliamentary Commissioner is superfluous. Another view is that the powers of investigation of the Commissioner are too narrowly restricted. He is deprived of personal initiative in investigating the administrative process; the discretionary decisions which are a more frequent source of dissatisfaction than maladministration are removed from his consideration. So limited are his functions that one wit has suggested that 'Ombudsmouse' would be a more appropriate title than 'Ombudsman'. It may well be, of course, that the powers given so far merely mark a first-stage reform and that they will be extended subsequently at central and local level. The acceptance by the Government and Parliament of the need for such an appointment at all does indicate an awareness that exclusive reliance on the traditional constitutional methods of dealing with redress of grievances is unsatisfactory. Increased Executive authority has made it more likely that individual grievances will require greater attention if the democratic system is to remain a reality. Abuses of Executive authority have been infrequent so far, but if panic is not justified neither is complacency.

FURTHER READING

D. N. Chester and N. Bowring, *Questions in Parliament* (Oxford—Clarendon Press, 1962).
T. E. Utley, *Occasion for Ombudsman* (Johnson, 1961).
Sir John Whyatt, *The Citizen and the Administration* (Stevens, 1961).
*The Parliamentary Commissioner for Administration* (Cmnd. 2767, H.M.S.O., 1965).
S. A. Walkland, *The Legislative Process in Great Britain* (Allen & Unwin, 1968).
J. D. Stewart, *British Pressure Groups* (O.U.P., 1958).
J. Blondel, *Voters, Parties, and Leaders* (Pelican Books, 1966).
R. Rose, *Politics in England* (Faber, 1965).
S. H. Beer, *Modern British Politics* (Faber, 1965).
See also Comments on Further Reading, p. 211.

# 6

# The House of Commons
## Some Procedural Problems

Shortage of time and the specialisation of knowledge are obstacles to full Parliamentary control. An analysis of legislative procedure suggests that there is little chance of time-saving. This is reinforced by a study of the Select Committee on Procedure proposals of 1958. The inability to adapt procedure to modern conditions has reduced the influence of the House of Commons. Financial procedure is the most conspicuous example of this weakness. Value of select committees.

THEME: The existing machinery for Parliamentary control is imperfect. Bolder use of Parliamentary committees is a possible solution.

The increasing responsibilities of the Executive would seem to lead to the conclusion that its greater power has been achieved by a reduction in the power of the Legislature. The situation, therefore, could be represented as a simple sum in subtraction. This would be a false simplification, for Parliament works harder than it did before the war, and there has been no formal decree depriving it of its ancient rights. It is possible, alternatively, that the extension in the powers of the Executive has been matched by an extension in the powers of the Legislature; in other words, both branches of government have greater responsibilities. The basis for this belief is that, though governmental control has widened, Parliamentary control, already supposedly strong through the use of questions and open debate, has been tightened still further by new committees, such as those on Statutory Instruments and on Nationalised Industries. It has already been indicated that some procedures, such as Question-time and those involving control of the issue of Statutory Instruments and of Special Orders, can leave loopholes which should be closed. It is fair to point out that the same concern is felt by some M.P.s themselves and has led to the frequent appointment of Select Committees on Procedure to consider suggestions for the more efficient examination of Parliamentary business. Clearly this has the greatest relevance to the extent to which governmental actions can be brought under the scrutiny of Parliament. There are two essential problems. One is how to make more time available to consider the increased volume of legislation of modern times. The second is how to secure stronger Parliamentary control over matters which modern specialisation has made intelligible only to the expert. An outstanding example of the latter problem is national finance. It will be convenient then to consider these two problems in order.

Saving of Parliamentary time is much more difficult to effect than it may appear at first sight. The frequent attempts made by the Select Committees on Procedure, consisting of experienced Parliamentarians, to find a solution suggest that there is little likelihood now of anything except slight changes. Parliamentary procedure, after all, is based on long experience, and for the most part has a sound practical basis. It would be difficult now to bring about changes without intruding on the accepted rights of Parliament. This can be illustrated by an examination of the legislative procedure for a public bill. This process, involving First and Second Readings, Committee, Report, and Third Reading may appear to involve some duplication of effort. There is little substance in this criticism. The First Reading is a brief formality, normally serving no other purpose than to give notice of the important Second Reading stage. This latter stage, the debate on the principles of the bill, is likely to rouse the greatest interest, both among M.P.s and the public. Most Government bills are allotted one Parliamentary day for their Second Reading stage; even a highly controversial bill is not likely to be given more than two Parliamentary days, a striking contrast with the leisurely Victorian approach when, for instance, the Second Reading of Gladstone's Irish Rule Bill lasted eight days. Plainly there it would be ill-advised to reduce much further the limited time currently available for this important stage of procedure. On the other hand legislation has increased voluminously in modern times so that there is a constant risk of a backlog of legislation accumulating unless there is close adherence to an exact timetable. In 1967 Standing Orders were amended to allow the Government to gain a decision on a guillotine motion (compulsory timetable) for a bill after only two hours of debate. Previously debate on a guillotine motion could take a whole day, and this added to governmental reluctance to use this procedure. It would clearly be undesirable if the new guillotine motion procedure were overused. The grounds for its use are that no agreement can be reached between the Government and Opposition on a voluntary timetable or that such an agreement, if it exists, has in the Government's judgement broken down. The procedure was first used in May 1968 for the Finance Bill. A second time-saving expedient has been the practice adopted in the 1965-6 session of allowing a Government bill to be sent to a Second Reading Committee. This cannot be done if twenty Members oppose this procedure. If there is no such objection the Committee considers the bill and recommends whether or not it shall be read a second time. The House then acts on this recommendation without further debate. This procedure is clearly only appropriate for bills which are distinctly uncontroversial.[1]

The Committee stage, involving detailed examination of the bill and consideration of amendments, is necessarily much the slowest. Delay at this stage may cause a blockage in the legislative 'pipe-line'. This careful scrutiny, however, is designed to protect the citizen against the hardships which badly-worded legislation can inadvertently impose. Even under the present system a bill which has passed through all its stages in the House of Commons may be heavily amended still further in the House of Lords, not from party interest but simply to make the bill a workable piece of legislation. Lord Morrison has indicated, for instance, how extensive and valuable the services of the House of Lords were over some of the nationalisation bills of the 1945-51 Labour Governments. The defects which may still exist in a bill after the Committee stage do not suggest that any shortening of the time available would be desirable. During the post-war period, however, it was sometimes felt that party politics intruded into Committee proceedings to an extent where Opposition members were more concerned with obstructing the Government legislative programme than with rational discussion of the detailed terms of the bills. On the other hand, Opposition members were apt to be equally suspicious that

---

[1] The article by C. J. Boulton, 'Recent Developments in House of Commons Procedure', in *Parliamentary Affairs* (vol. XXIII, no. 1, Winter 1969-70) gives a very useful summary of recent changes.

they were being stampeded into rushing bills through the Committee stage to suit Government convenience. The knowledge that the Government has 'reserve' powers to shorten Committee proceedings by forcing the closure of debate on particular amendments, by fixing a time-limit for the completion of the Committee stage (the guillotine procedure) and by only allowing discussion of selected clauses (the kangaroo procedure) made the fear of limitation of discussion more substantial than it would otherwise have been. Nevertheless, respect for the principle of thorough discussion is still strong and, apart from this, limitation of debate could damage the Government politically. The adoption in 1967 of the principle of timetables for the Committee and Report stages for selected bills, by agreement between the parties, has improved procedure. So too has the arrangement adopted in 1960, by which the membership of each Standing Committee consists predominantly of M.P.s expert in the matter under discussion. Party considerations are still a factor in choosing members of these committees, since Governments are understandably anxious to avoid defeat at the Committee stage, but the greater emphasis on expertise makes discussion more useful and less partisan. The theoretical maximum size of these committees is fifty. If this were the number actually present at Committee proceedings, discussion would be diffuse. In practice attendance at these proceedings is very much less than the maximum: within rational limits this is an advantage. A further suggestion is that more use should be made of an existing procedure by which the Committee stage of bills can be taken by a Joint Committee of both Houses, after which the Report and Third Reading stages take place separately in the two Houses. This would dispense with one Committee stage of the usual process. There is no objection in principle to this, but the difficulty is that it would be impracticable to secure sufficient synchronisation of the work of the two Houses to make this procedural device applicable, except on rare occasions.

The Report and Third Reading stages are unlikely to be greatly changed. The purpose of the Report stage is to make the House of Commons (or the House of Lords) aware of amendments made to the bill in Committee, and to give an opportunity to those who were not members of the Committee to add further amendments. The Government may also wish to introduce new clauses or amendments. Much of this work will be tedious, but it is necessary, both to emphasise the responsibility of the House for legislation and as an additional security against any loophole overlooked by the Committee itself. It was suggested to the Select Committee on Procedure in 1946 by Sir Gilbert Campion, himself an authority on Parliamentary procedure, that the Report stage could, with advantage, be taken from the whole House and dealt with by the Standing Committee concerned with that bill.[1] This Committee would have dealt with the Committee stage of the bill by delegation to sub-committees of its own members. The Report stage would then be signalised by these sub-committees reporting progress to the Standing Committee itself. This would save the fairly lengthy time, possibly one or two days, spent in reporting amendments and discussing new ones in the whole House. The Select Committee opposed this suggestion, however, on the grounds that the gain in Parliamentary time would not compensate for the diminished influence of the whole House over amendments. Nevertheless, if any change in legislative procedure for a non-financial public bill does come about it is the Report stage which is most likely to be affected; in practice it is clearly those who have already participated in the Committee stage who are most likely to make further contributions when the bill is reported to the whole House. If the Committee were to be given this further responsibility it would always be possible for members, if a sufficient minimum were stipulated, to ask that particular bills should be referred to the whole House for Report. The proposal appears reasonable, but the House of Commons has an understandable bias in favour of conservatism in Parliamentary affairs, since the present procedure has been devised from long experience, though scarcely in conditions comparable to those of the present day. The final stage in both Houses is the Third Reading. This is usually brief, and, since 1967, will usually be a formality, unless the Opposition particularly wants a last opportunity of stating objections before the bill passes to the other House. It would serve no useful purpose, therefore, to remove the Third Reading stage.

In general, it can be seen that there can be little expectation of shortening the legislative process for the non-financial public bill.

---

[1] A minor adaptation of this idea was the introduction in 1967 of Report Committees for bills which had undergone the Second Reading Committee procedure. Suitable only for uncontroversial bills, this method can be blocked if twenty Members object.

Turning to other types of legislation it is possible that time could be saved by allowing Private Bills to be considered exclusively by Committees, instead of the present system which allows public business to be interrupted at 7.0 p.m. for the consideration of matters unlikely to be of much interest to the vast majority of M.P.s. This interruption, however, may well provide a convenient lull between the two halves of a debate, and apart from this, Private Bill legislation has become much more rare, having been partly superseded by the issue of Government Department Orders; moreover, if a Private Bill is unopposed its stages in Parliament are so formal as to be negligible in its consumption of time. In respect of other legislation, such as financial bills and Private Members' Bills, the issue is not so much how time can be saved as how the time allotted can be put to better use. Private Members' time has already been reduced compared with pre-war days, and it would be undesirable to make still further inroads. It would be advantageous, perhaps, to review the somewhat haphazard procedure of selection of Private Members' Bills by ballot, but that is another matter. In financial matters the situation is much more complex. The importance of finance makes time-saving out of place unless it leads to greater efficiency. As will be seen later, an amendment to Standing Orders made it possible for the Finance Bill to be committed in 1968 to a Standing Committee with a maximum membership of fifty, but it would need a much more drastic reorganisation than was suggested, and a complete change of approach by the House of Commons, to bring about any drastic saving of the time at present given to financial matters.

Select Committees on Procedure have found it very difficult to secure any better use of Parliamentary time. The 1958 Committee, particularly was in no way hampered by scarcity of ideas. Among the suggestions considered were morning sittings of the House of Commons on Mondays, Wednesdays, and Fridays; the use of a specialist Colonial Affairs Committee, and of a specialist Defence Committee to consider the Estimates; use of the Standing Committees of the House for the consideration of the Report stage of most bills; the use of a Finance Committee to share the work on the Finance Bill with the House of Commons; a more even spread of Supply Days through the Parliamentary session, in recognition of the fact that Supply Days are used for general debate rather than for discussion of specific issues arising from the Estimates, and that the latter are not presented until February; the putting of questions before three Committees of the House of Commons on two days a week to reduce the pressures of the normal Question-time procedure (on Tuesdays and Thursdays, however, the existing procedure would be maintained); a reduction in the number of oral questions permissible for each member from three to two on any one day; an end of the practice by which Privy Councillors were given automatic precedence by the Speaker when more than one member rose to speak at the same time; the setting aside of one hour during major debates for five-minute speeches, and examination of various methods for reducing the time and energy lost in the division lobbies. This list of suggestions is not exhaustive but it is enough to indicate the amount of ingenuity expended.

Some of these ideas were dismissed by the Select Committee itself. Morning sittings, for instance, were rejected,[1] partly no doubt because of the claims of other Parliamentary duties during the morning. M.P.s need to deal with correspondence, help constituents, visit Government Departments, and serve on Committees. In addition, it has been calculated that approximately 60% of M.P.s have to combine their Parliamentary work with the continuance of their private employment. The increase in M.P.s' salaries from £1,750 to £3,250 a year in 1964 was overdue. Nevertheless, the need for additional outside paid work cannot be entirely removed, since every M.P. runs the risk of a General Election ending his Parliamentary career prematurely. Even now, the salaries and facilities granted to M.P.s compare unfavourably with those of legislators elsewhere in the world. Securing service to the community at bargain-prices is one of our less amiable national characteristics, but it exerts such inhibiting force that M.P.s, though they have the remedy in their own hands, have been reluctant to vote for themselves a salary adequate for their needs. A second suggestion rejected by the Committee was for the adoption of the method of voting by a push-button device operated by electricity. This system has been used in Sweden and would save a good proportion of the 10–15 minutes taken up under the present procedure while M.P.s troop in and out of the division lobbies. This 'electrical' voting might be particularly useful on the last of the twenty-nine Supply Days when there are many divisions

[1] Sittings on Mondays and Wednesdays at 10.0 a.m. were adopted in 1967 but have not been regularly used subsequently.

as the last of the Estimates are rushed through; this procedure is physically exhausting for the older member as well as being time-consuming. There is the traditional view however, once put by Mr. Baldwin to an earlier Select Committee, that the tour of the lobbies helps passions to subside. As much of Parliamentary procedure is directed towards moderating the strong feelings of M.P.s it is not surprising perhaps that this traditional view prevailed; moreover, it is not altogether established that mechanical voting would be immune from the attentions of the practical joker.

Although the Select Committee rejected some of the suggestions made, it approved in general those which involved fuller use of Committees, reduction in the volume of oral questions, and greater opportunities for back-benchers to speak in debates. These suggestions were debated in the House of Commons on July 13th, 1959, and on February 8th, 1960, and announcements relative to the matters discussed were given at various times during this period by Mr. Butler, the Leader of the House. For a variety of reasons few changes were made. The reduction of the number of oral questions from a permissible three to two a day from each questioner won favour. On the other hand, and perhaps predictably, no scheme which involved any delegation of House of Commons work by means of fuller use of Committees met with approval. The House of Commons generally shows a strong determination to keep most stages of its business in the hands of the House as a whole. The suggestion of a more even spacing of Supply Days secured general support, and sympathy was shown for the difficulties of the back-bencher. On the specific matters of five-minute speeches, and the automatic precedence of Privy Councillors in debates, the feeling was that these matters should be left to the goodwill of the House and of the Speaker. Changes, therefore, were few. There is no doubt of the innate conservatism of the parties over Parliamentary procedure, and, apart from this, the Government has to consider the possibility of its work being hampered by procedural changes which might lessen its authority.

There is one aspect of Parliamentary affairs, however, which may make far-reaching procedural changes unavoidable, if Parliament is not to be regulated to a merely subordinate role in the constitution. This is the crucial matter of the extent of Parliamentary control over national finance. The existing financial procedure has been under heavy critical attack for many years. It is not merely shortage of time which makes supervision sketchy, but also the difficulty of bringing to bear at the right time, and in the right way, the expert financial knowledge undoubtedly to be found amongst some members of the House of Commons. The present system too often condemns them to pass 'on the nod' huge sums in a manner which they would regard as intolerably inefficient in the management of their own businesses. The nationalisation of the Bank of England in 1946, followed by the abolition of the Ministry of Economic Affairs in 1947, when Sir Stafford Cripps moved to the Treasury as Chancellor of the Exchequer, gave the Treasury a dominance not challenged by later organisational changes. The secrecy which surrounds the preparation of the Budget and other aspects of economic policy has sometimes led Chancellors of the Exchequer to work with their Treasury advisers in isolation not only from M.P.s, but even from fellow-Ministers. The Governor of the Bank of England may offer advice to a Chancellor, but he is not bound to heed it. If the policies devised under the present system had been more demonstrably successful the dominance of the Treasury would be correspondingly acceptable. In fact, the 'stop-go' policies of the post-war years have caused widespread criticisms among City interests and industrialists who need stable policies giving a fair expectation of good returns from capital investment. Although Treasury influence is dominant, primarily on the grounds of the expert knowledge to be found there, its effectiveness as a planning organisation capable of forecasting the results of its actions has increasingly been called in doubt during its fluctuations in policy in recent years. This naturally has its impact on the general public as well as on business-men. The watch-dog for the general public ought to be the House of Commons itself, but a brief examination of financial procedure will show how slight is the influence which the House brings to bear.

Financial business is slight at the beginning of the Parliamentary session. There may be Supplementary Estimates to consider, if a Government Department, since the previous estimates were passed, has become involved in additional expenditure. Enterprises such as the Suez Canal attack, or, more recently, the help given to Anguilla may necessarily involve the Service Departments in unforeseen expenditure. The House of Commons sanctions the additional amount, but at this stage it is only able to discuss the sum being allocated as a Supplementary Estimate, not the general policy which made the expenditure necessary at all. Discussion, therefore, becomes largely a waste of time, since the only issue for debate is likely to be of more interest to an accountant than to an M.P. Sometimes, too, there will be Excess Votes to consider, when a Government Department has failed to calculate its requirements adequately and finds itself deficient at the end of the financial year. The sums involved are normally very small, otherwise it would be a serious reflection on the Department involved. Supplementary Estimates, therefore, are concerned with current spending and Excess Votes with the spending of the last completed financial year. In both the House of Commons is, in effect, confronted with a *fait accompli*. Even when the Excess Vote involves a large sum, as it did in 1959, when almost £95,000 extra was required for National Insurance and Family Allowances,[1] it could be claimed, with good reason in this instance, that exact forecasting of the sum required presented insuperable difficulties.

Of greater importance than these supplementary sums of money are the main estimates themselves. These are ready for examination by the House of Commons by February, and show in detail the proposed spending by Government Departments in the forthcoming year. They will already have been scrutinised very carefully by the Treasury. The Treasury will know, both from its records of previous departmental expenditure and from knowledge of current trends in the financial policy, which it so largely shapes itself, whether any adjustments are needed. Treasury examination, therefore, is concerned with the efficient spending of money in detail within the limits imposed by the Department's policy. This policy in turn is limited by the financial resources available and, in this, it is again the Treasury which is the expert authority. In view of the Treasury's paramount influence it is understandable that serious doubts have been expressed, both inside and outside the House of Commons, as to the ability of the House to control expenditure. Debates on the estimates have a sense of unreality since members can hardly fail to be aware that potentially the most effective contributors to the debate are the Treasury officials, who are debarred from participation in it. In recognition of this fact the House on its twenty-nine Supply Days shuns altogether any attempt at detailed scrutiny of the estimates; instead, the time is used at the

[1] See E. Taylor, *The House of Commons at Work*, p. 200.

discretion of the Opposition for general debates on the Government's administration of affairs.

Nevertheless, these debates could be a means of securing some measure of financial control if they were consistently directed towards their supposed objective of protecting the nation from wasteful policies. Relevant policy debates could be of the utmost value if they prevented the adoption of over-ambitious development plans divorced from any sense of financial reality. Although it has been said in criticism of the House of Commons that it does not scrutinise the details of expenditure, this matters much less than an adequate review of policy aims. Such a review, leading to amendments, could clearly save more of the nation's money than cutting down expenditure on a Government Department's stationery, for instance. Detailed examination of that kind could appropriately be left to the Treasury officials. The weakness of the present procedure in the House of Commons lies not so much in the lack of time for consideration of financial business as in the way debates stray away from what should be their major objective, namely the economical use of the nation's money.[1] The responsibility for this vital matter is apt in present circumstances to lie somewhere between the House of Commons, the Treasury, and the Government; divided responsibility is notoriously unsatisfactory and productive of uncertainty.

There is undoubtedly urgent need for continuous vigilance over Government expenditure, not only on the general grounds that it is the taxpayers' money which is being used, but also because of the great increase that there has been in recent years in Government expenditure. Between 1948 and 1958, for instance, expenditure rose by 50%. The root of the trouble is probably political, in that no party is anxious to give the impression of being niggardly over schemes for social development, but these schemes could well be nullified if they are not accompanied by financial stability. Attention has been called to this dangerous situation by Viscount Hinchingbrooke and by Mr. Peter Thorneycroft, who was himself Chancellor of the Exchequer in 1957-8.[2] They have both protested against the practice of giving formal approval to the very large sums comprising the vote on account, and then proceeding to a

[1] The changes in Supply Day procedure in 1966 and 1967 made the connections between the Estimates and Supply Days even more remote.
[2] See A. H. Hanson and H. V. Wiseman, *Parliament at Work*, pp. 271-8.

debate on matters which are of general national interest, such as unemployment problems, but which have little relevance to the spending of money by any particular Government Department, and still less to possible savings in Government expenditure. Even though the present procedure for the examination of financial policy may not be ideal it is still possible that better use could be made of it if purely financial considerations were given greater priority by all parties.

In April examination of the Estimates gives way temporarily to the announcement of the Budget resolutions by the Chancellor of the Exchequer. These arouse more public interest than the Estimates; they are in part based on the revenue needs of Government Departments, but in the post-1945 period, particularly, the Budget proposals have become very closely linked with the wider issue of management of the economy in the attempt to give Britain financial stability. The Budget is naturally devised in great secrecy by the Chancellor of the Exchequer and the Treasury officials to prevent speculators from gaining financial advantage. Even the Cabinet members are only told of the terms of the Budget shortly before it is disclosed to the House of Commons. Once it has been announced there are good opportunities for debate in the summer months, since the Finance Bill, in which the Budget resolutions are eventually incorporated, is regarded as 'exempted' business; this term simply means that the House can continue discussion beyond the normal time for the adjournment. Modifications can be made, therefore, to Government financial policy, but speeches in so large a body as the House of Commons tend to be discursive. This led the Select Committee on Procedure of 1958 to suggest that examination of the Finance Bill should be shared between the House of Commons and a smaller Finance Committee. This was put into effect in 1968.

The Finance Bill and the Appropriation Act (which authorises the allocation of money as the House of Commons has decided) are passed towards the end of the Parliamentary session; with their passage, scrutiny by the House of Commons, sitting as a whole House, is ended too.[1] There are, however, two small Committees,

[1] The Committees of the Whole House on finance were abolished between December 1966 and October 1967 because of their procedural artificiality in modern times. Committee procedure, applied to the whole House, is time-wasting.

the Estimates Committee and the Public Accounts Committee, whose work also deserves consideration. At the outset it should be stated that these two Committees can only partially remedy the present incomplete supervision of national finance. The Committee on Estimates consists of thirty-three members. Membership is roughly in proportion to the party position in the House of Commons, so that there is an assured Government majority in the Committee, and the chairman is drawn from the Government party. This does not make its supervision nominal since there is an obvious incentive for Government supporters to be vigilant over the estimates so that charges of waste and extravagance may not be made by critics later. Besides, the chairmen of the sub-committees into which the Estimates Committee divides for the more thorough examination of proposed spending may well be from the Opposition. The Committee has the power to summon officials before it to give evidence, and to ask for written statements from departments. K. C. Wheare in *Government by Committee* has pointed out that, though the members of the Committee are laymen and do not have expert assistance of the kind the Public Accounts Committee receives through the Comptroller and Auditor-General and his staff, they are very greatly helped by the preliminary work of the Clerk of the Financial Committees. This House of Commons official presents the Committee members with the information they require in a form which enables them to consider it with the maximum dispatch. Yet, when all these factors have been considered there are severe limitations to the effectiveness of the Committee. There is not time in a single session for the Committee to examine all the estimates, so it merely examines a cross-section of them, preferably those for services affecting several departments. Again, the Committee has no power to alter the policies on which the estimates are based. Sometimes, as Professor Wheare has pointed out, the Committee must infringe on policy matters if it is to do its work properly. In doing so, however, it is acting outside its terms of reference with a corresponding weakening of its position. Even within its terms of reference criticisms made by the Committee against a Government Department have no overriding force, and may well be answered in firm terms by the Government Department concerned. At the same time, if Departments are willing to accept criticism, improvements can be effected by the Committee's reports. The chief value of the Committee in fact lies in the

supervision of the work of the officials in the Treasury and other
Government Departments; it has no power to modify a policy
fundamentally since this is regarded as an infringement on the
functions of Government and Parliament. A basically extravagant
policy from a wider national point of view may, therefore, be put
into practice with only marginal criticisms, if any, being made by
the Committee on Estimates.

Somewhat similar considerations apply to the Public Accounts
Committee, though there are differences of detail. This Committee
of fifteen members has the expert help of the Comptroller and
Auditor-General and his large staff. It investigates irregular or
wasteful spending and is held in some awe by Department officials.
Its reports have been rarely debated in the House of Commons and
are for the information of the Treasury and of the Departments.
The Public Accounts Committee is generally held to be in a
stronger position than the Committee on Estimates for securing
effective action. The fact that the chairman of the Public Accounts
Committee is taken from the Opposition is also looked on as a
source of strength, though, as was pointed out, the choice of the
Estimates Committee chairman from the Government party does
not mean that criticism will be any the less effective. But, whatever
the opinion may be on this matter of the chairmanship, this is
merely a side-issue. The essential fact remains that, like the
Estimates Committee, the Public Accounts Committee is fundamentally inhibited by its terms of reference. It can only decide
whether money has been spent honestly and economically in
attaining certain political objectives. The desirability of those
objectives is not itself considered. It appears, therefore, that both
in Committees of the whole House and in the subsidiary committees there is little or no attempt to relate policy proposals to the
resources available. However, there has been some effort recently
to establish a firmer connection between Parliament and these two
financial committees. On July 26th, 1960, Mr. Butler advanced
proposals, to be put into effect in the following session, by which
three days would be provided for debate on the reports from the
Estimates Committee and from the Public Accounts Committee.
Two of these days would be taken from the time allocated to
Supply Days and the other would come from Government time.
This rearrangement of time was coupled with a reorganisation of
the Estimates Committee timetable to encourage the appearance of

the Committees' reports as early as possible in the session to give
more opportunity to the House for debate upon them. Even with
these changes, the size of the House of Commons and the varying
degree of financial knowledge to be found amongst its members
make the thrifty use of resources which a large business might
show out of the question. There is naturally a strong temptation to
leave these considerations to the Treasury. There are some
matters, in fact, such as investment programmes, grants to local
government authorities, and wage negotiations, which are not discussed at all in the House of Commons as financial matters, but are
decided by the Treasury and the appropriate Minister.

The House of Commons in the past has always been keenly
conscious of its financial responsibilities. In a sense it still is, since
it has clearly been most reluctant to delegate its duties over finance
to any subsidiary committee of the House itself. Yet there is the
curious contradiction that it has, in practice, delegated powers of
decision of the most vital financial importance to the Treasury in
particular, and to some extent to the nationalised industries. The
chief need within the House of Commons is for well-informed,
concentrated, and relevant criticism of policies involving large sums
of public money. This need might be partly supplied by the
Finance Committee set up in 1968. Its function is to deal with the
Committee stage of the Finance Bill. Committee proceedings on
this, one of the key bills of every Parliamentary session, are
invariably lengthy, and there has been a gain in time for the House
by the delegation of detailed scrutiny of the bill to the fifty M.P.s
who form this new Committee. It is probable that there has been a
gain in effectiveness, too, since discussion of financial detail by fifty
members, chosen for their specialist knowledge, is likely to be more
fruitful than maintaining the pretence that it is vital for the Committee stage to be dealt with by the House. The basis of this fallacy
was that the House of Commons must participate directly and fully
in all stages of the Finance Bill, partly because of the bill's importance, and partly because of the need to preserve the constitutionally vital doctrine that the Executive must be accountable to the
Legislature for its actions. Neither of these considerations pre-
cludes the use of the Finance Committee; on the contrary, Parliamentary control over the Finance Bill is likely to be strengthened
by the use of this specialist body at the Committee stage. Moreover, it is still possible at the Report stage for members of the

House who did not serve on the Committee to add their own amendments.

The powers of the Finance Committee fall well short of those advocated prolifically by reformers. Ramsay Muir's view in 1930 was that 'There is no Parliamentary country in which Parliament has less control over finance than in Britain'.[1] There is no reason to believe that the situation has changed markedly since, in spite of the creation of the Finance Committee. Chancellors of the Exchequer must necessarily be strongly influenced by the wealth of extra-Parliamentary specialist advice at their disposal, from Treasury officials, from the Bank of England, and from other professional advisers. As a counter-balance to this formidable array the creation of an Estimates Committee with much wider powers than the present one will be advantageous. It would still be valuable for the Committee stage of the Finance Bill to be dealt with by a relatively small group of M.P.s, but it is even more important to strengthen Parliamentary machinery for the examination of the Estimates. Since Finance Bill proceedings and discussion of the Estimates overlap in time to some extent in the Parliamentary year, it will be necessary to use two committees to deal with these separate issues of raising and spending money. There are practical difficulties to be faced in that the number of Parliamentary committees cannot be expanded indefinitely, otherwise M.P.s would be overloaded with duties to a ridiculous extent and attendance in the House of Commons might become farcically small. On the other hand, there are practical difficulties too about a system which made it possible for a business firm to make a profit of £4½ million out of Government contract work on the Bloodhound Mark I missile;[2] clearly there is a need for establishing priorities between the number of Parliamentary committees which can be adequately manned, and the relative usefulness of the work they are called upon to do. It is difficult to believe, though, that close Parliamentary scrutiny of the Estimates can ever be regarded as a low priority. The Estimates Committee is effectively hamstrung by the limitations of its powers over policy matters, and it suffers from other weaknesses (see p. 102) which substantially

---

[1] Ramsay Muir, *How Britain is Governed* (Constable, 1930).

[2] The firm concerned voluntarily refunded most of the profits, but the episode strongly emphasised the need for greater vigilance over the expenditure of public money.

reduce its effectiveness. Some of these weaknesses cannot be removed. Limitations of time and staff make it impossible for a Parliamentary committee to examine all the Estimates in detail; reliance on the vigilance of the Treasury, to whom the Estimates are submitted before they are examined by Parliament, will continue to be essential. Yet the Treasury, like the Estimates Committee, can only draw attention authoritatively to points of detail. It cannot recast policy itself, and it is not infallible even on points of detail. The suggestion is, therefore, that the Estimates Committee should not only be allowed to summon departmental officials to explain the details of the Estimates but also to ask Ministers, or junior Ministers, to explain the financial implications of their policy proposals to the Committee; furthermore those policy proposals, in their financial aspects, should not be regarded as being exempt from criticism at this stage. It could be answered that policy is a matter for the whole House, not for one of its committees. Yet a large committee is a microcosm of the whole House, with the parties approximately represented according to their strength in the House of Commons, and it has the duty of reporting its findings to the House which then has a further opportunity for debate. The House would not be deprived of its responsibilities; it would merely be asked to think again. This would make some inroads in the time available for discussion of other issues; if it led to widespread saving in departmental spending, without less efficiency, it is at least arguable that the loss of time for general discussion would not be greatly missed. The Government's intention, announced in October 1970, to set up an Expenditure Committee will, when implemented, remove most of the defects from which the Estimates Committee has suffered. It is expected to consist of forty-five members who will examine policy as well as costs; they will be allowed to ask Ministers to explain policy decisions and to examine public expenditure on a wide front, including the nationalised industries and local government. Apart from this, Opposition members who served on the Committee could gain invaluable information from Ministers, officials, and their own observation; this would canalise debate on Supply Days much more effectively than happens at the moment. Greater concentration on purely financial issues would avoid waste of Parliamentary time and of the taxpayers' money. It would also make it easier to ensure that the expert advice on estimates and public accounts, available admittedly under the present system but used too little and too belatedly, would be taken much more fully into account. While it would be undesirable to give the Expenditure Committee any power of decision its reports could be debated in the House of Commons. Since it would have more influence than the present Estimates Committee, and a wider range of work, its reports would be more likely to attract attention. Besides, its mere existence would constitute a more effective restraint on Executive control of finance than exists so far. Critics will have their own views on where money might have been saved in recent years, but, as an instance, expenditure on missile construction would seem to rank high among projects where closer Parliamentary surveillance might have saved money.

Parliamentary thinking on the extension of the powers of committees is undoubtedly influenced by the hostility several leading politicians have felt towards specialist committees. This hostility is based on the fear that committees of the American Congressional type will develop, powerfully composed, and able to bring such a weight of continuous informed criticism to bear upon the work of Ministers and Departments that they become policy-making bodies themselves, hampering Executive decisions, and making the Legislature seem almost superfluous. Undoubtedly these dangers exist, but to treat the idea of specialist committees as if it were as lethal to Parliament as Guy Fawkes intended to be is a mistake. The American system, based on the Separation of Powers, makes necessary the powers of investigation and criticism allocated to Congressional committees. In Britain, where Ministers form part of both the Executive and Legislature, and are regularly available for questioning and debate, the same need does not arise. Besides, the innate procedural conservatism of M.P.s makes it highly improbable that any specialist committee set up at Westminster will become a victim of megalomania; the way in which the specialist committees on Science and Technology and on Scottish Affairs have worked so far reinforces this view, though plainly a reformed Estimates Committee would have to have much more power than these committees if it is to be of any value.

Both the problems considered in this chapter—the time available for Parliamentary proceedings, and control of national finance —raise issues touching on the essential purposes of the House of Commons. Neither of these problems is insoluble. A greater

willingness to delegate work to its own committees and a greater
confidence in its own latent powers would do much to remedy
some of the present-day weaknesses. Confidence in its powers is
not helped by the fashionable cynicism prevalent among the public
towards politicians, nor by excessive preoccupation with party
warfare in debates. It serves little purpose to be a member of an
historic institution unless it leads to a full awareness of the significance of that history. The historic objective of the House of
Commons, since the seventeenth century, has been to protect the
community against misuse of power by the Executive. This is the
responsibility of the whole House of Commons, irrespective of
party. There is ample evidence that many M.P.s are keenly aware
of this responsibility. Yet there is no doubt that, if party allegiances
were to become too rigid, the House of Commons would not be
able to fulfil its historic role. This is of considerable relevance to
the future development of Parliamentary procedure. If procedural
reforms were habitually to be considered merely from the standpoint of securing a position of advantage which would help one or
other party to win the next election it is abundantly clear that this
could be a serious obstacle to national interests.

FURTHER READING

Lord Campion, *An Introduction to the Procedure of the House of Commons*
(Macmillan, 3rd Edition, 1958).
Eric Taylor, *The House of Commons at Work* (Pelican Books, 5th Edition,
1963).
A. H. Hanson and H. V. Wiseman, *Parliament at Work* (Stevens, 1962).
Peter Richards, *Honourable Members* (Faber, 1959).
K. C. Wheare, *Government by Committee* (Oxford—Clarendon Press,
2nd Edition, 1955).
B. Chubb, *The Control of National Expenditure* (O.U.P., 1952).
P. Einzig, *The Control of the Purse* (Secker & Warburg, 1959).
R. Butt, *The Power of Parliament* (Constable, 1967).
B. Crick, *The Reform of Parliament* (Weidenfeld & Nicolson, 1964).
Sir Ivor Jennings, *Parliament* (Cambridge University Press, 2nd Edition,
1961).
Hansard Society, *Parliamentary Reform 1933–60* (1961).
The Study of Parliament Group, *Reforming the Commons* (P.E.P., 1965).
H.C. 92–I of 1958–9. *Report from the Select Committee on Procedure.*
H.C. 153 of 1966–7. *First Report from the Select Committee on Procedure.*
H.C. 283 of 1966–7. *Third Report from the Select Committee on Procedure.*
See also Comments on Further Reading, p. 211.

# 7

## *Voting Systems*

Characteristics of the British voting system. Other systems: cumulative voting, party lists, second ballot, alternative vote, single transferable vote. Merits of proportional representation. Reasons why it has not been adopted. Assessment of the possible effects if post-war elections had been by proportional representation. Retention of the existing system coupled with the emergence of a single Radical party would give the best solution.

THEME: No voting system combines fair representation with the certainty of stable government. The existing system works best when there are only two parties, but, even in the present situation, it is preferable to the alternatives.

Voting, as it is conducted in Britain, is looked upon as the climax of the democratic process. Because of its quasi-sacrosanct nature it merits rather more attention than it is sometimes given. The freedom of the voter to use his vote as he chooses, or not at all, is a feature of the system which can be taken for granted. Apart from this, the usual defence of the British method of voting is that it is simple, expedient, and, by and large, fair. The least controversial aspect of the system is its simplicity. All British subjects over the age of eighteen are allowed to vote, with certain self-evident exceptions such as peers, lunatics, and various categories of law-breakers. On the appointed and well-publicised day the voter merely has to go to the polling-station and place a cross on the ballot-paper against the name of the candidate he favours. The choice will generally lie between two or three candidates; it would be unusual for there to be more than four candidates. The system needs little understanding, and the number of spoilt ballot papers is negligible.

The simplicity of the system is easy to establish, but the claim of its expediency is another matter. It is said to provide a stable government since it favours a two-party system. The party forming the Government will have a working majority, and the other party will form a strong Opposition, ready at the shortest notice to take over if internal divisions should bring about the downfall of the Government. The suggestion that the British system of voting encourages the two-party system is probably true. The 1920s provide some exceptions, but this was a period when the challenge to Conservatism was being taken over from the Liberals by the Labour Party. This produced situations such as the election of December, 1923, when Britain experienced in an extreme form difficulties imposed by a three-party system. The Conservatives gained 256 seats, Labour 191, and the Liberals 158. The two latter parties combined to defeat the Conservatives in January, 1924, when Parliament met, and the Labour Party came to power as a minority government. The near equality between the three parties did not last. By 1929 when the Labour Party formed its second Government Liberal representation had shrunk to 58 seats, the Conservatives had 260, and the Labour Party itself 288. The Labour Government was still a minority one, but the pattern emerges of one radical party being squeezed slowly but decisively out of prominence while another takes its place. Supporters of the British system look on the situation in the 1920s as a purely temporary phenomenon therefore, but it should be realised that it may recur if there should be a revival of Liberalism. A repetition of the election results experienced in the 1920s might then be expected, though there is no certainty that it would resolve itself as quickly as it did then by the virtual disappearance of one of the radical parties.

The British electoral method may not automatically produce a two-party system, but the elections of this century, with the exception just mentioned, show that it tends to do so. Experience of the three-party system in the 1920s, producing two minority governments, established an understandable preference in Britain for the two-party system. Coalitions in Britain in the twentieth century have not been notably popular, excluding war-time when a common objective unites the parties. The coalition of 1918–22 of Liberals and Conservatives under Lloyd George's leadership developed such strains that it broke down. The National Government of 1931 began as an all-party government, but in the House of Commons, and eventually in the Cabinet, the Conservatives were so preponderant that it hardly qualifies for the description of a coalition. Coalitions then, whether voluntary as in 1918, or involuntary as in the 'Lib.-Lab.' alliance of 1924, have not been associated with stable government in Britain. The advantage claimed for the existing system that it makes coalitions unlikely is therefore an important one.

Since the inter-war years could perhaps be regarded as a period when the Liberal Party was giving way to the Labour Party it would be fairer to consider the working of the system in the post-1945 period. Advocates of the system would no doubt agree that the situation had then stabilised itself with the virtual disappearance of the Liberal Party. Five elections, those of 1945, 1955, 1959, 1966 and 1970, created governments with sound majorities, so that there was no need to consider the possibility of a coalition. Three of the elections, however, gave very narrow majorities indeed to the Labour and Conservative Parties respectively. In 1950 Labour had 315 seats, Conservatives 297, and the Liberals 9. In 1951 the Conservatives had 320, Labour 296, and the Liberals 6. In 1964 the figures were Labour 317, Conservatives 304, and the Liberals 9. Even when the third party has been reduced to numbers which are artificially small in relation to its general support in the country, it is obviously still quite possible under the British system to obtain a result where the Government majority is very precarious. Furthermore, had the Liberals gained only a few more seats they would have been in a position to hold the balance between the two parties, and to select whichever party they chose to form a Government with Liberal support. The weakness of the system is that it is based on the assumption that a two-party system meets the needs of the great bulk of the electorate. With only two parties to choose from the existing method is ideal, but the third party is a distinct embarrassment to the system, and the difficulty it poses has not yet been solved.

The strongest claim made for the British method of voting is that it is expedient since it leads to the formation of stable governments. This is held to justify some of the imperfections in the system which will be examined later. Yet, as has been seen, the evidence in favour of the present system is inconclusive. Even if the transitional period of the 1920s is ignored on the assumption, possibly fallacious, that the Liberal challenge was then ending, the post-1945 elections have produced governments in 1950 and 1964 which did not stay the course, and another in 1951 which could have been ended by a very slight alteration in the number of seats gained by the respective parties.

The charge against the present system that it is unfair is based on the large number of votes which in one way or another are ignored. In industrial areas a Labour candidate may easily have a surplus of some 20,000 votes over his nearest rival. These surplus votes are wasted. Conservative majorities tend to be smaller, so that a situation can eventuate in which the Conservative Party wins more seats than the Labour Party, but has fewer total votes. This happened in the 1951 election. The Conservatives polled 200,000 fewer votes than Labour but gained twenty-four more seats. The anti-Conservative vote, taking the Liberals into account also, was 920,000 more than the Conservative vote. These figures do not fully represent the situation. The anti-Conservative vote, for instance, does not take into account the fact that party bargains were made in some constituencies so that by agreement some Conservative voters would support Liberal or Independent candidates; nor does it allow for the fact that the Labour Party did not contest some Ulster seats so that vast Tory majorities were not counted in these figures. A full assessment taking factors of this kind into account would show some reduction in the anti-Conservative vote. Clearly, too, the trend was in favour of the Conservatives and their supporters who increased their vote by 1,225,000 approximately compared with the 1950 election, while the corresponding Labour increase was 635,000. It is relevant in this connection to realise that the 1950 election, which was rather more favourable to Labour, had only secured a very slender majority for that party, insufficient in fact to make the survival of the Labour Government possible. It may, therefore, have been sound politically that the Conservatives took office. The fact remains that by the workings of our electoral system it became possible for a minority government representing less than half the number of those who voted to stay in power until it sought re-election in 1955.

There is nothing freakish, historically, about this situation. Governments representing less than half of the voters are commonplace in recent times. In 1959, when the Conservatives had an overall majority of 100, they polled only 49·4% of the votes recorded. Between elections the swing of public opinion against the Government intensifies, as by-elections show. For most of its life, therefore, a Government will have the support of considerably less than half of the voting population. This comes about not only through the wastage of votes, where an Opposition candidate has a large majority, but also through the large number of seats which are won on a minority vote. Peter Richards, in *Honourable Members*, quotes a perfect example of this from the 1945 General Election result in the constituency of Caithness and Sutherland.[1] The figures were:

| | |
|---|---|
| E. L. Gandar Dower (Con.) | 5,564 |
| R. McInnes (Lab.) | 5,558 |
| Rt. Hon. Sir A. Sinclair (Lib.) | 5,503 |
| Conservative majority | 6 |

Approximately 66% of the voters were opposed to the candidate who was returned to Westminster as their representative. The existence of the third party in this century has made similar situations commonplace, even if not quite to the same degree as in the Caithness election. In 1951, and 1955, 6% of M.P.s were elected on a minority vote, but this has been the lowest figure in post-war years. In 1945 the number was 28%, in 1950, 30%, in 1959, 13%, in 1964, 37%, in 1966, 29%, in 1970, 38%. These figures demonstrate the unrepresentative nature of the present system. They can be justified only if it produces a more stable government than any other voting system. This is a powerful consideration. Its claims to do so are not invincible. It remains to be seen whether any of the alternative voting schemes offers a better solution.

Some of these systems are unlikely to win much favour in Britain, either because of intrinsic defects or because they are so alien to our tradition. Cumulative voting, for instance, which would require large multi-member constituencies, allows each elector to have as many votes as there are seats. The voter can give all his votes to one candidate or can distribute them amongst candidates according to his preference. It is possible that minority parties would gain by this system. The larger parties would presumably put up two or three candidates for each constituency. Their supporters would be tempted to share out their votes. A small party, on the other hand, would only put up one candidate, who would gain by the fact that his supporters, with no divided

[1] *Ibid.*, p. 36.

allegiance, would give all their votes to him. This might be circumvented by systematic organisation of the voters by the large parties, but the complexity of the scheme, coupled with its undue partiality for minority parties, makes it altogether undesirable.

Another suggestion is the party-list system. If frequency of use were any criterion of the merit of a voting system this would be the best of all, judging by Continental example. Apart from Eastern Europe it has been used in Germany, Italy, Belgium, Greece, and France, for instance, in one form or another. It is a form of proportional representation. Multi-member constituencies are used. The parties each draw up a list of candidates and the elector votes for the particular list he prefers. Seats are then allocated to the parties in proportion to the number of votes obtained. The parties then fill the seats from their lists by choosing their candidates in order. Sometimes this order has been decided by the party organisations themselves; sometimes the electors may vary the order of the party list according to their personal preference for candidates. The latter method involves considerable complications. On the other hand, selection by the party organisations alone suggests a remoteness from local feeling which would not be acceptable in Britain. A similar objection would no doubt be felt to the large multi-member constituencies. Selection of suitable candidates by the central party organisations does admittedly take place in Britain, but it is apt to be unpopular locally as the 1962 by-election in Orpington proved.[1] There is the further objection to the party-list system that it is firmly associated in the minds of many with election proceedings in totalitarian countries with single-party systems.

Two other schemes, the second ballot and the alternative vote, used in single-member constituencies, are very similar to each other. The aim of both of these is to eliminate the winning of seats by a minority vote, which bedevils the British system. The second ballot, as the name implies, may require two elections. If no candidate has an overall majority at the first election the last candidate is then withdrawn and the voters proceed to the polls a second time, when a final decision is reached. In a country where there are

---

[1] In this constituency, traditionally Conservative, the local candidate, Mr. Lubbock, a Liberal, decisively defeated Mr. Goldman, who was chosen as the Conservative Party candidate primarily because of his services to Conservatism at their national headquarters.

virtually only three parties this seems a pre-eminently fair system.
A possible result in a first ballot might be as follows:

Con.        25,000
Lab.        20,000
Lib.        10,000

Since the Conservative candidate has no overall majority a
second ballot would then become necessary. The Liberal candidate would accordingly be withdrawn, and after much canvassing
for the floating 10,000 votes, a second ballot might give the
following result:

Lab.        28,000 (8,000 from the Liberals)
Con.        27,000 (2,000 from the Liberals)

The Labour candidate would then be declared elected. This system
would greatly reduce the likelihood of minority victories in elections; it would increase support for the third party, in this country
the Liberals, since potential supporters of the Liberals would see
more hope of their votes counting. The defect in the system, which
became apparent when it was used in France, was that the delay
between one ballot and another led to intrigues and party-bargains
in order to catch the floating vote. Apart from this there is the
expense and interference with normal routine involved in a second
election.

A simple way of overcoming these last objections is to use the
alternative vote system. The principle is the same as the second
ballot, but only one election is necessary. The voter shows on the
ballot paper his first and second choices, simply by putting the
figures '1' and '2' against the names of candidates. If no candidate
has an overall majority of first preferences the last candidate is
withdrawn. The second preferences of his supporters are then
examined and allocated to the other parties. This is a simple system
and fair to the three main parties, if not to the very small minority
parties. The effect it would have on government in Britain will be
examined shortly, after considering a further scheme which is the
logical extension of the alternative vote method, namely the single
transferable vote system.

The aim of this latter system is to remove completely all the
inequalities of the single-ballot system. Large constituencies,
returning possibly four or five members, would be necessary.

There would be several candidates. Voters would show their preference, as in the alternative vote system, by putting a figure '1' opposite their first choice and '2' opposite their second choice, but then they would continue to show their preferences in order until they came down to candidates whom they felt they could not possibly support. Thus voters might return ballot papers showing as many as six or seven preferences in descending order of popularity. The next stages concern the electoral officials. They have to determine first of all the 'quota'. This is the necessary minimum number of votes required in order to secure election. To determine the quota presents no great difficulty. In a constituency of 90,000 voters, for instance, where there are five candidates contesting for two vacancies, the minimum number of votes required to ensure election would be 30,001; (this number is secured by dividing the number of voters (90,000) by one more than the number of vacancies (2) i.e. divide by 3. To this result (30,000) simply add 1.)

A count of the first preferences of voters will then establish which candidates have secured their quota. Any votes they secure beyond this number are superfluous. This obviously has some relevance to the Labour Party's complaint of the large number of votes wasted in industrial constituencies where the Labour majority may be very large. The remedy for this in the system described is to distribute the surplus votes of successful candidates in accordance with the second preferences shown on their ballot papers. If 40,000 is the quota, and the successful Labour candidate has 50,000 first preference votes, then 10,000 of these are spare. The 50,000 votes are then examined for the second preferences shown. These second preferences could be in the ratio of 4:1 for the second Labour candidate and for a Liberal candidate respectively. The 10,000 surplus votes are accordingly distributed in the same ratio. Thus 8,000 would go to the second Labour candidate and 2,000 to the Liberal candidate. These additional votes may be enough to bring one or both of them up to the necessary quota, so that those successful could then be declared elected.

In a multi-member constituency there may still be additional seats to be filled. In order to give other candidates the requisite quota to ensure election the candidates at the bottom of the list are eliminated in turn. The second and other preferences shown on their voting-papers are examined, and distributed as the papers indicate. This will continue until all the vacant seats have been filled when candidates, still in the running, have received sufficient additional votes by this distribution to reach the electoral quota.

If the overriding purpose in a voting system is exact representation of the voters' wishes then the single transferable vote method is the fairest of all. There are no wasted votes, either for candidates at the top of the poll with large majorities or for candidates at the bottom of the poll who are eliminated. In both these eventualities voters know that their second preferences will be taken into account, and possibly later preferences too, so that their personal wishes will almost certainly have some bearing on the result of the election. Although the proportion of voters who actually use their right of voting at General Elections seems quite high under the present system—over 70%—this still means that many citizens do not vote. In the 1970 election nearly eleven million failed to do so. Some of them would not do so whatever the system but others certainly abstain from realisation that in some constituencies their vote is likely to be wasted. The Liberals, in particular, have suffered from this feeling. Voters who would have supported the Liberals were deterred from doing so by the set-backs of the post-war period. Since a Liberal victory in almost any constituency was usually unlikely, the choice for the 'floating voter' with general Liberal sympathies was either to vote without real conviction for the Conservative or Labour Parties or to abstain. The Liberal vote during these years was not entirely representative of the support which existed for them, as the by-elections of 1962 would seem to show. These successes were brought about not by any marked change in the policy of the Liberal Party, nor in the policies of the other two parties, but simply by a change of mood, a belief that the Liberal Party was not defunct after all. Under the single transferable vote system there would have been no need for the Liberal Party to have been quite so much at the mercy of the fickle moods of public opinion. The system itself would have secured accurate representation of Liberal support. The extraneous factors which gave a false picture of Liberal support in the post-war years would have been removed.

The features of the system which make it beneficial to the interests of the third party, at the moment the Liberals, also help other minority parties to secure fair representation. The three main parties would still be dominant under any of the suggested reforms, but it is possible that other parties could gain a few seats under the single transferable vote system. Minority parties are apt to compensate for their small numbers by their vigour and this could well lead to livelier debate in the House of Commons.

In view of the undoubted merits of the single transferable vote system it is of interest to know why it has not been adopted. A cynical answer is that no government which has come to power under the existing system would wish to court the risk of defeat at the next election by changing the system. The last Liberal Government came to an end in 1915 when a coalition was formed. The Conservative and Labour Governments since then have obviously had no motive to support a change from which the Liberal Party was by far the most likely to gain. But consideration of party advantage is not the only reason why the system has not won support. The crux of the matter is whether the single transferable vote system, or the somewhat similar alternative vote system, would provide stable government. Admittedly, stable government is not a certainty under the present system either, but the evidence suggests that there is a better chance of stability with our present method than by means of the various forms of proportional representation. These latter methods would certainly have the effect of increasing support for the Liberal Party. In 1945, for instance, Labour won 396 seats, the Conservatives 200, and the Liberals (including the Liberal Nationalists) 25. If seats had been allocated in proportion to the votes cast, and this is the idea of proportional representation, Labour would have won 307 seats, the Conservatives 256, and the Liberals 58. In fact, of course, under proportional representation the Liberal Party would be much stronger than these hypothetical figures show. Voters would no longer regard a Liberal vote as a wasted vote, and there would be many more Liberal candidates to take advantage of a system so encouraging to their interests. Even from the figures shown for the 1945 election it is obvious that if proportional representation had been used Labour would have needed Liberal support to keep the Government in being, instead of the large majority which it had in practice. In the elections which have followed it is easy to see by comparable calculations to that for the 1945 election that the effect of the system in practice would have been to give the party which came third in the polls the opportunity to place in power whichever of the other two parties it wished. No single party since 1945 would have had a working majority on its own.

It is not difficult to visualise the deadlocks, frustrations, party-bargaining, compromise, and rapidly recurring elections, which would have been brought about by this situation. This, moreover, was at a critical time in world politics, when the cold war was dominating attention, when alliances were being constructed of vital strategic importance, dependent territories were seeking their freedom, plans for nuclear development and defence were being devised, while at home urgent problems of reconstruction demanded attention. The Liberal Party could hardly have accommodated itself both to the Conservative and the Labour policies over these issues; on the other hand, failure to do so would clearly have produced a deadlock on some occasions. This would have been prejudicial in the extreme to our interests, and to those of our allies. The present system may lead to the tyranny of the majority, but that is preferable to the tyranny of the minority which proportional representation is likely to produce in this country. It cannot be acceptable to put the third party with the smallest number of seats into a position where it can nominate the Government itself, merely by granting it its support. Yet the post-war voting figures show that this situation would happen more often than not if seats were proportional to the votes cast.[1]

The real need is not for a change of voting system but for a realisation that three parties are one too many. As a means of choice between two parties the British system is excellent. It is simple; it does not require large multi-member constituencies, where contact between M.P.s and their constituents is likely to be lost; it is likely to produce a Government with a sound working majority. The ideal solution, therefore, would be for the emergence of a single Radical party to oppose the Conservatives. The Conservatives represent one philosophy of government, the radicals, in their different ways, another. But the latter can hardly do themselves justice while they are divided. Obviously politically extreme parties would find themselves unable to accept the degree of compromise which the creation of a single Radical party would

[1] Employing similar calculations D. E. Butler, in the second edition of *The Electoral System in Britain since 1918*, published in September, 1963, has also pointed out the drawbacks of the system of proportional representation (pp. 189–94, *ibid.*).

entail. Nevertheless, an alliance of Labour and Liberal interests would be the most important step in the formation of a single Radical party; the suggestions made to this effect in the early 1960s showed that it was a political possibility, and though the idea has subsequently fallen into disfavour it may be revived. The central problem is that the present electoral system undoubtedly imposes almost total frustration on the Liberal Party who, to give merely one recent instance, gained 7·4% of the votes cast in 1970 but were rewarded with less than 1% of the Parliamentary seats. Those who support proportional representation will argue that the solution is to adopt a fairer electoral system than the present one, but the risks of adopting proportional representation have already been indicated, and it is unrealistic to ignore also the political factors which make its adoption extremely unlikely. The remaining alternatives for the Liberals are these, assuming that the present electoral system is maintained. They can hope that by their efforts Liberalism will attract such widespread support that they can one day form a Government. More modestly, as an interim aim, they may have to be content with the hope that for many years the most they can achieve is that electoral chance will give them a position where they have enough seats to make a Conservative or Labour Government dependent upon their support. Lastly there is the possibility of a 'Lib.-Lab.' alliance, or even, in the shifting world of politics, of a Conservative–Liberal alliance. Political factors will be a far stronger influence in shaping the Liberals' choice from these alternatives than considerations of electoral arithmetic on polling day.

### FURTHER READING

Enid Lakeman and J. D. Lambert, *Voting in Democracies* (Faber, 2nd Edition, 1959).
D. E. Butler, *The Electoral System in Britain since 1918* (O.U.P., 2nd Edition, 1963).
D. E. Butler and Anthony King, *The British General Election of 1964* (Macmillan, 1965).
D. E. Butler and Anthony King, *The British General Election of 1966* (Macmillan, 1966).
D. E. Butler and M. Pinto-Duschinsky, *The British General Election of 1970* (Macmillan, 1971).
J. F. S. Ross, *Elections and Electors* (Eyre & Spottiswoode, 1955).
   See also Comments on Further Reading, p. 211.

# 8

## *The House of Lords*

Long-standing nature of the criticisms of the House of Lords. Modification of the Labour Party view of the House of Lords is significant. The use of Second Chambers in other countries. The functions and value of the Second Chamber in Britain. Attempts at reform of membership and powers of the House of Lords 1910–69.

THEME: There are anomalies in the present powers and composition of the House of Lords, but the dilemma of reconciling strong membership with limited powers has so far defied solution.

It is probable that to criticise the British constitution effectively it is necessary to be a foreigner. Only then would it be possible for the anomalies in the constitution to strike the understanding with full force. To those brought up in Britain familiarity surrounds our apparently curious constitutional habits with a haze, which we seldom attempt to penetrate. A foreigner, unfortified with our mystical certainty in the wisdom of our constitution, might well be baffled by many aspects of our system. We have a monarch who is head of all government, but with virtually no powers; we have a governing party, which, even at election-time, only occasionally represents more than half the voting population; in a democratic country we have a Prime Minister whose influence between elections is comparable to that of a dictator. Above all, we have the House of Lords still with effective powers, but with a membership qualification based on the social order of the Middle Ages.

But even in Britain, where antiquity and wisdom are so often regarded as synonymous, there have been some penetrating criticisms of the membership of the House of Lords, not least from the Lords themselves. Lord Samuel's witty remark on the composition of the House of Lords, to the effect that the efficiency of that House was secured by the almost permanent absenteeism of most

of its members, was a more telling blow than the clumsier attacks
sometimes aimed at the Lords. There is nothing new about these
criticisms. The radicals from at least the 1870s onwards were
bitterly antagonistic towards the House of Lords, and criticism
rose to a crescendo over the events leading to the Parliament Act of
1911. The close association of the House of Lords with the Conservative Party was used openly by Balfour and Lord Lansdowne
to achieve a degree of negative control over legislation, in spite of
the huge Liberal majority in the House of Commons. The indig-
nation of the Liberals led to the cleverly conducted political campaign between the 1909 Budget and the 1911 Parliament Act, by
which the absolute veto of the House of Lords was reduced to a
suspensory veto of two years, later, in 1949, reduced to one year.
Among the many attacks made on the Lords in the heated atmosphere of 1909-11 the invective of Churchill, then a Liberal, stands
out still with characteristic force. He called the House of Lords 'a
one-sided, hereditary, unprized, unrepresentative, irresponsible
absentee'.

Although the powers of the House of Lords have been greatly
reduced, its composition has not been substantially changed by the
influx of men and women who have joined it since the 1958 Act
providing for the appointment of Life Peers. Considering the
violence and long continuance of the criticisms made of the
membership of the Lords, it is surprising at first sight that more
radical changes have not been made. The most radical change would
be abolition of the House of Lords. This would show the social neatness of the guillotine, and would be based also on the apparently
logical approach that as the Lords' powers have been progressively
reduced in 1911 and 1949 all that remains is the completion of the
process by abolishing the House altogether. It is sometimes argued
that its powers are now so trivial that abolition would make little
difference. For a time this outright solution commended itself to
the Labour Party, and was put forward as part of their programme
in the 1935 election. Experience of office between 1945-51 modified
Labour opinion.[1] The Lords were able to show their usefulness by
the non-partisan approach they showed to some of the nationalisation bills, where their concern was not to challenge the principle of

[1] See *Government and Parliament*, pp. 176–8, for Lord Morrison's views
on the attitude of the House of Lords to the Labour Governments of this
period.

the bills, but to help in making them workable in practice. So long
as this approach prevailed repetition of the 1909–11 events was
unlikely. The Lords may not have approved of the schemes proposed, but they were recognising the prior right of the House of
Commons, as the popularly elected body, to impose its will over
legislative matters.

There were some controversial issues in the Labour Party
legislative programme, however, where it might have been unwise
to count on the House of Lords adopting this attitude of benevolent impartiality. This applied particularly to the Iron and Steel
nationalisation bill. The Labour Government was naturally
anxious to make full use of its period of office, and it would have
been frustrating in the extreme if its legislation of the 1948–50
period were brought to nothing by the imposition of the Lords'
two-year veto, followed by a General Election which the Conservatives might win. Accordingly a bill was introduced, which became
law in 1949, reducing the power of veto of the Lords to one year.
Among some quarters of the Labour Party it is regarded as intolerable that the Lords should have any power of veto at all. They
would like to see the Second Chamber used as an amending and
advisory body, whose suggestions could be overruled if they were
unwelcome in the House of Commons. There does not, however,
appear to be any great pressure from any quarter for the abolition
of the House of Lords. It is possible, therefore, that if many of its
enemies are prepared to allow its continued existence the House of
Lords may have merits to commend it. Some of these have been
implicit in the description of its relationship to the Labour
Governments of 1945–51, but it would now be fitting to consider
more fully the arguments in favour of keeping this much-abused
House.

As a beginning, it is worth realising that the existence of a
Second Chamber is not unique in the Governments of the world.
The existence of two Chambers in the United States, the Senate
and the House of Representatives, is familiar enough, but, apart
from this, bicameral government once adopted has been retained in
nearly all the countries of the world. New Zealand, in 1950, and
Denmark, in 1954, have abolished their Second Chambers, but
these are small countries and their example is outweighed by the
acceptance of the two-Chamber system in Canada, Australia,
Sweden, and surprisingly, perhaps, the U.S.S.R., as well as in the

United States and Britain itself. These countries differ in the division of powers between the two Chambers. In Sweden, for instance, the two Chambers are of equal strength, and solve differences either by use of a Joint Committee, or, in respect of the Budget, by a simple majority taking the total number of votes in the two Houses combined. The urgency of Budget legislation makes this a more appropriate system than delegation to a Joint Committee. There are interesting points of difference of this kind, therefore, but it is a chastening thought for the outright abolitionists that so many of the countries of the world with a variety of political systems still find it necessary to make use of a Second Chamber, even if the membership qualifications are very different from those prevailing in Britain.

Apart from this general justification for the House of Lords there are several specific points to be made on its behalf. According to the Bryce Commission report of 1918 the chief functions of the House of Lords were to share the burden of legislation with the House of Commons, to use its power of veto to prevent over-hasty legislation, to act as a forum for debate, and to act as the final court of appeal. This last use has no relevance to the political functions of the House of Lords, and by custom only the Law Lords attend when the House is meeting in its judicial capacity. The major justification for the House of Lords is the assistance it is able to give to the Lower House in the work of legislation. Viscount Hailsham, in a Parliamentary debate, pointed out that it would be a mistake to regard the House of Lords as 'a decorative appendage'.[1] His view would command support among all the major parties. The Labour Party leaders, for instance, were far more appreciative of the usefulness of the House of Lords after 1945–51 than they had been before. The Lords during that period introduced many amendments to the complicated nationalisation acts, not primarily with any obstructive purpose, but simply to ensure the production of an efficient piece of legislation. The number of amendments made it evident that, in spite of the careful scrutiny of most legislation by the House of Commons, there is need for a vigilant Second Chamber as well. The House of Lords may also initiate

[1] Report of House of Lords' Debate, April 10th, 1962, col. 374. Viscount Hailsham renounced his title in 1963, and returned to the House of Commons as Mr. Quintin Hogg. It would be unfair, however, to regard this action as a contradiction of his own words, especially as in 1970 he accepted a life peerage on becoming Lord Chancellor.

legislation, if it is of a non-controversial nature. In the 1968-9 session, for instance, Government bills on Customs Duties, Family Law Reform, Genocide, the Sea Fish Industry, and Trustees Savings Banks were introduced in the House of Lords. Obviously, public legislation is frequently controversial, but there is much wider scope for the non-party approach in private bill legislation, and in the scrutiny of provisional orders. Work of this subordinate but useful nature is ideally suited for relieving the House of Commons of some of the increasing burden of legislation. The work of acting as hand-maid to the House of Commons should, therefore, be a cause for gratitude rather than complaint; it is essential to realise, too, that since the Parliament Act of 1911 the Lords have been shorn of the claims they unwisely made at that time to tamper with financial legislation from the Lower House.

The function of acting as a forum of debate also deserves favourable consideration. The nucleus of regular attenders at House of Lords proceedings consists either of ex-Cabinet ministers who have earned their titles through their political work, of life peers, or of members of ancient families in whom a sense of public service is ingrained by long traditions. The presence of the latter may require more justification. Obviously there may be exceptions, but a willingness to attend House of Lords' sittings regularly is one criterion of a genuine concern for national progress; moreover, a long family record of service in national affairs ought not automatically to be a matter for censure. The other gibe levelled against the Lords is that many of its regular members are old to the verge of senility, a chage made on the grounds that changing economic circumstances have required younger peers to take on a full-time career. They have not the time to attend the House, and the small sum of daily expenses allowed for attendance there is no very great incentive. The creation of life peers has not greatly altered the position, since, as Lord Salisbury pointed out in a 1962 Lords' debate,[1] the life peers themselves tend to be elderly. It is admittedly, then, the older members who predominate, but it has yet to be demonstrated that this is harmful. Age and experience may not necessarily be interchangeable terms, but they are more likely to be so in political matters than youth and wisdom. Experience of politics and of public service provides a sound background for effective Parliamentary debate. These characteristics are to be

[1] Report of House of Lords, Debate, April 10th, 1962, col. 405.

found in good measure among the minority who make it their business to attend regularly. It has been asserted that the standard of debate in the House of Lords is in fact superior to that in the House of Commons, partly because of the greater experience to be found in the Upper House, and partly because party discipline weighs more lightly upon its members. Besides, without the need to placate constituents, or to win votes for the next election, peers can speak their minds freely, so that debates gain in pungency and relevance. Even the normally cursory accounts of proceedings which appear in the Press make this apparent. It is true that the House of Lords is likely to lose some of its most active members to the House of Commons following the 1963 legislation on the surrender of peerages, but hardly in sufficient numbers to weaken its debating merits greatly.

The remaining function of the House of Lords—its power to impose delay on legislation from the House of Commons—is the one which has aroused the most doubt. The power of veto has been used with great discretion since 1911. The Lords have realised that, since they have no mandate from the people, they must be content with a subordinate role in the constitution. Some Government legislation has been rejected, such as the Government of Ireland Bill of 1912, the Parliament Bill of 1948, and the Rhodesian sanctions order of 1968. In general, however, under a Labour or a Liberal Government, the House of Lords has resorted to heavy amendments rather than rejection. During most of this time, in fact, there were Conservative Governments in power, but it can be said in defence of the Lords that, as was seen earlier in the chapter, they generally did not adopt a partisan attitude towards the Labour Government legislation of the post-1945 period. Naturally, with a Conservative majority ever available in the House of Lords, Conservative Government bills are better placed than those coming from Liberal or Labour Governments. The last time a specifically Conservative bill of major importance was rejected in the House of Lords was in 1823. This apparent partiality has called forth the defence that the Conservatives are less in need of restraint than their rivals, because Conservative reforms are unlikely to be characterised by the undue hastiness which is alleged to be the weakness of radical parties. This suggestion seems intolerable to sections of the Labour Party who feel quite able to take their own decisions on the timing and desirability of legislation. They feel that a purely nominal delay, of one month for instance, would be entirely adequate. They are on strong ground, too, in pointing out that a Labour Government is under an unfair disadvantage in that it cannot count on pushing all its measures through in its last year of office. There is always the threat that the Lords may use their power of veto though the 1949 Act has greatly reduced the effectiveness of this device. The Conservative Party, on the other hand, can bank with certainty on the help of the Lords if ever it is urgently needed.

The reform proposals put forward in approximately the last fifty years have occasionally glanced at this question of the veto, but have been much more concerned with the question of membership. The veto after all is only very occasionally applied, but the special nature of the membership of the House of Lords is much more frequently apparent. Naïve critics, ignorant of the useful functions performed by the Lords, base their attacks entirely on prejudice against any aristocratic share in the work of government. It would be foolish, however, to jettison the experience of many of the Lords simply from devotion to the ideal of levelling-down. The chief reform schemes, therefore, all take account of the valuable nucleus of knowledgeable peers, and, in their different ways, try to blend them into their new proposals.

The earliest official proposals of this century to reform the membership belong to the period of the Lords-Commons quarrel which culminated in the 1911 Parliament Act. These suggestions for reform came from the Lords themselves, but they were belated, and too closely bound up with the issues at stake at this time to be regarded as anything else but attempts by the Lords to divert attention from the crucial point, namely, which House was to have constitutional dominance. This criticism does not apply to one of the reformers, Lord Rosebery, who had made earlier attempts to reform the House's membership, but the fact that the Lords had shown little interest in these proposals until late in 1910 savoured too much of deathbed repentance. The proposals themselves are of some interest, however. They are much more open-minded than one would expect, when controversy was so heated. Lord Rosebery in November, 1910, proposed that the House should consist of 'Lords of Parliament'. Some would be elected by the peers from their own number; some would be nominated by the Crown; some would be automatically members by virtue of their office; some would be nominated by the Government, on behalf of the Crown, from distinguished members of the community who were not already in the House of Lords. This was a reasonable compromise, though the question of the number of members from each source needed to be resolved. A similar willingness to accept quite drastic modifications in membership is evident in Lord Lansdowne's proposals in 1911. One hundred members were to be elected by, and from, the peers themselves, one hundred nominated by the Crown in proportion to party strength in the House of Commons, and one hundred and twenty chosen by M.P.s organised on a regional basis. The period of appointment was to be for twelve years, with retirement at three-year intervals. The probable membership, including Princes of the Blood, Bishops, and Law Lords, would be three hundred and fifty. Both these schemes came too late and did not arouse much genuine enthusiasm in the Lords. For a time the matter remained in abeyance. The Parliament Act was duly passed, excluding Money Bills as defined by the Speaker from amendment by the House of Lords, and reducing the absolute veto to a suspensory one of two years. There were vague references in the preface to the Act to the idea of reforming the membership, but these ideas were temporarily shelved in deference to the more urgent events of the pre-1914 period.

The next reform scheme was that put forward in the Bryce Commission report in 1918. The proposals are sound enough, and recognisably similar to the Lansdowne proposals of 1911. Two hundred and forty-six members of the Second Chamber were to be elected by the House of Commons, sitting in territorial groups, and voting by proportional representation. Eighty-one peers (later reduced to thirty) were to be nominated by the Joint Committee of both Houses (five members from each); the basis of choice for them was to be their historical claims to membership. Members were to retire after twelve years, one-third being retired at four-year intervals. Again, the scheme seems a fair compromise with the selection of members weighted much more heavily in favour of choice by the House of Commons than the Lansdowne scheme. Naturally, one is left wondering why these eminently reasonable schemes were not adopted. They may be defective by ideal standards, but they clearly appear to be a great improvement on the present anomalous system. It will be seen shortly, though, that there are powerful political reasons that make it far more probable than not that any scheme for wholesale reform of the House of Lords, whatever its intrinsic merits, will be rejected.

Meanwhile, there are two much more recent proposals for reform to be considered. One of these is most ingenious. It is contained in a Fabian pamphlet 'The Privy Council as a Second Chamber'[1] by Anthony Wedgwood Benn. The author's personal objections to his transfer, then obligatory, from the House of Commons to the House of Lords should not prevent his scheme from being considered on its merits. The idea of using the Privy Council as a Second Chamber has several advantages. Historically, the Privy Council, from which the Cabinet once stemmed, has a strong claim to importance in the constitution. The change-over would be comparatively simple since no elections would be involved, and the Privy Council already has a Judicial Committee, expertly composed, which could take over the appellate functions of the House of Lords. The Judicial Committee is now mainly concerned with appeals from colonial and church courts, but its functions could be easily widened. The quality of the membership of the Privy Council is high; it includes, for instance, all ex-Cabinet ministers, so that the attacks made on the political inexperience of the majority of the present peers could not be levelled against Privy Councillors. There are difficulties in the scheme, since Privy Councillors may not wish to be dragooned into the Second Chamber, but these difficulties are fairly considered in the proposal. Hereditary peers, who were also Privy Councillors, would present no difficulty. They would receive a writ of summons in the normal way; so, too, would hereditary peers who were not Privy Councillors, but they would only attend on ceremonial occasions. Privy Councillors who were not in the Lords or the Commons would receive a writ of attendance. They would not be numerous, and many of them would have sufficient leisure and interest to attend a newly-constituted Second Chamber. The greatest difficulty would come in recruiting the Privy Councillors serving in the House of Commons. They would be given the power to apply for a writ of attendance to the Second Chamber if they wished—no doubt Mr. Wedgwood Benn was aware of his own similar situation in this respect at the time of writing. It is doubtful whether many would make use of this opportunity. The main objection would be that compared to the House of Commons,

[1] Fabian Tract No. 305, 1957.

the House of Lords is very much a backwater. The House of Commons is demonstrably more active and powerful. For the Privy Councillor attempting to bring his political career to a climax his presence in the House of Commons gives much better hope of advance. Such a man would be reluctant to transfer himself to the Second Chamber.

Apart from these major groups Mr. Wedgwood Benn advocated that the Prime Minister should have the power to recommend anyone else as a Privy Councillor, including women, Commonwealth statesmen, and churchmen of the various denominations. This proposal is obviously very similar to the present-day appointment of Life Peers. The appointment of churchmen from different denominations is of particular interest, since, previously, Church representation in the House of Lords only took account of the Established Church, the Church of England; it is desirable to have ecclesiastical representation, but it also seems to be reasonable to allow some representation to other faiths outside the Church of England. The adherents of these other faiths are numerous; acknowledgment of their right to representation as special interest groups in the House of Lords is clearly in keeping with the present movement in the Church towards unity, rather than insistence on the superiority of one religion over another. There are, after all, a number of social matters, having no bearing on the establishment and ritual of the Church of England, on which churchmen of all denominations have strong opinions; the Life Peerages Act of 1958 has widened church representation only a little.

A few special difficulties remain. Reluctance on the part of some Labour members, particularly, to join the Upper House, and the conspicuous shortage of Liberal Privy Councillors, would give the Conservatives an undue preponderance in the House of Lords. This difficulty could only be overcome by the creation of new Privy Councillors by the Prime Minister, by agreement with the leaders of the other two parties. It is improbable still that there would be anything else but a Conservative majority. This would matter less in view of the reduction in powers of the Lords also suggested in the scheme. A point of detail of some interest is that peers would have to be given the right to vote, and to stand at elections for the House of Commons, since many of them would not qualify for this newly-composed Second Chamber.

Mr. Wedgwood Benn also suggests some changes in the functions of the Second Chamber. It would be simply an advisory body with no effective power of delay. If a bill should be rejected in the Second Chamber then three months after it was sent to the Second Chamber by the House of Commons it would be put down in the latter for a fourth reading and automatically passed. Otherwise, amendments made would be reported to the House of Commons and settled by the Commons vote. The Lords would not be in a position to press amendments, therefore, as they can now. This reduction in powers of the Upper House looks as if it may be a further weak point in the suggestion. The power of delay would be so slight that it would virtually cease to matter. The present arrangement of a possible year's delay seems more reasonable. Although it is understandable that the Labour Party is concerned about the Conservative majority in the House of Lords, and this is likely to occur under this scheme too, the need for the existence in the constitution of some form of brake on hastily passed legislation is of considerable importance. The increasing burden of legislative work makes mistakes more likely. The quality of membership which this scheme would secure should lead to intelligent application of the power of the veto; it seems undesirable, therefore, to reduce it from the statutory one year to a mere three months. The unduly short veto period, coupled with the doubts about the number of Privy Councillors who could be recruited from the House of Commons, are the chief defects in an otherwise ingenious scheme.

The schemes for reform mentioned so far have mainly been of academic interest, though it can be seen that when the Government made possible the appointment of Life Peers in 1958 that idea already had a lengthy pedigree, dating back at least to the Lord Rosebery proposals at the beginning of the century. In the 1950s an idea developed which gained readier acceptance. This was for some differentiation between the regular attenders in the House of Lords, whose work there is frequently of great value to the community, and the 'backwoodsmen' for whom politics are of lesser interest. It would be unreasonable to bar the latter altogether from attending since they would then have neither voice nor vote in the country's affairs, unless they renounced their peerages. Various schemes were proposed to solve this problem. Differentiation on any permanent basis between the regular and occasional attenders would almost certainly involve a system of selection on a somewhat

invidious basis; this prevented the acceptance of some of the suggestions made. Eventually it was the Lords themselves who solved
the dilemma through their acceptance of a plan advanced by a
committee under Lord Swinton. The essence of the plan was that
at the beginning of every Parliament the Lord Chancellor should
ask every peer whether he wishes to attend; if he says that he does
not, or if he fails to reply, he is on his honour not to attend, and not
to vote without notice. This suggestion has been incorporated in
the standing orders of the House of Lords, and is a useful step
towards rationalising the composition of the House of Lords.

Nevertheless, this change was only a partial reform compared
with some of the far-reaching schemes previously mentioned. The
accumulating pressure of suggestions for reform, coupled with
annoyance over the Lords' rejection in 1968 of the Rhodesia sanctions order, led the Labour Government to issue a White Paper[1]
which became the basis of the Parliament Bill published in December 1968. This bill might have become a constitutional landmark
comparable to the Parliament Acts of 1911 and 1949. Hereditary
peers, owing their membership of the House simply to the right of
succession, were to lose their voting rights. They could still attend
the House; if they were sufficiently active and useful there they
might, by being appointed life peers, gain the right to vote.
Voting rights were to be exclusively confined to life peers and to
peers of first creation. Peers would be allowed to vote in Parliamentary elections since they would no longer have an automatic
vote in the House of Lords, and hereditary peers who, in future,
were not members of the Upper House would be able to stand for
election to the Commons. The Government envisaged a House of
about 200 to 250 members, distributed among the parties in such
a way as to give the Government a small majority of about 10%
over the Opposition parties combined. This would not be a
majority necessarily in the House as a whole, because of the
presence of 'cross-bencher' voting peers having no particular
party allegiance. Incoming governments would have to create new
peers to secure a majority over Opposition parties. The Prime
Minister would be responsible for recommending to the Queen the
names of those who should be created peers, though he was to be
assisted by a committee, widely based in terms of party and
knowledge, which would report to him, or to Parliament, on 'the

[1] *House of Lords Reform* (Cmnd. 3799).

balance and range' of membership. Voting peers would have to attend at least one-third of the sittings of the House, and, according to the White Paper, were to receive some remuneration; the stipulation about payment was not included, however, in the Parliament Bill itself. Serving law lords would have the right to vote, and were exempted from the rules governing attendance. Long-term changes envisaged in the White Paper were compulsory retirement of voting peers at the end of the Parliament in which they reached the age of seventy-two, and a reduction of episcopal representation from twenty-six to sixteen. The Government was strongly in favour of securing the presence of peers in the House who could represent authoritatively science, industry, the trade unions, Scotland, Wales, Northern Ireland, and the English regions.

These proposals for a reform in the membership of the House of Lords had a good measure of support among the members of the main political parties, except for fears that Prime Ministers might use their influence in the creation of 'cross-bencher' peers, particularly, to minimise independent opposition to the Government's policies; this extension of Prime Ministerial patronage, it was argued, would dangerously strengthen the dominance of the Executive over the Legislature. Admittedly, the dominance of the Executive over the House of Lords was more conspicuous under a Conservative than a Labour Government. The remedy lies not in giving a Labour Government the same 'built-in' majority in the Upper House which the Conservative Governments tend to enjoy, but to ensure that the cross-bencher peers are sufficiently independent in outlook to prevent a Government having an automatic majority in the Upper House. It might be safer, constitutionally, to leave the power of recommending the creation of peers entirely to a committee rather than to Prime Ministers themselves.

Proposals for alterations in the powers of the House of Lords aroused stronger opposition still, from back-benchers on both sides of the House. It was proposed that the Lords' power to delay legislation should be reduced from the present right to delay public bills by one year, from the date of the Second Reading in the House of Commons, to the right to delay a bill for six months from the date of rejection by the House of Lords of a bill from the House of Commons. This would still apply even if the six months' delay overlapped into the next Parliament. Subordinate legislation, such as the Rhodesia sanctions order, could not be rejected by the House of Lords. All it could suggest was that the Commons should think again; if the Commons still refused to modify this type of legislation, the Lords could do no more. The hostility to these proposals of many back-benchers on both sides sprang partly from those who felt it would be dangerous to reduce the powers of the Lords still further, and partly from those who wanted a more radical reform than the one proposed. The proposals for reform were well received in the House of Lords itself, but the resolute opposition to the bill of back-benchers in the House of Commons, and the need for speedy legislation on industrial relations in 1969, induced the Government to drop the bill. Since the general principle of the reform of the House of Lords would have commanded widespread support, the breakdown of the bill over the details of the reform was unfortunate. 'This is a chance', said Lord Butler 'to have a good practical Upper House': in the end the chance was not taken, and, though the reform proposals are sound enough to serve as a basis for eventual reform, this is not much consolation for a lost opportunity of valuable constitutional reform. The proposals would have ended the farce of hereditary succession entitling a peer to a vote in the Upper House, they would have reduced the powers of the House of Lords a little, they would have put party representation in the Upper House on a rational basis, they contained valuable detailed reforms, and they would have succeeded in creating a House of Lords which would have been neither a rival to the House of Commons nor a constitutional non-entity. The breakdown of the bill meant a reversion to the *status quo*. Although the Life Peerages Act of 1958 introduced a greater flexibility of membership (by July 1968, 143 life peers had been created), and although the idea of 'backswoodsmen' Lords pouring into Westminster to thwart Government legislation is a myth, the case for a methodical revision of the membership and, possibly, the powers of the House of Lords is strongly established.

FURTHER READING

Lord Campion (Ed.), *Parliament—A Survey* (Allen & Unwin, 1963).
Martin Lindsay, *Shall We Reform The Lords?* (Falcon Press, 1948).
P. A. Bromhead, *The House of Lords and Contemporary Politics, 1911–1957* (Routledge & Kegan Paul, 1958).
See also Comments on Further Reading, p. 211.

# 9

## *Problems in the Administration of Justice*

Recent uneasiness over the administration of justice. An outline of criminal court procedure gives some insight into the principles of justice. Difficulties in dealing with semi-political offences. The importance of the idea of the accountability of the Government to the people. The dangers of the constitutional dependence of the Judiciary on the Executive. Suggested reforms need to be judged from the standpoint of basic principles.

THEME: The working of the British judicial system is soundly based, but its present virtual independence of the Executive should not be taken for granted.

Until very recently concern over the administration of justice was not strongly marked in the community. Those concerned with the law at close quarters knew that it was a conservative profession, that the procedure of relying on an overworked Lord Chancellor and on understaffed Law Revision Committees for the production of reforms was unsatisfactory, and that the political parties were unlikely to be attracted to making legal reforms of little general interest to the electorate. Amongst the general public there was some concern over the high cost of civil law procedure, but on the more fundamental matter of the rights of a citizen when facing charges which might lead to the loss of his liberty or life there was a feeling, perhaps a little smug, that English justice was a model for the world. The better-informed members of the public, however, were becoming conscious of the risk of some loss in independence of the Judiciary in face of the expanding authority of the Executive. In theory the Judiciary is subservient to Parliament and, hence, in modern times to the Executive; in practice the Judiciary has for long been characterised by an impartiality which is the main reason for the high respect in which it is held. However, the peculiar circumstances of the post-war world have given national security an importance which may, in the Government's estimation, override all other considerations. The dangers are too obvious to need enumeration, but one of them manifestly is the risk that governmental pressure on judicial decisions may be more strongly felt than ever before. These feelings crystallised in 1963 in the proceedings which stemmed from the Profumo crisis. The right of the police to detain people for questioning, the right of a defendant to be able to call any witnesses necessary to his defence, the powers of the Court of Criminal Appeal,[1] the position of the Attorney-General who has both a quasi-judicial and a political role, all roused controversy. The best corrective to disproportionate alarm is to study the system itself, particularly the procedure in criminal law. Obviously, the system cannot be better than the people who administer it and there will be occasional individual failings for this reason. Lord MacDermott has pointed out in *Protection from Power under English Law*[2] that a sound system of law is inadequate in itself. It must be reinforced by a general sensitivity to the spirit of the law. This cannot be achieved by legislation. The primary purpose of this chapter, therefore, will be to consider the more tangible matters of judicial procedure in cases of a criminal or political nature, since these are the issues over which most concern is felt.

One of the most crucial tests of a judicial system lies in the provisions made for the treatment of the accused person from the time of the arrest onwards. A brief account of criminal law procedure, therefore, will give some insight into some of the principles which pervade the English judicial system. The outstanding feature is the thorough way in which the interests of the defendant are safeguarded. When a man is arrested he must be told what the nature of the charge is, he must be cautioned against making remarks which might be construed to his disadvantage later on, and any statement taken from him must be voluntary or else it loses its validity in court. At the earliest possible opportunity the accused must be brought to court, when the charge is stated, evidence of arrest given, and, in the more serious cases, matters of bail and

---

[1] Since 1964 the Court, renamed the Criminal Division of the Court of Appeal, may order a retrial for a convicted person if fresh evidence becomes available after the original trial.

[2] p. 41, *ibid*. See pp. 25–40, *ibid.*, for an excellent and reassuring analysis of the Attorney-General's relationship to the Executive.

legal aid are decided. Legal aid is always given in criminal cases whenever there is the least doubt about the ability of the accused man to pay for his own defence. The privilege of being granted bail depends on the judgment of the police and the gravity of the charge, but if the defendant is remanded in custody he must be brought to court again within eight days. The purpose of this delay is simply to allow both sides to assemble evidence and witnesses. The accused will then appear again in the magistrate's court where witnesses are heard, the accused is given the opportunity to state his case or reserve his defence, and the magistrate then decides whether the prosecution has produced enough evidence to give sound reason for committal of the case to a higher court. The purpose of this procedure is, again, to safeguard the accused. If the charge against him has no substance it can be dismissed at this early stage without keeping him in custody until the time for trial in a higher court arrives. In addition, the magistrates can order that these proceedings should be conducted in private if publicity is likely to damage the rights of the defendant in a higher court. Whether private or not, Press reports of the proceedings will be purely formal so that no evidence is disclosed which might prejudice those who may be jurymen in the case later.

There may be a delay of approximately one month before the case is heard in a higher court. During this time the accused is likely to be remanded in custody. Procedure in the higher court is based on the same principles applied in the previous hearings. The accused is given every opportunity to put his case to the best advantage. He is given expert legal aid, he is allowed to produce witnesses, there are strict rules of evidence to protect the interests of the accused, and a summing-up by the judge to present the issues to the jury as clearly and as fairly as possible. The jurors must not be known to the accused, and he has the right, on their first appearance, to object to any number of them either because they are known to him or because they may be prejudiced, for religious or racial reasons for instance. The jury's decision requires at least a 10–2 majority. If the finding is one of guilt the jurors must be satisfied beyond all reasonable doubt. The accused is then sentenced, and only then is his previous criminal record, if any, taken into account. He may appeal to the Criminal Division of the Court of Appeal on matters of fact, law, or sentence. If there are special grounds for doing so the Appeal Court may allow him to appeal again to the House of Lords. It is well-known, too, that in murder cases the accused often appeals for mercy to the Queen who exercises this prerogative power through the Home Secretary.

This outline of criminal procedure has merely touched on the chief safeguards for the accused. In fuller detail there are other safeguards also, but all with the same purpose. There are occasional criticisms of the procedure. The long delay between the preliminary hearing and the hearing at the higher court has caused concern since it is possible that a man subsequently proved innocent may spend a month or more in custody before his case is fully heard. It should be remembered, however, that it will already have been established at the preliminary hearing that the prisoner has a case to answer. Furthermore, the judges whose experience best fits them for trying cases at the higher courts cannot be made instantly available to deal with one particular case out of many others. There is the alternative of allowing the accused out of custody on bail, but this will involve police surveillance and the risk of the accused escaping justice. A second criticism lies, significantly, in the fact that the defects in the procedure arise less from the fact that an innocent man may be wrongly found guilty than that a guilty man may be wrongly found innocent. Most of this criticism springs from the use of the jury. The purpose in using a jury is to widen the approach to the facts of the case to embrace the ordinary man's concept of natural justice. This concept is apt to be more generous —possibly too generous—to the accused than the purely legalistic approach to guilt or innocence. If the law is out of touch with public opinion the jury is a valuable means of correction. Lord Devlin in *Trial by Jury* describes the jury as 'the lamp that shows that freedom lives'.[1] The way in which juries frequently refused to bring in a verdict of guilty in spite of the evidence in the early nineteenth century when the penal code was absurdly harsh is a well-known example of the humanity of the system. The jury system is sometimes valuable precisely because the jurer is likely to know very little about the law; his decision may be shaped by his own sense of natural justice which can occasionally be more enlightened than statutory law. Consequently jury decisions might again be a way of forcing the amendment of the penal code. It is true, admittedly, that juries are more prone to be mistaken in their decisions than judges, but their mistakes are more likely to be in

[1] *Ibid.*, p. 164.

favour of the accused than against him. Besides, in trying a case it is difficult for mere human beings, whether trained or not, to be completely certain about the rightness of their decisions. It is reasonable, therefore, to weight the balance in favour of the accused.

Criminal law proceedings are clearly based on eminently sound principles which ought to apply, wherever they are appropriate, to all judicial proceedings. They give a standard by which all judicial proceedings can be judged; hence the value of knowing the procedure in some detail. The principles which ought not to be infringed without demonstrably good reason can be briefly stated. No arrest should take place without a specific charge being made both at the time of the arrest, and as soon after as possible at a public court. This would preclude the use of the 'lettre de cachet' system employed in France in pre-Revolutionary days by which men could be placed in prison without trial by purely arbitrary methods. It would not, however, preclude a dictatorial state with an entirely subordinate and docile judicial system from following these same procedures precisely in form if not in intention. There are further principles, therefore, to consider. There must be no coercion of the accused. He must be given every facility to conduct his defence effectively. This means that, even if kept in custody, he must be allowed communication with the outside world. He must be given the opportunity of receiving legal advice, paid for by the State if necessary. He must be allowed to produce witnesses who are free from any fear of victimisation. These are not principles which would commend themselves entirely to a dictatorial state anxious to secure the conviction of political opponents, for instance. But this is not all. The crucial matters of guilt and sentence, in serious offences at least, are not settled in secret by a small tribunal whose members might easily be the obedient instruments of the will of an arbitrary state. The verdict is given by a jury of fellow-citizens chosen at random. The sentence is imposed by the judge, but there is the possibility of appeal to at least one higher court so that the sentence may be reduced or even quashed altogether. Apart from this, in a free country an unduly harsh sentence may cause a public outcry in Parliament and in the Press; knowledge of this is likely to militate against severity. Yet more important than all the points enunciated so far is the underlying principle that all procedure should be based on the presumption of the innocence of the accused. The onus of proof of guilt rests with the prosecution who must perform the task in strict accordance with rigidly prescribed rules of procedure.

It would obviously be wrong to assume that because of the soundness of the English judicial system in one respect, it is as equally effective in others. There are some offences where the courts are not so well fitted to reach a wise judgment. These are offences committed primarily for political motives. Constitutionally they are more interesting than other offences. A Government, whatever its nature, has no political interest in safeguarding or ill-using the small number of criminals in society, but it has a much closer interest in offences which spring from political differences. Political agitation with its occasional undertones of violence sets a particularly difficult problem for the courts. Since the eighteenth century Britain has been fortunate, compared with the Continental countries, to experience relatively little political disorder. When it has occurred the judicial system has been put under a heavy strain, and has operated with greater uncertainty than it does in the normal way. The disorder of the post-1815 period, the early Trade Unionist agitation leading to the Tolpuddle Martyrs case of 1834, the attempts in the 1870s to break the strike weapon by imprisonment and fines of the ringleaders, and the attempts to control the activities of the suffragettes, are instances of the peculiar difficulties confronting the courts in dealing with crimes stemming from political motives. In each of the examples mentioned the true remedy lay not in judicial action at all, but in constructive political action, such as recognition of the lawfulness of Trade Union organisation and of the right to strike.

Obviously the mere existence of agitation does not necessarily justify the demands being made. Until it has become clear whether those demands are in the national interest or not, the judges have to deal with the problems of the awkward interim period by enforcing the law as it exists at the moment. This is also difficult, partly because of the problem of deciding at what point a lawful attempt to influence Government policy has strayed over the border-line into criminal action, and partly because the Government itself is so closely concerned in cases of this kind and has special powers which may make it impossible to apply the ordinary procedure of the courts. These points have been given specific significance by the arrest of members of organisations opposed to all forms of military force. As part of a policy of civil disobedience actions have been carried out involving obstruction and threats to the security of Government property, in particular the aerodromes used as bases for possible nuclear operations. Apart from deciding the exact nature of the offences involved, trial by the normal procedure has been hampered by the difficulty of assessment of evidence. A full defence would necessitate a detailed examination of the rights and duties of State and citizen; it would partake more of a debate on political theory than of the normal proceedings which the courts are best fitted to conduct. It reinforces the belief, which the earlier instances quoted tend to confirm also, that court procedure is not adapted to the trial of basically political offences. Meanwhile, the judges have to do their best to protect the community with the means to hand. It needs to be pointed out also, that the present system, if not ideal, is certainly preferable to the setting up of political courts by the Executive itself, which is the probable alternative.

The other feature of the trial of these political offences which diverges from normal practice is that the Government is not obliged to state in full its case against the accused. To safeguard national interests (of which it is itself the sole judge) the Government can, on the advice of a Minister, withhold evidence which might ordinarily be considered essential for the establishment of a case. The courts have no powers to compel the Crown to produce this evidence, and accordingly have to take these aspects of the Crown's case on trust.[1] Most people can appreciate the dilemma in which the Government is placed, since national security is an overriding interest, as the emergency powers taken in wartime illustrate. Now that the world is living in a state of half-peace, because of the tremendous speed and power of modern weapons, it is only to be expected that citizens cannot have the same freedom of action which was reasonable when war was conducted in a more leisurely manner. The new problem is to define the limits of national security. Since the Government must be judge in its own cause on this subject the situation is both difficult and potentially dangerous. The only solution is to ensure by every available means that Governments are kept as fully accountable to the people as possible.

It is still possible to secure that this idea of accountability should be applied with reasonable effectiveness. 'In a democracy,' writes Sir Ivor Jennings, in *The Law and the Constitution*, 'Government

[1] See, however, footnote, p. 84.

must necessarily be carried on in such a manner as to secure the active and willing consent and co-operation of the people; for a Government that fails to persuade public opinion will be overthrown at the next election'.[1] He goes on to say that the difference between a dictatorial and a free country rests, to some extent, on intangibles since 'the existence of a free system of Government creates an atmosphere of freedom which is more easily felt than analysed'. However, there are also specific principles at work in the judicial system which the general public would expect to see applied in any court case. These principles are those previously mentioned (see pages 136–8), such as the right of the defendant to state his case fully. They derive part of their strength from their long continuance. Some of them stem from statutes such as the Habeas Corpus Act of 1679. Some stem from the decisions of judges. It was the notorious Lord Chief Justice Jeffreys, for instance, so often pilloried for his harshness after the Monmouth Rebellion of 1685, who refused to accept the validity of hearsay evidence. A great deal of law and judicial procedure in England has a strong practical basis. Much of English law has been formulated as a result of innumerable decisions in individual cases. This is a better guarantee of individual rights than the phrases of a written constitution. Words change their meaning with the passage of time, so that a written constitution, however carefully devised, cannot anticipate all the circumstances which may develop in later years. Precedent, on the other hand, has a dual advantage. It makes it more obvious when a breach of customary procedure occurs; secondly, since it is not static, it can be adapted to changing circumstances without losing contact with the essential principles of justice. In brief, therefore, there are standards of conduct in judicial procedure which are generally familiar; they are not absolute and in exceptional circumstances may be infringed, but the risk of serious abuse is slight so long as Governments remain accountable to the people.

It is important to realise that these comforting reflections do not altogether preclude abuse of the judicial power by the Executive. Some of the law springs from precedents created by the judges themselves, but much of it is statutory. Statutory legislation, devised by Parliament, has absolute authority in the courts. The judges may interpret statutory legislation when it is ambiguous, as

[1] Sir I. Jennings, *The Law and the Constitution*, 5th Edition, p. 61.

they did in reaching their unexpected decision over the Taff Vale
strike of 1900, but that is the limit of their authority. They cannot
flout the wishes of Parliament. It was the Bill of Rights of 1689 and
the Act of Settlement of 1701 which brought this about by pre-
venting the monarch from exercising the undue judicial influence
practised by James I and James II. These Acts increased the
influence of Parliament. The purpose was to limit the power of the
Executive. Now that modern conditions have so enlarged the power
of the Executive that effective Parliamentary control is again endangered, the risk of Executive influence in the courts once more
emerges as a potential, if remote, threat. What was once a security
against abuse of power by the Executive could now make that abuse
more easy. There is no full Separation of the Powers in Britain;
the executive, legislative, and judicial functions of Government
overlap, and the Judiciary is not independent; there is no Supreme
Court in Britain, as there is in the United States, to nullify acts
by the Executive which are a breach of the constitution; in this
sense, we have no constitution. The dangers are protentially tremendous. Control of the courts is one of the first objectives of a
despotic system; in Britain there would be far less technical
difficulty in achieving this than in many countries which we
regard as less democratic than our own.

If Parliament wished to proscribe a political party and imprison
the leaders, judges who wished to retain their position would have
no option but to put these laws into effect. The appointment of
judges and of Justices of the Peace is by the Prime Minister and
the Lord Chancellor, in practice by the latter.[1] The office of Lord
Chancellor is a political appointment. He is a member of the
Cabinet and has a political allegiance to it, to the Prime Minister,
and to his party. This does not influence the choice of judges and
Justices of the Peace at the present time, but, clearly, it could do so
if a political party with little respect for precedent gained power.
Political prejudice could then strongly influence appointments
made, without any need at all to change the method of appointment. Dismissal of judges would present greater difficulty. By the
Act of Settlement of 1701 judges may only be dismissed by a joint
petition to the Crown from the two Houses of Parliament. To alter
this under our present constitution would require a new Act of

[1] The Prime Minister, however, may well use his overriding authority
in making the major judicial appointments.

Parliament. An intending despot would want the power of dismissal to be placed in the hands of the Executive, but only a Parliament far more docile than can be visualised at the moment would allow this dangerous power to pass out of its own hands. In general, however, it would not need any radical change in the present organisation of the judicial system to put it completely at the mercy of the Executive. The dangers which result can be illustrated by the political trials which have taken place in Europe and the Middle East since 1945.

In practice, the Judiciary in Britain is far more independent than a study of its organisation alone would lead one to expect. Its long history and high reputation for impartiality make it relatively safe against usurpations of its authority by the State, though, as has been seen, the formal barriers against State domination are negligible. This independence is well worth preserving. Its preservation should be a primary consideration in examining proposals for reform. It has been suggested at various times that juries should be abolished, and that Justices of the Peace should be replaced by professional magistrates. Very convincing reasons can be advanced for both these ideas. Justices of the Peace and jurors represent an amateurism in the judicial system which is out of touch with the prevailing movement towards professionalism and specialisation. It could reasonably be replied that if it is out of touch so much the better, particularly in a sphere of life where a man's freedom and reputation in the community are at stake. The besetting weakness of the specialist is that his specialised knowledge can become of greater interest to him than the people to whom he is applying it. Considering the very large number of cases with which Justices of the Peace deal—obviously an asset in itself in widening their experience—the number of appeals from their decisions is significantly small. Juries may sometimes irritate legal specialists by their apparent perversity, but there is no strong case for reducing the number of occasions when juries are used, still less of abolishing the jury system altogether. Jurors have the advantage of having the legal issues in a case summed up for them by a judge, a process incidentally which may help to clarify the arguments in the judge's own mind. The judge in his summing-up may stress the significance of particular evidence, but the jury may ignore his advice and it is not a self-evident proposition that they would always be wrong to do so. When jury verdicts required a unanimous decision there was the risk that, through corruption or through irrational obstinacy, one or two jurors might frustrate the working of justice. The reduction of the requirement to a 10–2 majority has largely eliminated this risk. The view that Justices of the Peace and jurors form a useful counterbalance to a narrowly legalistic outlook in the courts has much to commend it.

The total replacement of unpaid by paid magistrates and the abolition of the jury are far too extreme as reforms to win general support. A reform of a milder nature, which correspondingly has been more strongly pressed, is that Britain should imitate the practice of many other countries and appoint a Minister of Justice. This would be more clear-cut than the present system in which responsibility to Parliament for the workings of the Judiciary is shared between the Home Secretary and the Law Officers of the Government. It might lead to a rationalisation of judicial adminis-tration in other ways too, notably in reducing the long delays which occur in civil law actions, and an extension of the number of courts in provincial areas. Yet even if this administrative activity marked the limit of the Minister's powers, it would still make a small inroad into the independence of the Judiciary. If the powers of the Minister were ultimately to become more extensive, involving, for instance, the sole power of appointment of judges and Justices of the Peace, then obviously the dangers would be very great indeed. Independence of the Judiciary is one of the key principles of the theory of the Separation of Powers. Although the Judiciary is theoretically vulnerable to an extension of Executive control, in practice its independence is accepted. The creation of a Minister of Justice would be a powerful instrument, potentially, for limiting the independence of the Judiciary. If efficiency can only be bought at the expense of increasing the possibility of direct State control, it is a price not worth paying.

FURTHER READING

F. T. Giles, *The Criminal Law* (Pelican Books, 1963).

F. T. Giles, *The Magistrates' Courts* (Pelican Books, 1963).

L. Page, *Justice of the Peace* (Faber, 2nd Edition, 1947).

F. Milton, *In Some Authority* (Pall Mall, 1959).

Lord Devlin, *Trial by Jury* (Stevens, 1956).

A. V. Dicey, *The Law of the Constitution* (Macmillan, 10th Edition, 1959).

Sir Ivor Jennings, *The Law and the Constitution* (Univ. London Press, 5th Edition, 1959).

R. M. Jackson, *The Machinery of Justice* (C.U.P., 4th Edition, 1964).

See also Comments on Further Reading, p. 211.

# 10

## Local Government
## Some Recent and Prospective Changes

The present period is one of great change. The importance of
local government to the citizen. The need for reorganisation.
Why changes are slow. The reports of the Local Government
Commissions. The Royal Commission on Greater London. The
Redcliffe-Maud Report, 1969. Present methods of financing local
government. Suggested reforms.

THEME: The proposed changes are overdue and may strengthen
local government.

There are many controversial issues which arise from a study
of local government. In a short space only a few of them
can be considered. The issues of the greatest topical interest
are those involved in the Government's recent or prospective
legislation on the subject. Reforms affecting finance have already
been put into effect by the general grant system, imposed by the
Local Government Act of 1958, and structural changes have taken
place in the organisation of local government in London; the
Redcliffe–Maud Report of 1969 emphasised the structural and
administrative weaknesses of local government in England. If its
reforming proposals are acted upon by the Government of the day,
the 1970s will witness a wholesale alteration in the status and
powers for many local government authorities. Nor do the changes,
present and prospective, only affect the administrators themselves.
Local government clearly involves every citizen. Police, fire
brigades, and Civil Defence services exist for his protection; the
home in which he lives may be council-owned; he is likely to have
the keenest interest in the number, variety, and efficiency of the
schools in his district; the pleasantness of the area in which he
lives may be greatly improved by an enterprising council which
provides parks, ornamental gardens, and recreational activities.

These and other services provided by the Council are under the constant close scrutiny of the citizens of that district. The quality of these services can be assessed much more readily and accurately by the citizen, from his close contact with them, than the more distant policy decisions of the central Government. For this reason alone then, changes in local government, which may affect the efficiency of the services provided, are of interest to every citizen.

There are other factors, too, to be borne in mind in assessing the wisdom of changes. For most people local government means paying rates and receiving services. Fortunately, there are many thousands of citizens about the country who also give services. These are the councillors. Motives for becoming a councillor are no doubt very mixed. A keen sense of social service, a desire for prestige, the use of local politics as a preparation for an eventual Parliamentary career, may all play their part for different people. Yet, whatever the motives, local government service itself is the same for all in that it closely associates large numbers of people with the business of government. The desirability of doing so in a democracy is obviously very great. It is of value not only to the councillors themselves, but to the whole community, since it touches on the fundamental issue of the relationship of the central Government to the citizen. Local government, with the voluntary element preponderant (for councillors receive no salary), is potentially a very strong barrier against domination of the community by central Government. The power of the latter in local affairs has increased in this century, but the limits of central control are closely defined and any infringement would be very obvious to councillors, and to the Opposition in the House of Commons. The changes proposed in the structure of local government have brought to the fore this question of the central–local relationship; with the whole system likely to be in a state of flux for some time to come it is worth being clear about the essential features which ought to be preserved.

That some changes are necessary is indisputable. The organisation of local government in England and Wales gives a wonderful opportunity to the tidy-minded administrator to display all his talents, for the system is both anomalous and anachronistic. There are far too many small authorities whose boundaries have been fixed neither by convenience nor logic. The post-war Local Government Boundary Commission reports have shown what

huge discrepancies in size there are between local government
authorities of the same status. A County Council may be large,
such as Lancashire which provides services for a population of over
two million; on the other hand, it may be extremely small, like
Rutland with a population of 29,000, or Westmorland with 68,000.
A County Borough may, like Birmingham, have a population of
over a million, or it may, like Canterbury, have a population of
33,000. Yet the desirable status of County Borough, with complete
independence from the County Council, was long denied to a
Borough as large as Ilford with a population of 180,000. In all there
are fifteen non-County Boroughs of about 100,000 inhabitants in
England and one, Rhondda, in Wales. At the other end of the
scale are tiny Boroughs, such as those which cluster round the
Kent coast: Lydd with 4,000 inhabitants, Rye with 4,500, and New
Romney with 3,600. The same discrepancies can be seen in the
size of Urban District Councils. Lynton in Devon has a population of 1,680; Thurrock in Essex has 121,670; both are Urban
District Councils. In fact, a change in status from Urban District
Council to Borough does not matter greatly, since their powers are
virtually the same, but the independence given by county borough
status is of the greatest importance.

The teeming population of Greater London poses special problems. Most of the growth is taking place outside central London
where, in all except a very few Boroughs, population has been
falling since 1931. A glimpse of the nature of the problem can be
seen in the fact that the City of London, the square mile at the
centre, has about 5,000 permanent householders, but a daytime
business population of 500,000. Huge dormitory towns have grown
up on the outskirts of London to accommodate the great masses of
London workers. Several of these towns had sufficient resources
to be County Boroughs in their own right; this made it possible to
delegate extensive powers to the Greater London Boroughs in the
London Government Act of 1963. Some of this area had previously
been administered by the London County Council whose constituents numbered over 3 million out of the 8 million population
of Greater London. The remaining 5 million inhabitants had their
local services administered through the Home Counties of Surrey,
Kent, Essex, and Middlesex. This division of responsibility was
thoroughly unsatisfactory as the report of the Royal Commission
on Greater London made very plain. Problems of local government

administration in the area have very much in common. The splintering of authority outside the L.C.C. area caused too parochial an approach, which was obviously inefficient for a service such as roads, where an overriding planning authority was needed for the whole area.

The illogicalities of the present system, in the conurbations and elsewhere, spring from a failure to adapt the organisation to the needs of modern times. The present-day administrative areas of the County Councils are largely the same as those which were set up at the time of the Norman Conquest. A tract of land which could be conveniently controlled by a Norman sheriff is not automatically going to be ideal administratively for the provision of an efficient fire service, nor for coherent development of a road system suited to modern traffic. Even in 1888, when the County Councils and County Boroughs were set up by the Local Government Act, it was a little doubtful whether the existing county divisions were entirely suitable for all the services provided. Since then the local authorities have taken on new responsibilities for education, the Welfare State has been created, leading among other things to a great variety of health services, there have been large movements of population to London and the South-East, services such as gas and electricity are administered by nationalised boards, and modern improvements in transport have made nonsense of boundaries appropriate to the days of the horse and carriage.

In spite of these vast social changes, the essential framework of local government remained unchanged throughout the twentieth century until the structure of local government in London was radically altered by the Act of 1963. Urban and Rural District Councils were set up in 1894, while Boroughs and Parishes have a much more ancient history. Even within the system detailed changes have been few. Several County Boroughs were created between 1888 and 1926 but since then the system has ossified. The County Councils, with their huge variations in size, are virtually the same as they were in 1888. The immobility of the system may seem curious but opposition to any change is bound to be strenuous. The problem is not simply one of attaining administrative neatness. Local government is an important arena in party politics. Only a peculiarly altruistic Government would pioneer a scheme for a revision of boundaries from which it is likely to lose politically. Besides this, local pride seems to be felt in inverse proportion to the size of the area so that schemes for amalgamation which seem desirable administratively are likely to stir up a hornet's nest of protest from the small authorities. In these circumstances the reluctance of governments to interfere with the present structure becomes undersandable.

Amongst the larger authorities the practical obstacle to a change of status has been finance. This was most apparent in the way in which large Boroughs such as Ilford, Luton, and Ealing were frustrated for so long in their attempt to gain County Borough status.[1] In a county such as Bedfordshire the grant of County Borough status to Luton in 1964 removed at one blow a very large proportion of the rate revenue for the whole county. The standard of services in the rest of the county may easily suffer, in spite of the likelihood of additional Government grants. Thus Luton, with a population of 140,000, that is 40,000 more than the prescribed minimum for County Borough status, was heavily penalised under the present system. In the neighbouring county of Cambridge there is a similar difficulty. The city of Cambridge, numbering just over the 100,000 suggested for County Borough status, has a greater population than the whole of the rest of the county put together. The Cambridge householder, therefore, depends for many of his services on a County Council which, in proportion to the relative populations inside the city and outside it, is insufficiently representative of his interests.

These problems have been well known for years, but action to remedy them has been slow, for the reasons previously given. A Local Government Boundary Commission investigated the situation in 1946–7 and made radical suggestions for recasting the present structure, but alarm at the likely reaction of local opinion prevented these proposals from being put into effect. In 1958, under the Local Government Act, Commissions were set up for England and Wales. The first duty of these Commissions was to examine what changes were necessitated by the shift of population to the large conurbations. In England this involved detailed consideration of five Special Review areas, the West Midlands, Tyneside, Merseyside, S.E. Lancashire and W. Yorkshire. The proposals on the West Midlands and Tyneside gave some insight into the likely pattern of local government, since the problems of

[1] Ilford and Ealing became London Boroughs by the London Government Act, 1963.

all these areas are very similar. Towns have spilled over their old boundaries and coalesced, so that the divisions have become purely arbitrary. At the moment local government services are largely provided by the County Councils whose areas these conurbations happen to overlap—in Tyneside, the County Councils of Northumberland and Durham, for instance. These Councils have the strangely mixed responsibility of looking after rural areas, small towns, and sections of the swollen urban communities. The first step suggested was the removal of these communities from the control of the present County Councils; in their place the ideal arrangement would seem to be a directly elected central planning authority for the whole conurbation, using the subordinate local authorities as agents. These local authorities would be entirely responsible for the type of service now performed by the non-County Boroughs, but greater independence than this would be likely to prejudice unified development of the area. The recommendations of the Commission made this partly possible in Tyneside where it was suggested that there should be four Boroughs, Newcastle, Gateshead, Tynemouth, and South Shields, all included in a new Tyneside county. In the West Midlands, on the other hand, the conurbation was to split between six County Boroughs, Wolverhampton, Walsall, Dudley, West Bromwich, Smethwick, and Birmingham, but there was no mention of a county authority. These proposals then, although an improvement on the existing arrangement, still did not seem to allow fully enough for large-scale planning of the conurbations. The creation of a strong overall planning authority would undoubtedly diminish the powers of the smaller local authorities, but this need not be undemocratic in the least, rather the reverse. Apart from London, the population figures in these areas do not differ markedly from those in the larger County Councils today, so that the size itself would be no new problem; the planning authority would be directly elected, so that councillors would be conscious of their responsibility to their constituents; finally, the fact that services are likely to be more efficiently managed under this unified control would make any interference by the central Government less justified.

The Commission on Wales published its draft proposals in 1961. The interest of its proposals lay in the fact that they were planned for the whole country of Wales and, therefore, were a possible pointer to the arrangement to be expected in England when the areas other than conurbations are reorganised. The proposals were that the existing thirteen Welsh counties should be abolished and replaced by five large administrative areas, North-West, South-West, North-East, and South-East Wales, and Glamorgan. The general pattern was for a richer county to form the nucleus of each area, which would also include a few of the poorer counties to be propped up by the support of their richer neighbour. Since some of the counties of Central Wales are extremely poor this scheme had obvious benefits for them. The scheme looked sound, at first sight, but it was attempting to go to its objective too quickly. The urgency for reconstruction of the Welsh system is possibly less great than it is in the densely populated English conurbations, and this will give added force to the usual objections based on local feeling. The Welsh are strongly conscious of their history so that they can hardly be expected to take kindly to the new administrative areas with highly unimaginative names. The Fabian slogan of 'the inevitability of gradualism' could very well be applied to changes in local government structure where there is no desperate urgency.

Greater London was not included in the Special Review areas designated in the 1958 Local Government Act for investigation by the Local Government Commissions. Instead, its problems were examined by a Royal Commission under the Chairmanship of Sir Edwin Herbert.[1] The Government believed that changes in the structure of local government in Greater London were urgent. This view was challenged and controversy has centred also on the form the changes have taken. The first need, according to the Commission, was to achieve unity of control for the whole of the Greater London area by the creation of a planning authority with overriding powers for the provision of the main local government services. The boundaries of the London County Council dated back to the nineteenth century. More of the inhabitants of the Greater London area lived outside the L.C.C. boundaries than within, so that in its existing form the L.C.C. could not give the unity of direction required for the whole area. To provide this unity of direction the Commission proposed the setting up of a Greater London Council, directly elected, to be responsible for such services as education, traffic, town planning, and fire and ambulance services. This Council would replace the L.C.C. which

[1] Report of the Royal Commission on Local Government in Greater London (Cmnd. 1164. H.M.S.O.).

accordingly, together with the Middlesex C.C., would be abolished. The Government's acceptance of the abolition of the Labour-controlled L.C.C. was criticised as a political manoeuvre, but it is fair to point out that the setting up of a larger authority is in keeping with the general movement towards larger authorities and greater unity of control visible in the proposals for the other conurbations in England. Another objection naturally came from the counties such as Surrey, Kent, Essex, and Hertfordshire, which have lost prosperous rate-producing areas under the new scheme. The Commission stated that these counties would still remain financially viable, and subsequent evidence suggests that this was a fair assessment. Costs of local government have risen, but rates, particularly since the revaluation of industry, shops, and private houses, and other sources of local income, such as house rents, still produce enough revenue to give the counties a degree of financial independence, though large Government grants are needed too. It needs to be remembered also that financial arrangements should be determined by structure, not the reverse. It is easier and better to adapt financial organisation than it is to be saddled with an outdated administrative structure for the provision of local government services.

The Government, itself, raised one objection to the Commission's proposals on the functions of the Greater London Council. The Commission proposed that the Council should be responsible for education in the whole area with help from newly created Greater London Boroughs. Education, like some of the other services, suffered from the splintering of responsibility in the previous system. The L.C.C. was organised into large divisions for education of up to half a million inhabitants. Yet adjoining the L.C.C. boundary there were, for contrast, two divisional executives, one, Penge, serving a population of 25,000, and another, North Central Surrey, serving a population of 203,000.[1] Variations of this kind were numerous. The Government, while accepting the need for reorganisation, baulked at the idea of giving overall responsibility for the whole area to a single council.[2] Their suggestion was that there should be a single education authority in central London serving a population of some two million inhabit-

[1] These figures are taken from an article 'The Government of London' in *The Times Educational Supplement* of May 15th, 1959.
[2] Cmnd. 1562. H.M.S.O. paragraphs 38-44.

ants. Outside this area the Greater London Boroughs should act as the education authorities for their own areas. The large authority in central London will continue to make possible the freedom of choice of schools for pupils which has been taken for granted there for years. How effectively the Government's scheme for making education a Borough service works is now beginning to emerge. It has certainly removed some of the oddities of the previous system, which were imposed by purely geographical considerations with so many counties fringing on London. One of the difficulties was that education had become a political battle-ground since the L.C.C., with a Labour majority, seemed to incline towards replacing the grammar schools in its area by comprehensive schools. The Conservatives, on the other hand, wished to retain the grammar-school system.[1] From the Conservative point of view in 1962 it would have endangered the grammar-school system much more gravely still if a Labour-controlled Greater London Council, responsible for the whole area, had made a great extension of the comprehensive-school system. The issue closely resembled the nationalisation controversy in that once the conversion is made it is almost impossible to reverse the process.

In general, the Commission assigned a lower status to the Greater London Boroughs than the Government gave. The Commission's suggestion was for the formation of Boroughs, ranging from 100,000 to 250,000 in population. These Boroughs should be responsible for housing (with some guidance from the Greater London Council), personal health, welfare, child care, environmental health services, apart from refuse disposal which was to be a Council responsibility, and sundry other normal Borough services. To these functions, as has been seen, the Government added the great responsibility of the education service, but suggested no other change of function. It did, however, require an increase in the size of the Greater London Borough, raising the minimum population from 100,000 to 200,000, presumably with the needs of education chiefly in mind. Amidst all this welter of change the City of London, alone, reinforced by its ancient history, has remained intact. The view of the Commission

[1] *Report of House of Commons Proceedings*, February 20th, 1962, col. 245. Sir David Eccles, then Minister of Education, referring to the Labour plan, stated 'They know that this plan will not go through so long as there is a Conservative Minister of Education.'

was that 'Logic has its limits and the position of the City lies outside them',[1] and this the Government supported. The City has received the additional powers given to Boroughs in the London area.

These changes are most far-reaching. The full effects must still be a matter of speculation. It is reasonable to believe that some services have gained greatly. The organisation of an efficient road system into central London has long been hampered by the parochial nature of the present structure. On this subject the Commission said 'the only possible solution to the present administrative muddle is for the organisation to be firmly in the hands of the Council for Greater London'.[2] The Greater London Council has, therefore, become responsible for the main roads in the area, and has the help of a strong traffic engineering department. One result has been a more ambitious traffic scheme for the area than would once have been possible. Splintering of authority still persists in that the Ministry of Transport is responsible for trunk roads, the Greater London Council for metropolitan roads, and the Boroughs for other roads; nevertheless, the new system does mark an advance, and the expensive but necessary new ringway round London, designed particularly for heavy through traffic, looks as if it may at last become a reality. The need for an overall authority to deal with the overspill problem is also apparent; the difficulties over housing in central London, great though they are, would become intolerable if the London Boroughs had unlimited powers to oppose overspill housing programmes in their own areas. The London Government Act was the first modern attempt to deal comprehensively with the complex administrative problems of this heavily populated city. Naturally, there have been difficulties, particularly in services such as roads, housing, and planning, where there is some sharing of powers between the Council and the London Boroughs. The system has worked sufficiently well, however, to have become the model in the Maud Report for other conurbations.

In the early 1960s the conurbations were the main focus of interest in the attempt to reform the structure of local government; the outstanding result of this activity was the London Government Act of 1963. At the same time there was a general awareness that

[1] Cmnd. 1164. H.M.S.O. paragraph 935.
[2] Cmnd. 1164. H.M.S.O. paragraph 779.

the larger issue of recasting the whole structure of local government was becoming increasingly urgent. Consequently in 1966 a Royal Commission on Local Government in England was set up with Lord Redcliffe-Maud as chairman; the work of the Local Government Commission for England set up in 1958 was discontinued. There was little likelihood from the outset that the Maud Commision would find much to say in favour of the existing structure. The absurd discrepancies in size between units exercising the same functions, and the illogicality of the boundaries of local government units in relation to the functions they had to perform, were acceptable to those who assumed that society had not changed since the end of the nineteenth century, and to those whose authority and prestige rested on the continuance of the existing system, but not to anyone else. The decisive comment on this issue by the Commission was that 'Local authorities, we are convinced, cannot under the present system grapple effectively with their problems. This was generally admitted to us.'

The possibility of retaining the existing structure, with minor modifications, could thus be dismissed, but there were still several alternatives from which the Commission could choose. One possibility was to divide England into large regional units and to make regional councils, assisted by subordinate councils, the key unit of local government. There had been a spate of books and articles in the 1960s suggesting various forms of regional government for the United Kingdom. The economic planning regions set up by the Government suggested a pattern for regional boundaries which might be adopted, but there were other suggestions, too, ranging, as far as England was concerned, from five to eleven regional areas. A second suggestion was that England should be divided into some thirty to forty 'city-regions'. The Ministry of Housing and Local Government in its evidence to the Commission explained the merits of this idea. The basic pattern of settlement now, and hence the natural area for most local government services, consists, it was said, of a single large town or conurbation, surrounded by smaller towns and villages of which it is the focus. The city-region, therefore, was a more logical administrative unit than the county.

The Commission was plainly influenced by these various suggestions, but modified them. Its chief proposal was that 58 elected 'unitary authorities' should be created responsible for all services.

In addition there should be three metropolitan authorities, Mersey-side, the West Midlands, and 'Selnec' (south east Lancashire, and north-east Cheshire), which would share the responsibility for services with their district councils. The arrangement for these metropolitan areas obviously bore a close resemblance to that which prevails in the Greater London area; Greater London itself was excluded from the consideration of the Commission. Above the unitary authorities there would be eight provincial councils indirectly elected by the unitary and metropolitan authorities, and also including some co-opted members. They would be responsible for the broad planning of economic and social development within their areas in collaboration with the central Government and also, presumably, with the unitary authorities; the vague definition of the powers of the provincial councils was influenced by the fact that until the Crowther Commission reports on constitutional reform there is not much point in an interim definition of the powers of the provincial councils. To soften the blow a little of the wholesale removal of functions from county borough, borough, urban district, and parish councils, the Commission proposed that elected local councils for each of these areas should continue to represent local opinion, to be consulted on matters of special local interest, and to improve local amenities. These councils might acquire greater powers, on housing and highways for instance, if the unitary authority agreed.

Local taxation would be in the hands of the unitary authorities who would collect revenue on behalf of the provincial councils and the smaller local councils too. This is a simplification of the system by which county boroughs, boroughs, district, and even parish councils can levy a rate, and should lead to a reduction in the overhead costs of local government. Rates would still be the chief local tax. The Commission pointed out the danger implicit in the inelasticity of rate revenue in that, since there can be no expectation by councils of substantial increases in rate revenue, the cost of expanding services will increasingly be met by Government grants. It was calculated that by 1970–1 local councils would be dependent for 57% of their finance on Government grants; in 1963–4 the corresponding figure was 38%. Increasing dependence on central Government grants might make local authorities sub-servient to central Government policies to such an extent that it would make democracy meaningless at local level. Yet unless more productive sources of local revenue are found, this unpleasant prospect might become a reality. The suggestions from the Commission that capital value rating should replace rental valuation and that the anomaly of exempting agricultural land and buildings from rates should be ended do not go far enough. One financial advantage which should ensue, however, if the Commission's proposals are adopted, is that the sharp reduction in the number of local government authorities with direct responsibilities for finance will simplify the working of the general grant system[1] and lead to larger-scale and longer-term planning of financial resources.

Important though the financial issues are, the main interest roused by the Report was in the proposals for structural change. At Westminster the Report was favourably received, naturally enough perhaps, since it is easier to co-ordinate Governmental policies through a relatively small number of large local authorities than through a mass of small ones. In the Press and in the country at large the Report created the anticipated mixture of hostility and support. Although the boundaries of the unitary authorities coincided quite closely with many of the county boundaries, the changes proposed were still sufficiently numerous to make opposition from local loyalists inevitable. Those who judged the Report's proposals from the wider viewpoint of national development were by no means wholly convinced that the Commission had found the right solution, though as *The Times* pointed out, 'There is no ideal or "correct" structure of local government which can be deduced from close study of the facts.'[2] The salient criticisms were that the unitary authorities were too large, too powerful, and were town-dominated to such an extent that country interests would suffer. Local government would cease to be local, and the almost derisory limitation of the powers of local councils to expressing opinions accentuated this feeling. It seemed likely, too, that the quality of local councillors would not be improved if the powers of councils were whittled away to vanishing-point, since there would be little incentive to take part in an activity having such slight significance. Furthermore it was felt that a unitary authority, unlike a borough or county borough, was not a natural centre of local loyalty.

One of the members of the Commission, Mr. Senior, produced a minority Report which would remove some of the criticisms

[1] See p. 163.          [2] June 12th, 1969.

levelled at the main Report, but is itself liable to others. Mr. Senior accepted the city-region concept but proposed that there should be 35, not 58, as the main Report proposed. To meet the objection that the city-region proposal would make local government meaningless, Mr. Senior suggested that there should be 148 local authorities dividing services and functions with the city-regional authorities. He felt that the Commission was mistaken in relying so exclusively on the unitary authorities, which were too small for services such as transport which required large-scale planning and too large for the personal services. He suggested that there should be five rather than eight provincial councils. This was a logical corollary of the reduction in the numbers of city-regional authorities in his proposal, but, as in the main Report, proposals about the provincial councils are bound to be nebulous until the Crowther Commission reports, prospectively in 1972, on constitutional reform. In effect Mr. Senior's proposals involved a compromise between the adoption of regional planning and the retention of many of those units of local government which are believed to be the natural foci of local loyalty. The English have a constitutional preference for gradual transitions, for the old surviving alongside the new; their strongly-marked belief that in the long-run individualism is more important than administrative neatness, and that, meanwhile, compromise is more important than either, is well illustrated in Mr. Senior's proposals. Administratively, however, one weakness of Mr. Senior's suggestions is that it would be difficult, in practice, to devise a satisfactory division of services between the city-region and the district authorities; the line between large-scale development planning and personal services is not clear-cut. Secondly, the minority Report would lead to a more complex system of local government than that proposed in the main Report, since Mr. Senior proposed a two-tier division of local units by which effective powers would be given both to city-regional authorities and to district councils. This would be more confusing for the citizen than the system proposed in the main Report where, except in the metropolitan areas named, the unitary authorities would be directly responsible for all services.

When the structure of local government is reformed there seems little doubt that the present splintering of authority will be brought to an end. Even Mr. Senior's proposals involve a vast reduction in the number of local authorities, some 1,200, having powers of

decision. The Commission's view was that the appropriate size for
a local government authority even for the 'smaller' personal
services should be 250,000 to one million. In education, for
instance, its recommendations were that the existing 280 authorities should be reduced to 78. For planning, development, and
transportation, the need for still larger areas was apparent; these
functions, the Commission reported, are shared between 79
county boroughs and 45 counties 'often in an atmosphere of
hostility'. The vulnerability of the main Report is that it takes too
little account of local loyalties, in spite of the partially successful
attempt to make the boundaries of the unitary authorities coincide
where possible with county boundaries. It could be retorted that
these local loyalties are dying, as indifference to local elections
seems to show, that the population is much more mobile and
adaptable than it was, and that the radical recasting of local
government in the London area took place with remarkably little
fuss even in areas outside the boundaries of the L.C.C. Local
loyalties may prove to be something of a myth; on the other hand
the constitutional and administrative need to keep a balance
between central and local government is a matter of fundamental
importance.

The first formal reaction to the Maud Commission Report was the
issue of a Government White Paper in February, 1970. The
recommendation that unitary authorities should be created was
accepted, though the number of these authorities was to be
reduced from 58 to 51. They would be all-purpose authorities
except in so far as they chose to delegate functions to lesser
authorities; the suggestion for the creation of eight provincial
councils was shelved until the Crowther Commission reports.
Within each unitary authority there were to be local councils. The
existing councils were to decide in each area whether to retain the
existing single council system, or whether local representation
should consist of local groups to advance the interests of particular
districts or communities. Local councils could, at their own expense, improve the comforts and amenities of their areas, and they
must be consulted by the unitary authorities on matters in which
they were directly concerned. Local councillors would continue to
serve on the governing bodies of schools and other institutions;
they would also serve on committees set up to assist the unitary
authorities in their work. They were to be chosen by their fellow

councillors for this service, not co-opted by the unitary authority. Local councils were not to share powers with the unitary authorities since this would produce confusion.

To the three metropolitan authorities originally proposed two more should be added, West Yorkshire (Bradford, Leeds, Halifax, Huddersfield and mid-Yorkshire—most of which have severe housing problems), and South Hampshire, centring on the Isle of Wight, Southampton, and Portsmouth. These are areas where industry and population are expanding rapidly, but where there is also outstanding scenery to be preserved.

In the metropolitan areas the Government proposed that education should be controlled by the main authority rather than by the metropolitan districts. The object of this was to provide a greater flexibility of educational opportunity within these areas; it differed from the greater separatism to be found in educational administration in Greater London. The housing service was to be divided between the metropolitan authority and its subordinate districts. The metropolitan authority was to be responsible for planning, transport, and major development; it was also to be the rating authority for the whole of its area. The metropolitan districts were to be responsible for personal social services, but if their house-building programme should fail to reach a satisfactory standard then their work will be taken over by the higher authority.

There were several other isolated but important suggestions in the White Paper. The names for the unitary authorities were to be decided locally. Special arrangements were to be made for the organisation of the police, fire, water, and public transport authorities, national parks, and youth employment; committees had already been set up to examine these problems. The Health Service was not to be administered by local authorities, but would be reorganised on the basis of the new areas. Regional Economic Planning Councils, set up in 1965 by the Government, were to continue their work until the Crowther Commission reports, and to co-operate with local authorities. Scotland and Wales were to have separate reports. Rates would remain the principal local tax but a Green Paper was to be published on supplementary forms of revenue. Councillors were not to be paid but allowances were to be improved. At least ten local Ombudsmen were to be appointed, including one for London to investigate complaints and to report directly to councils. The new system was to take effect in 1973 when elections were to be held for the new authorities rather than in 1975. Talks were held on having single-member divisions in the elections, a common voting day for all main authority elections, and a plan to make it easier for local government staff, such as teachers, to serve on councils.

These proposals were designed to simplify and rationalise the system of local government. The reduction in the number of authorities and the increase in their size would, it was hoped, make Government intervention in local affairs less necessary. There would, for instance, be half the present number of education authorities, and less than one-tenth of the number of housing authorities; it was expected, therefore, that fewer Civil Servants would be required for the work of co-ordination.

Another major development has been the revival of the general grant system by the Local Government Act of 1958. In conjunction with the structural changes likely to take place the grant could be of the utmost value in strengthening local authorities. From April, 1959, the County and County Borough Councils have received a general grant, often referred to as a block grant, for education (except school meals and milk), agricultural education, health, fire services, and child care. Housing, roads, and police have been excluded from this system,[1] but even so the general grant caters for some highly important services. The assessment of money to be allocated to each service is a matter for the councils, but the Ministers lay down minimum standards to prevent unbalanced use of funds, obviously a necessary proviso. The calculation of the amount of the general grant is based on a formula which takes into account the level of prices, costs, and pay, development plans, probable fluctuation in needs, and population figures, with special reference to the numbers of aged people and of schoolchildren in the area, since their dependence on the social services is greater than for the rest. The grant is made for three-year periods (except that the first one was for the period April, 1959–April, 1961) thus making it possible to plan ahead. The other

---

[1] Housing is financed by unit grants. Central Government pays a basic amount for each house; local government pays the additional costs involved in building houses of better quality than the basic unit. Grants for the police and roads are on a percentage basis, central Government providing 50% of police expenditure, and between 50% and 75% of road expenditure depending on the classification of the road.

sources of revenue—rates, trading services, and loans—are not affected by this change in the grant system; rate deficiency grants will continue to be paid by the Government to poor areas.[1] General grants, by giving some latitude of choice to local authorities in their allocation of money to particular services, encourage initiative at that level. If, in addition, large authorities of the kind envisaged in the Redcliffe-Maud Report are eventually created, then it may seem that local government authorities, possessing a degree of financial initiative and being of a large enough size to speak authoritatively to the central government on local needs, will be an effective counterbalance against any attempt by Whitehall and Westminster to dominate local affairs unduly. This optimism is unjustified so long as the notoriously inadequate rating system remains an essential component in the financing of local government. The burden of rates falls far more heavily on the aged and on the poor with large families than on the rich, as the Allen Committee Report[2] of 1965 conclusively proved. In the sixteenth century, when the rating system originated, to tax a man on the basis of the land and buildings he possessed was reasonable; to retain the same system in the totally different circumstances of the twentieth century is not only absurd but also dangerous. Its absurdity is apparent in the crudity of the means of assessing the contributions which citizens are presumed to be able to make to local revenue. Rates are assessed on the notional rental value of a house after minor deductions for insurance and repairs. This system takes no account of the great differences which exist between occupants of houses of the same rateable value in income, capital resources, commitments, and the number of their dependants. Knowledge of the arbitrary inequality of the rating system inhibits councillors from raising rates to the level which would otherwise be imposed. The system therefore is inelastic, as well as regressive and archaic. Even within its own illogical limits it has not been consistently applied. Until 1967 the owners of unoccupied land and property paid no rates on them, though they required the protection of police and fire services. Agricultural land has been exempt from rating since 1929, though the circumstances which justified this then apply with less force now, in spite

---

[1] The rate deficiency grant and the general grant, combined in 1966, are collectively known as the rate support grant.

[2] *Impact of Rates on Households* (Cmnd. 2582).

of the undoubted hardships of small-scale farming. Rating valuation assessments are more likely to be out of date than not, yet property values change rapidly with gains or losses in amenities affecting prices within an area, or even within a given road. In spite of this there was a gap of almost thirty years between the housing valuation of 1934 and the next full valuation in 1963. This cannot be wholly explained away by reference to the 1939–45 war and its consequences. The only flexibility within the system is the negative one that if a householder improves his property by building a garage, for instance, his rates will be increased. There have been some modifications to the system so that industry, shops, and offices pay a fuller share of rates than they once did, and the burden on the householder has been increased too. Councils also rely for revenue on house rents and trading, but these are largely self-paying activities and cannot provide the large-scale additional revenue required. The point has been reached, in short, where expansion of revenue from existing local sources cannot be reasonably expected. Since the range and cost of local government services are increasing, the need for finding other sources of local revenue has become urgent. The alternative of relying increasingly on central Government grants is undesirable since it adds substantially to the risk of central control.

Much ingenuity has been expended on proposing alternative sources of local revenue. Assignment to local authorities of the proceeds of the Motor Vehicle Licence Duty, which is collected locally but paid to the central Government; the institution of a local sales tax, which is a system used in Canada; the proceeds of taxation on gambling, entertainment, and advertising; finally, the adoption of a local income tax, as in Sweden and the United States, are among the more prominent of the suggestions made. Many of these suggestions have the merit, unlike the rating system, of being a means of financing local services from money which is surplus to the ratepayer's needs. It could be objected that all of them will tend to be more productive in richer areas than poorer ones, and that the use of rate equalisation grants by the central Government will lead to inequalities in the degree of independence experienced by rich and poor areas respectively. One answer is that this is inevitable; a more encouraging one is that as local authorities become larger, and this is conspicuously the trend, differences between area and area will become less strongly marked since individual authorities will contain both rich and poor districts. Obviously exact uniformity in this respect will never be attained, but there will be a nearer approximation to it than under the existing system. Even so, none of the taxes mentioned, except local income tax, would produce enough revenue to make it possible to dispense with the rating system. To impose all the taxes mentioned to make up the total collectively would be administratively complex to the point of absurdity. In the end, therefore, most informed opinion favours the idea of a local income tax. There are difficulties to be faced. To avoid the wasteful-ness of a duplication of central and local income-tax authorities, the suggestion is that income tax should be increased and the additional money raised should be allocated to the local authority. This tax increase would be substantial; if the present over-dependence on Government grants is to be reduced, an addition of about 15p. in the pound would be needed. If it is felt, as is likely, that this would be a staggering increase, a disincentive to work, and a proposal which no political party would risk making, then the alternative is the one already mentioned of relying on raising revenue from a variety of sources of which a local income tax would be one, but not the only one. As a last resort, education and health, or some particular item such as teachers' salaries, could be taken out of local hands entirely and administered at national level. Such a drastic curtailment of the responsibilities of local authorities might ease their financial difficulties, but is entirely out of keeping with the frequently expressed view that local govern-ment ought to be strengthened, not weakened.

The structure and financing of local government are so in-adequate to meet modern needs that drastic reform seems certain. Reform will involve losses and risks, but also chances of gain. Some sacrifices of existing local loyalties are inevitable. Critics of change will also argue that the creation of larger and fewer local authorities will facilitate control by the central Government to the detriment of local interests. If the Jeremiahs are wrong, however, the upshot of reform may be the setting-up of large authorities, strong enough in composition and knowledge to hold their own in dealings with the central Government, and possessing some degree of financial independence if a sensible alternative to the rating system can be found. If this proves to be so, then councillors of good calibre will be attracted to serve authorities which they feel to have a worth-while role in government and the apathy of local government electors may be dispelled.

## POSTSCRIPT

The Conservative Government published its plan in February 1971, for the reshaping of local government. England is to be divided into 38 administrative counties and 6 metropolitan areas (Merseyside, south-east Lancashire and north-east Cheshire, West Midlands, West Yorkshire, South Yorkshire, the Tyne and Wear areas). Below the county authorities will be 370 district councils. The county boroughs will lose their independence and be merged into the county and district framework. Wales is to have 7 administrative counties and 36 district councils. Scotland is to have 8 regions and 49 district councils. In all three countries the major functions have been allocated to the county councils. The new organisation is expected to be operational by April 1974.

### FURTHER READING

J. H. Warren, *Municipal Administration* (Pitman, 2nd Edition, 1954).

L. Golding, *Local Government* (English Universities Press, 1959).

W. E. Jackson, *Local Government in England & Wales* (Pelican Books, 1959).

Sir J. Maud and S. E. Finer, *Local Government in England and Wales* (H.U.L., 2nd Edition, 1953).

M. Cole, *Servant of the County* (Dobson, 1956).

J. P. Mackintosh, *The Devolution of Power* (Penguin Books, 1968).

*Report of the Royal Commission on Local Government in England* (Cmnd. 4040) (H.M.S.O., 1969).

*Memorandum of Dissent* by D. Senior (Cmnd. 4040–1) (H.M.S.O., 1969).

H. V. Wiseman, 'Regional Government in the United Kingdom' (*Parliamentary Affairs*, vol. XIX, no. 1, Hansard Society, 1966).

R. M. Jackson, *The Machinery of Local Government* (2nd Ed., Macmillan, 1965).

See also Comments on Further Reading, p. 211.

II

# The Commonwealth
# The Problem of Independence

---

Attitudes to the Commonwealth and Empire. Factors in granting independence: political maturity, social development,
industrial organisation, multi-racial problems, economic stability,
the problem of the small dependencies. Federation—its limitations and value. Can the Commonwealth survive?

THEME: The methods of training dependencies for self-
government were soundly conceived, but have not been fully
applied.

---

A balanced assessment of Britain's relationship with the
Commonwealth and colonial territories is peculiarly difficult. Present issues are apt to be clouded over with a haze
of emotion. There are some who feel a sense of guilt over the way
in which the Empire was acquired. They dislike the acquisitive
instinct so evident in its formation, the jingoism of painting the
world map red, the commercial exploitation of the colonies in the
eighteenth and nineteenth centuries, the bitter fighting in India,
North America, South Africa, and the Gold Coast, and the overriding of native interests experienced by the Maoris, for instance,
in New Zealand; above all they dislike the bland assumption of a
divine right to rule by small groups of white settlers over vastly
greater numbers of native inhabitants; nor are they reconciled to
the situation by the attempts in the nineteenth and twentieth centuries to create governments on the Westminster model in the
dependent territories. Conditioning dependent communities to
accept a form of government alien to their own traditions is
regarded by these critics as simply another example of British
arrogance.

Others, however, regard British policy as simply one of paternalism. Just as a father prepares his son in the manly virtues and then

launches him in adult freedom on the world so, too, Britain coaches dependent territories in the arts of democracy, and grants full self-government when the ideal moment has been reached. The newly-fledged Commonwealth country is then free in all aspects of government but, influenced by this benevolent treatment, will, it is hoped, mix a proportion of filial respect with its new equality of status, and co-operate on the whole with British policy out of gratitude. Admittedly, there may have been incidents in the past which native populations find it hard to forget. But these are wiped out by the dedicated services of British administrators, missionaries, and social workers, labouring together to train the dependent territories to accept one of the best forms of government in the world.

Both these views contain elements of truth, but both are far too simple to be accurate. For those who are hag-ridden by guilt and who have no faith in the right of the British to train native populations in our own habits of government the only justifiable policy is to cut the links abruptly, leaving the Commonwealth territories to work out their own salvation with some assistance from the United Nations. This suggestion was more popular before the tragic events in the Belgian Congo, where the consequences of a sudden withdrawal of a colonising power have been clearly demonstrated. British withdrawals from colonies have been less abrupt, but the disorders following the grant of independence to India and Pakistan in 1947 and to Nigeria in 1960 give an indication of the dangers of leaving territories to manage themselves when there is a risk of internal conflict. Empires, as Thucydides knew over two thousand years ago, are even harder to lay down than they are to acquire. To jettison an Empire creates more problems than it solves.

The idea of paternalism has more to commend it as it is an attempt at a constructive policy to deal with present problems. Yet the 'paternal' analogy is a very imperfect one. It is obvious when a son attains his eighteenth birthday, but not at all obvious when a state becomes adult. The son comes of the same stock as his father; his circumstances and habits of thought are intrinsically very similar, but there are vast differences in these respects between Britain and the dependent territories. Moreover, it would be a singularly unfortunate father whose son's emergence to adulthood was preceded by the agitation and violence which are commonplace in Commonwealth history. Canada in the nineteenth century, South Africa, India, Eire, Ghana, and Cyprus in the twentieth century, all achieved self-government soon after periods of violence, and there is little doubt that the violence accelerated the process.

Paternalism, therefore, is a loose description of the relationship, but the policy which has been applied towards the colonies has been strongly influenced by the desire to make the transition to self-government as painless as possible. Between 1957 and 1964 Ghana, Cyprus, Nigeria, Sierra Leone, Tanganyika, Uganda, Kenya, Zanzibar, Malawi, Zambia, Jamaica, Trinidad, Cyprus, and Malta all became independent. The pace of the change was almost certainly quicker than the Colonial Office wanted, but pressure from world opinion and explosive agitation for independence within the colonies themselves hastened the process. Even so, without the guidance given for many years by the Colonial Office, the task of the leaders of the newly independent territories would have been much harder.

Ideally, certain requirements need to be fulfilled before a colony attains independence. The aim of British colonial policy is to prepare the dependent territories as fully as possible for self-government, though this work often cannot be carried through to its completion, because of the various pressures mentioned. One of the first requirements is that the colony should be politically mature, by which we tend to mean that it is ready to adopt a democratic form of government. Although dependent territories are free to establish whatever form of government they choose on attaining independence, their training under British administration is in democratic procedures with the hope that they will adopt a government of this type. Parliamentary democracy is not necessarily relevant, however, to the political needs of these new states which, in their historical background and present circumstances, differ so sharply from Britain. Democracies cannot work effectively unless there is an electorate sufficiently well-informed and critical to be able to make an intelligent choice between the contending parties. Any colony on the verge of independence should be able to provide all its citizens with a basic education. In practice, this ideal cannot be fully attained in the time available. In Britain itself the standard of general education lagged far behind political development for centuries; it was not until 1891 that it could be said that there was a free, national, compulsory system of elementary education, although the vote had been widely extended by the Acts of 1867 and 1884.

The gap between political development and the educational development which gives substance to the forms of democracy is equally apparent in the newly independent Commonwealth territories. Nor is this surprising. The size of the Commonwealth countries—Nigeria, for instance, is nearly four times the size of Britain—the dispersion of their populations, the sheer physical difficulty of getting to schools, and the rapidity of the movement towards self-government have all contrived to make it peculiarly difficult to organise a satisfactory system of primary education. These problems are particularly relevant in India, Pakistan, and the African territories.[1] Ghana, the first of the native African states to gain Commonwealth status and a possible leader of the pan-African movement, provides a good example. Its secondary and higher education is of fairly recent origin, but it is of good quality; on the other hand, it was not until after independence was given that a comprehensive attempt was made to build primary schools in sufficient numbers for the country's needs. The top-heaviness of the system helps to explain some of the political actions in Ghana which have caused so much disquiet. The rulers have been educated to a high standard, often reinforced by a period of further education in Britain. The masses, who have moved at bewildering speed from the primitive context of tribal life to the complexities of modern civilisation, have lacked the education to adapt them to the change. Measures taken by Dr. Nkrumah may have seemed distasteful by our standards, but circumstances are very different there, as he was often at pains to point out. More-over, if so basic a service as primary education is inadequate, the re-sponsibility is in some measure our own. The critics of the Nkrumah regime were sometimes those who were most insistent that our continued presence in the Gold Coast was wrong; yet, ideally, a longer period of British rule might have been justified to ensure a balanced development of the social services before independence was given. An essential preliminary should be a complete framework of primary and secondary schools together with university colleges for higher education. The education

[1] See *Parliamentary Affairs*, Spring 1964, pp. 160–71, for an instructive article by John Day on the problems of democracy in Africa.

sections of the Commonwealth Office and of the United Nations have worked towards this objective, but the pace of events, politically, has left them stranded.

Political education of the African administrations has proceeded more successfully. British officials stayed on briefly after independence, as they did in Ghana, but their role was an entirely subordinate one. African leaders, such as Nkrumah in Ghana and Balewa in Nigeria, did not need to be propped up by Civil Servants. This was partly due to their own natures, but partly also to the political training which has been one of the best features of the British Colonial system. Early political development in colonies destined for independence follows a set pattern. Nomination by the Governor of a few native members to join the British representatives in the Legislative Council, the embryo Parliament, is the first step. By gradual stages, usually based at first on property qualifications, a full electoral system is introduced. The British officials in the Legislative Council are reduced in numbers until the Legislative Council consists entirely of native elected members. Meanwhile, a similar process is at work in the Executive Council, which is the embryo Cabinet. The Governor, by selection from the Legislative Council, includes a few native members in the Executive Council which previously would have consisted entirely of British officials. Eventually, native members are given charge of some Government departments until, finally, a full Ministerial system is introduced on the British model. The Governor's powers then gradually recede until his functions are the same as those of the Queen in Britain. By that time the Colony is ready for independence. The process may often be less gradual than would be ideal, but it gives enough time for the leaders to study the techniques of law-making, debate and administration. Political leaders in the newly independent African and Asian territories have been facing problems, which, in their different context, are quite as testing as those which face the statesmen of western Europe; without a sound political training they would be quite unable to do so. Administrative mistakes are made of a kind which one would not expect in Brttain. Matters involving expertise of a specialist kind such as clear wording of parliamentary bills are sometimes not very well managed. But it is more to the point that the administrative system works so remarkably well, considering the brief duration of independence of the post-war Commonwealth countries.

In local administration Africans are well fitted to manage their own affairs. Local government under the tribal system had been firmly established in Africa for centuries when the British arrived. The wise guidance of Lord Lugard, who by the doctrine of Indirect Rule adapted the existing system of local government in Nigeria to fit in with the central administration, created a relationship which has since been imitated in East and Central Africa and in the newer territories of the Commonwealth. Since independence occasional changes have been made affecting local government structure. Ghana, for instance, has been divided into nine regions, each under an African politician, and Nigeria into twelve states, but no radical regroupings have been necessary. This is natural enough since the existing units of local government follow racial, territorial, and religious boundaries, so that local government does not present any great specific difficulties. It is a natural growth of long duration; central Government, on the other hand, is a forced plant and correspondingly fragile.

The physical needs, relating to health problems and working conditions, require as much forethought as matters of education and political training. One way of gaining increased awareness of the social problems of the newer Commonwealth territories is to visualise the somewhat similar problems which faced British politicians in the nineteenth century. During the course of that century there were many social reforms affecting public health, local government, industry, and the trade unions. These reforms provided protection for the citizen against bad management. Similar problems face the colonial administrators. Medical aid and training are given through the World Health Organisation of the United Nations, and through the Medical Section of the Commonwealth Office. These organisations are not large enough to meet all the needs of the situation—no existing organisation could be—as the outbreak of serious diseases in India and Pakistan has shown. Although great progress was made from the time when West Africa, for instance, was known as 'the white man's grave' the level of training in matters of health and hygiene is still appreciably lower than in Britain; admittedly, climatic conditions accentuate the difficulties. The fact that health problems have little bearing on politics is an advantage, however, since it makes little difference whether the doctors are European or African so long as the diseases are cured. Trained medical experts can stay on in ex-colonies much longer than European administrators without their presence there providing an affront to national pride.

Trade Union organisations able to secure fair hours, reasonable wages, and good working conditions, also need to be firmly established before independence is given. Since industrialisation is a comparatively new phenomenon in the post-war Commonwealth countries it might be expected that the principles of Trade Unionism would not be readily understood. If that were true it would militate against the grant of independence since the future welfare of the mass of the workers is an important consideration. In fact these countries have adapted themselves with surprising speed to the ideas of Trade Unionism. This may be caused, in part, by the fact that the idea of concerted action, as a protection against any abuse of workers' interests by the employers, has something in common with the mass sentiment of nationalism often directed against political authority as a preliminary to independence. Apart from fitting in with current moods and attitudes Trade Unionism has also gained strength from the specific guidance which has been given by the Commonwealth Office and by the Trades Union Congress. In areas where there is extreme poverty, as in parts of India and in some of the West Indian islands, the objectives for which the Unions strive are naturally limited by the acute hardship of living conditions there; Trade Unions by their nature work far better where there is wealth inequitably distributed than where there is no wealth at all. Africa has its slums and poverty too, but with its great natural resources provides a situation favourable to the rapid growth of Trade Unionism. Trade Unions there have in fact made rapid advances towards federation, a more sophisticated level of development than is involved in the existence merely of Unions for the separate industries. There has been strong support for the All-African Trade Union Conference, though there is another school of thought which favours support for the Socialist International Confederation of Free Trade Unions. The aims of Unionism are broadly the same as in Britain. Where differences occur they are in method as in Ghana, where Union membership has been compulsory, an instance of the more authoritarian approach visible in the newer Commonwealth countries.

Whether suitable political and social organisation has been developed or not, additional factors can influence the pace of the movement towards independence. Multi-racial communities, in particular, have problems which may seem incapable of solution without the serious risk of oppression of minorities. The racial factor has not greatly hampered the movement towards independence of Ghana; in Nigeria, however, in East and Central Africa, and in Cyprus, racial considerations are of the utmost importance and they have a strong bearing, too, on the policies of the Malaysian Federation. In Kenya the problem is partly how to reconcile the interests of a small minority of educated Europeans, accustomed to political and economic dominance, with the interests of a large African population, often illiterate, but inspired by their native leaders to secure independence. But there is also the complication involved in the presence of other races, such as Indians and Arabs. In the Central African Federation the grouping of the two Rhodesias and of Nyasaland illustrated that unions of this kind cannot be solidly based merely on geographic and economic convenience. Racial separatism is too strong an emotion to be outweighed by material advantage, as Dr. Banda's determined opposition to federation showed, for Nyasaland (Malawi) seemed scarcely viable economically as a separate state. The basic antipathy of black men towards white rule, and of white men towards black rule cannot be overcome by the belief that it has been outgrown; in the shifting pattern of political structures in Africa there is hope of solution, as will be seen later, but not by making assumptions that racial antagonisms are purely superficial. In some areas the situation is less flexible than in Africa, so that the only possibility is to work out a *modus vivendi* on the existing basis. Racial differences in Cyprus between Greeks and Turks, and in Malaysia between Malayans and Chinese cannot be obviated by territorial regroupings.

In these multi racial communities it will require an imaginative and adaptable approach to achieve any solution to the problem of government. The hope of a friendly constructive agreement has often been destroyed before the delegates sit at the conference table by the bitterness of the struggles which have gone before. Archbishop Makarios, Jomo Kenyatta, and Dr. Hastings Banda have all had experience of prison or exile because of their association with militant nationalism. Yet, paradoxically, the violent nationalist desire for independence can be an obstacle to its success. There is a natural wish to ensure that minorities will not be victimised upon the withdrawal of British rule, but this is difficult to guarantee where long-standing hatreds have eaten away respect for individual freedoms; violence directed against British rule could swiftly be turned upon other alien minority groups. The outbreak of violence in India and Pakistan, when they were given their independence in 1947, led to many deaths of Hindus in Pakistan, and of Moslems in India. It would be culpably irresponsible to grant independence to a country if it led to a repetition of these 1947 events. Yet time is short, nationalism is explosive, and it is wildly optimistic to hope that in a few years it can be possible to inculcate native populations in dependent territories with the traditional restraints shown in Britain towards minority groups. Clearly, the multi-racial communities are posing problems which are difficult even to comprehend in Britain, and which are certainly likely to prevent a perfect solution, or even a very satisfactory one, in some parts of the Commonwealth and Empire. In this connection it is important to realise that the existing frontiers in Africa are largely the result of European imperialism in the nineteenth century. Once the controlling hand of the European is removed the old tribal frontiers will acquire a new relevance and old hostilities are likely to revive. This has been seen already in Uganda, Kenya, and Nigeria. The conventional war for adjustment of frontiers, which appears to be outmoded in modern Europe, may take on a new lease of life in Africa unless the new states there show a more international outlook than has been common in Europe.

A further factor to consider in granting independence is the economic stability of the dependency. Where there are good natural resources, as there are in Ghana and Nigeria, independence was economically justifiable. Ghana in particular has launched an ambitious development scheme involving improvements in communications, the £200 million Volta River project—made possible by exploitation of the well-established trade in cocoa—research into newer sources of wealth such as oil and minerals, and the erection of many modern buildings. Enough confidence has been created to attract foreign capital from America and from West Germany among other countries. Most of the African territories have enough natural resources to provide reasonable security for the future, except Malawi and small somewhat isolated territories like Sierra Leone. Yet in India poverty is tragically rife, and in another quarter of the world, the West Indies, the break-down of the Caribbean Federation means that the Windward and Leeward group of islands, remote and deficient in resources, must remain dependent on British help. An undue dependence on outside aid is a great source of weakness since it can make political independence an empty form. The subsidies which Britain provided through the Colonial Development Corporation gradually ceased to flow when independence was attained. In 1958 the Government made it plain that after independence projects already started would continue to be helped through the Corporation but not new ones. Help may come through the World Bank, but in general the new Commonwealth territories cannot launch out on the new developments they need unless British and foreign investors can be filled with enough confidence to risk their capital in the hope of a good return. The chances of their doing so can be estimated with reasonable accuracy by the British Government before self-government is granted; this factor of economic stability is yet another consideration in the grant of independence. The main interest of investors is profit, and they cannot be expected to make contributions out of altruism.

The factors which have been studied so far relate primarily to the large dependencies with sufficient resources in population and wealth to be self-sufficient ultimately if not immediately. There still remain a large number of scattered small dependencies, some placed in a special category because of their strategic importance, like Malta, Gibraltar, and Singapore, and others, relics of our history, which are very tiny, like Pitcairn Island with its 130 inhabitants, Mauritius, and the Seychelles Islands. The strategic reasons which one made Malta and Singapore of such great significance have lost some of their importance through changing methods of warfare. The American emphasis on powerfully armed, thoroughly organised task forces, such as their Seventh Fleet, and on an underwater fleet depending for its needs simply on a mother ship, has led recently to some re-assessment of the need for the retention of British bases overseas. They are expensive to maintain and it may be that some of them are outmoded. Each needs to be judged on its own merits. Singapore is very vulnerable; it is possibly less vital now as a base in view of the firm establishment of American forces in the Far East. The isolation of Singapore was only temporarily removed by its membership of the Malaysian Federation, since tension between Malays and Chinese led to the secession of Singapore in 1965.

These considerations apply to some extent to Malta and Gibraltar. Malta was used as a base during the attack on Egypt, and for the limited operations which may arise in the Middle East it might continue to be useful. Retention of a base there, however, ought not to rest merely on habitual thinking where preparations are made to meet situations which no longer exist. Egyptian control of the Suez Canal and the diminished influence of Britain in Arabian countries have detracted from the value of Mediterranean bases. The fluidity of politics in the Middle East is probably the best reason for maintaining the *status quo* in Malta and in Gibraltar; it may be that their significance will revive, even though at the moment the practical value strategically of Malta in particular seems very slight. Complete political freedom for these strategically placed dependencies is not yet likely simply on the grounds of their potential military importance.[1] Since Malta has close ties with Britain, springing from her part in the last war and the number of Maltese who have come to Britain, it was often suggested that the best political solution would be integration with Britain. Presumably this would have placed Malta in the same constitutional position as Northern Ireland. She would have sent two or three members to Westminster to participate in debates there. The scheme does not sound very convincing. The closeness of Northern Ireland to Britain, and economic and social factors give its union with Britain some reality. British and Maltese interests do not overlap sufficiently to have made it worthwhile for Malta to have separate representation at Westminster.

Even if integration had proved to be the best solution for Malta's future there remain many small territories for whom neither integration nor federation is feasible. The Labour Party's proposal in 1957 was that these small territories should be given Dominion status and they would presumably have complete control over internal and external affairs, including the right to withhold the use of bases from Britain. The aim of the proposal was to give these small areas the same right as independent nations to manage their own affairs and to take on commitments of their own choosing. One weakness in the scheme is that the complete freedom envisaged can hardly be possible where economic aid continues to be required. There is abundant evidence in recent history of the

[1] Malta's independence (September, 1964) leaves Britain's military rights there intact.

way in which economic aid has been the prelude to political infiltration. It is also extremely debatable whether a small dependency
would have leaders sufficiently knowledgeable to chart a course
through the intricacies of foreign relations. This is particularly so
if it had value as a military base as a result of which it could easily
become the victim of the ingenious pressures which larger states
can bring to bear. In internal affairs, on the other hand, there is no
reason why these small powers should not be able to manage the
great bulk of their own affairs through Legislative and Executive
Councils. Admittedly this approach means that the small dependencies will never be able to attain complete self-government, but a
passion for exact equality of status amongst all Commonwealth
countries from Canada to Pitcairn Island appears to be misguided
in placing a greater burden on the smaller dependencies than they
are able to carry. If in addition they became the objectives for the
great powers manoeuvring for positions of advantage the dangers
involved for them would be much greater than anything they are
experiencing at the moment. The recent granting of Associated
Statehood to the smaller West Indian islands, with Britain responsible only for defence and foreign affairs, appears to be a
reasonable solution.

The problem of the small dependencies shows how necessary it
is to maintain some flexibility of approach towards these greatly
varying territories. To visualise the movement towards independence as a process in mass production is unrealistic. Another
instance of the need for broad vision lies in the recent suggestions
for federation. Difficulties in the Caribbean Federation and in the
Central African Federation have brought the federal idea into disrepute. Yet in each of these areas the break-down was produced by
specific local factors, economic in the Caribbean Federation and
racial in Central Africa, which need not apply elsewhere. Canada
and Australia provide examples of territories where federation in its
present-day form has produced relatively little disorder and
discontent. To make federation work there must be a real community of interest, especially racially; the geographical unity of the
area needs to be sufficiently a reality to make communication
reasonably easy, unlike the islands of the West Indies scattered
over a thousand miles of sea; above all, post-war history has shown
that federation has little chance of success if it is imposed against
the wishes of large numbers of the inhabitants. Economic advantage

is not sufficiently powerful a factor to compensate for the slights on nationalist feeling which an imposed solution continually produces.

Bearing these factors in mind, two federal schemes, the one being merely suggested, the other an established fact, deserve examination. The first one, put forward by Dr. Nyerere from Tanzania, has the initial advantage of emanating from an African rather than a European leader in a continent where the former are so preponderant. His suggestion was that the East African territories of Uganda, Kenya, Tanganyika, and Zanzibar, the first three already having some experience of working together under the East African High Commission,[1] should federate with Zambia and Malawi, thus combining territories where African nationalist feeling might be a powerful unifying force. Possibly the Federation could become larger still with the addition of the former High Commission territory of Botswana which shares a common frontier with Zambia.[2] Encouragement of the scheme would be a positive way of showing sympathy towards African nationalism, nor are the difficulties insurmountable. The territories are adjacent to each other and, although communications between Central and East Africa would need to be improved, that problem in modern times is not so intractable as it once was. Economically, Zambia, Tanzania, and Kenya have sufficient natural resources to make the Federation prosper. Political problems would present difficulties, particularly the allocation of power to the Central Federal government. Problems of this kind are greatly eased by good-will, however, and if at first anyway the Federal government were a guiding and advisory body, especially on matters of common interest involving economic affairs and communications, the scheme should have a good chance of working well. A second political problem is that the creation of such a Federation would inevitably tend to harden the division between the white-dominated southern states of South Africa and Rhodesia and the proposed federation, increasing the risk of conflict. A further difficulty lies in the

[1] The leaders of Kenya, Tanganyika, and Uganda agreed on June 5th, 1963, to establish a federation which they hoped would be the basis of a wider grouping still. Tanganyika and Zanzibar were federated in April, 1964, as the Republic of Tanzania.

[2] The article by C. Legum, 'Doom and Promise' in the *Observer* of November 27th, 1960, contains a stimulating analysis of the Nyerere scheme.

internal disagreements in Uganda, though the creation of a larger unit may submerge local discords. Ideal solutions for the complexities of the African situation are likely to be endlessly evasive, but the Nyerere scheme shows a breadth of vision and, at the same time, a respect for the realities of the African situation which deserve sympathetic appraisal. It is more soundly based in principle than the Central African Federation and more worthy of trial.

The second scheme, which has been put into effect, was for an extension of the Malayan Federation to bring in Singapore and the dependencies of North Borneo (Sabah), and Sarawak.[1] The scheme has several weaknesses. One of the mainsprings of the suggestion was Malayan concern over Singapore, partly because Commonwealth use of it as a base might involve Malaya itself in the repercussions of conflict, partly because the large number of Chinese in Singapore might be a threat to Malaya if Singapore gained independence separately. The situation is made more complex by the fact that Singapore is still a base for the Commonwealth powers in fulfilling their obligations to the South East Asia Treaty Organisation; this may remain so in spite of the build-up of American strength in this part of the world. These matters of high policy are apt to obscure the fact that in modern times an imposed Federation has little chance of success, and that ultimately the most cogent factor of all is the willingness of inhabitants to accept a federal scheme. The swift withdrawal of Singapore from the Federation after only two years strongly emphasised this point. A further difficulty lies in the scattered nature of the federation. Sarawak at its nearest point is some 400 miles from Malaya and North Borneo 900 miles. Federation has some superficial attractions in that it groups together with an appearance of neatness territories which would otherwise be isolated, but in relation to the other issues involved this is a secondary consideration. Each scheme has to be considered on its own merits. In Africa circumstances favour the idea of federation if it is based on African nationalism; the Malaysian scheme, on the other hand, has much less to commend it, except expediency.

The issue which captures the greatest popular attention about the Commonwealth is whether it can survive at all. The differences between the newly independent territories and Britain in their political outlook are so conspicuous that the idea of a liberally

[1] This federation was set up on September 16th, 1963.

minded Commonwealth, united by a common belief in democratic government and acting as a single unit in external affairs, seems wildly divorced from reality. Freedoms and rights which are regarded as indispensable in Britain, such as the equality of citizens before the law and the freedom to express open criticism of Government leaders and policies, are not necessarily respected or even accepted at all in the new territories. It is true that in one instance, that of South Africa, the racialist policies followed there led to such strong pressure from the Afro-Asian countries that South Africa was obliged to withdraw from the Commonwealth in 1961. Yet racialism is not the only issue in which there have been departures from the standard expected in a democratically organised society. Pakistan was under martial law from 1958 to 1962 and the powers given to the President both during that period and in the 1962 constitution far exceeded those which would be accorded to any one man in the British system. President Ayub Khan's blunt and significant comment on the Parliamentary system was as follows: 'This we tried, and it failed. Not that there is anything inherently wrong with it. The trouble is that we have not attained several sophistications that are necessary for its successful operation.' In an article in *The Observer* (June 3rd, 1962) Julius Nyerere expressed a similar opinion. 'We recognise that the system of "checks and balances" is an admirable way of applying brakes to social change. Our need is not for brakes—our lack of trained manpower and capital resources, and even our climate, act too effectively already. We need accelerators powerful enough to overcome the inertia bred of poverty, and the resistances which are inherent in all societies.' The comments of these two leaders are not produced by megalomania but by a realistic appraisal of the habits of mind of their own countrymen. Set in the context of the national histories of the newly independent Commonwealth territories British occupation has been a relatively brief interlude for many of them. The 'scramble for Africa', for instance, did not develop until the last quarter of the nineteenth century. The period of training in democratic conduct has been briefer still, and it is not surprising consequently that the idea of an Opposition has been considered synonymous with treason in several African territories particularly. Nor is it surprising that Ghana, Tanzania, and Malawi, amongst others, have all made use of a one-party system of government. All this is understandable, but it does nothing to improve the relationship between Britain and these countries particularly when, as so often happens under an authoritarian Government, the boundary between the exercise of legitimate power and the exercise of tyranny becomes blurred or forgotten altogether. An outstanding instance was the way in which opinion in this country and eventually in his own, steadily hardened against Dr. Nkrumah in Ghana. The early limitations on individual freedom could perhaps be justified by the kind of arguments used by Ayub Khan and Dr. Nyerere about their own countries. Eventually, however, the power of Dr. Nkrumah became irrational. As *The Observer* (October 8th, 1961) drily commented on the eve of the Queen's visit to Ghana, 'President Nkrumah might be reminded that, when the Queen makes a State visit to a member of the Commonwealth, it is customary for her to meet the leaders of the Opposition at Government House, and not in prison.' In the end however, it needed a military coup rather than dry comment to remove Nkrumah from power, but before this was achieved, in 1966, his career had followed the classical course of dictators, with the suppression of opponents, a one-party state, concentration of the powers of decision into the hands of one man, and a semi-religious glorification of the leader by the party machine as *Osagyefo*, the Redeemer. Dictatorships, military coups, as in Ghana and Nigeria in 1966, civil wars, and assassinations represent a state of affairs from which Britain had safely emerged by the end of the seventeenth century. In 1948 the official Report on Colonial Office work stated that 'The central purpose of British colonial policy is simple. It is to guide the colonial territories to responsible self-government within the Commonwealth in conditions that ensure to the people concerned both a fair standard of living and freedom from oppression from any quarter.' The gap between the admirable intention and the often tragic results is only too plain. It is still too early to say that the experiment has wholly failed; Ghana itself, for instance, has shown signs of moving back to parliamentary democracy after her experience of dictatorship followed by military rule. Nevertheless it is difficult for Britain and the older Commonwealth countries to feel that the internal policies in some of the Afro-Asian territories contribute towards any sense of political kinship with them.

Differences between the Commonwealth countries are by no means confined to clashes of opinion over internal policies. India and Canada were prominent in condemning Britain's war against Egypt in 1956. India and Pakistan were at war with each other in 1965 over the Kashmir issue. Ghana and Tanzania broke off relations with Britain following the latter's refusal to use force to defeat Rhodesia, whose unilateral declaration of independence in 1965 had been an attempt to preserve white minority rule there. Britain's financial difficulties have contributed to the feeling of disillusion, partly because it is no longer possible to feel certain that loans, grants, and investments from Britain will continue indefinitely on the same scale, and partly because of doubts over the economic effects on the Commonwealth if Britain eventually succeeds in her intention of joining the European Economic Community. There are manifestly other sources of capital in the world than Britain. If, as some assert, economic self-interest is the only effective link within the Commonwealth, then that link may seem to be a very thin one indeed.

There is ample evidence, in short, to justify the dismal view that in the wide context of history the Commonwealth concept is sentimental, misguided, and, prospectively, a failure. Nor is it any answer to this charge to compile, as can easily be done, a lengthy list of the organisations which foster cultural exchanges and provide technical and scientific advice for Commonwealth members. These gossamer connections could all be blown away, their existence and usefulness forgotten in a few months, if political events made it a matter of self-interest for a Commonwealth member to break with Britain. The same applies to the Commonwealth Secretariat, set up in 1965, mainly at the request of President Nkrumah of Ghana, President Kenyatta of Kenya, and Prime Minister Williams of Trinidad and Tobago. The Secretariat merely has the function of disseminating information, assisting existing agencies of co-operation, and organising future conferences. Its powers are slight and it is clear that one of the reasons for setting it up was to reduce still further the influence of the British Commonwealth Relations Office upon the course of affairs in member states. It is sometimes stated, too, that the member states have the bond of the English language which is widely used even where it is not the mother tongue. To believe that this automatically creates an atmosphere favourable to co-operation is patently false. George Washington spoke English; so does Ian Smith.

The central argument for the continuance of the Commonwealth is that it is to the advantage of its members to keep the association in being. This is evident in several ways. Quite apart from loans and grants from British Governments, public authorities and private firms in the Commonwealth have been able to acquire capital by heavy borrowing through the London money market since the war. Financial connections built up there are too useful to the Afro-Asian members, engaged in large-scale development projects, to be jeopardised by abandonment of Commonwealth membership. Investors would be much more cautious about providing capital for a country experiencing the political uncertainty and isolation which would almost certainly follow a withdrawal from the Commonwealth. The doubts about Britain's financial position do not mean that the Commonwealth will have exhausted its usefulness in the near future as a source of credit. Even if Britain's position were to be gravely weakened, she is only one member of a Commonwealth whose potential wealth is very great indeed. Maintenance of the connection is a long-term investment in itself. Furthermore, since financial support can be a prelude to political infiltration, the Commonwealth members are well aware of the advantages of using the existing sources of capital within the Commonwealth, simply on the basis of the axiom 'Better the devil you know than the one you don't'. Other sources of capital are used, of course, such as the United States and West Germany, but the sums advanced are not so large as to give either of these countries, or any other, the feeling that they can exercise any influence over political affairs in the Commonwealth.

It would be equally pointless, politically and strategically, to break up the Commonwealth. The members rarely feel inhibited in their actions by belonging to the association. There are no restraints other than those of opinion on the external or internal policies of members. Flexibility in this respect is so well established that it is possible to break off relations with Britain, or with any other Commonwealth country, and still to remain a member. Tanzania, for instance, broke off relations with Britain in 1966 over the latter's handling of the Rhodesian problem, but President Nyerere was at pains to point out that his state still wished to retain Commonwealth membership. The point is that complete independence is an anachronism in a world dominated politically, economically, and strategically by great powers and by large-scale international groupings. The Commonwealth survives because it is

politically realistic that it should continue to do so. There would
have to be radical changes in the world situation, far more radical
for instance than Britain joining the European Economic Community, to induce the Commonwealth countries to forgo the major
advantages they gain from membership at the moment. It may be
thought, however, that the advantages of the Commonwealth
association are much less marked for Britain than they are for the
newly independent members. Why then should not Britain herself
leave the Commonwealth? Even at the level of crude self-interest
the argument for doing so betrays a myopic insularity; without the
Commonwealth Britain might become merely one of the larger
Channel Islands off the coast of Europe and correspondingly vulnerable, economically and politically. Surely, too, the unselfish
reasons for British membership of the Commonwealth deserve
consideration. In spite of the cynics and its occasional failures, the
Commonwealth is a unique, vast, and valuable experiment in multi-
racial co-operation. Furthermore, whether we like it or not, there is
a moral obligation imposed on Britain by her history to take thought
for the military, financial, and social welfare of those peoples whose
countries in the past provided the raw materials and bases upon
which Britain's economic and military power was partly founded.
Nor should it be forgotten that there are some twenty Commonwealth countries which are still dependencies and which have to
rely on Britain and the Commonwealth for financial and military
security. For Britain to abandon the Commonwealth would be
neither responsible nor sensible.

FURTHER READING

J. Coatman, *The British Family of Nations* (Harrap, 1950).
Sir Ivor Jennings, *The Approach to Self Government* (C.U.P., 1956).
M. Wight, *The Development of the Legislative Council 1606–1945* (Faber, 1947).
Sir C. Jeffries, *The Colonial Office* (Allen & Unwin, 1956).
D. Austin, *West Africa and the Commonwealth* (Pelican Books, 1957).
J. Strachey, *The End of Empire* (Gollancz, 1959).
K. C. Wheare, *The Constitutional Structure of the Commonwealth* (Oxford —Clarendon Press, 1960).
H. V. Wiseman, *Britain and the Commonwealth* (Allen & Unwin, 1965).
W. D. McIntyre, *Colonies into Commonwealth* (Blandford, 1966).
See also Comments on Further Reading, p. 211.

# British, American, and French Constitutions
## —a Comparison

Changing conditions are leading to stronger Executive control.
Formal restraints on the Executive are negligible. The only
counter-balance is public opinion. The degree of freedom of the
Judiciary, of local government, and of the citizen, in relation to
central Government. Comparative study of the British, American, and French systems of government.

THEME: British constitutional flexibility may lead to imitation of
American or French methods.

The inability of constitutional commentators to isolate the
British constitution, to dissect it, and duly hold up the
parts for inspection, is often a source of insular satisfaction.
The constitution of Britain is unknowable, like its weather, and the
pride taken in both has a similar quality. It may be that there is
merit in a constitutional flexibility which makes Governments con-
tinuously responsive to the wishes of the people, and it is still possible to take this optimistic view of the working of the British
system of government. But flexibility carries with it dangers too.
In a constitution resting ultimately on the intangible factor of
public opinion the guarantees of individual freedom are extremely
fragile. Habits of thought change. The degree of State control
which has become commonplace now would have seemed an out-
rageous intrusion on private rights one hundred years ago, and
there is good reason to believe that the strengthening of the
Executive in the modern state is a process which has by no means
reached its culmination. The speed and ease with which the
traditionally slow-moving British democracy can transform itself
into an authoritarian state in war-time, without any need to
diverge from normal constitutional usage, is a sharp reminder that

governmental methods in Britain can easily be akin to those of dictatorship.

In the emergency of war these methods are necessary, for the preservation of the state is the first duty of government. The current problem, however, is that emergency conditions have far outlasted the war itself. The close-knit relationship and rivalry of so many nations of the world in politics, strategy, and finance have produced the now familiar situation in which distant threats, or stock-market fluctuations, produce repercussions throughout great sectors of the world with the utmost speed. Recurrent crises in the post-war era have conditioned Governments into a frame of mind where the possible use of emergency powers is always close to the surface. Peace is a misnomer for the conditions which have applied since 1945, when it would be difficult to point to any time when fighting was not going on in some quarter of the world. This may always have been true in world history, but now the risks are incomparably greater. The destructive power and speed of modern warfare have undoubtedly given some justification for the increase of Executive powers not only in Britain but elsewhere.

Recent tendencies in internal policies have accentuated this movement towards greater Executive control. The precariousness of the economy in Britain since the war has increasingly made it evident that the freedom of Victorian times is entirely inappropriate to efficient management of the country's finance. The uneven way in which governmental wage-restraint policies have had to be applied shows the essential difficulty in Britain of working towards objectives which are nationally desirable without infringing individual freedom. There is strong reason to believe that this dilemma is much more likely to be solved by a further extension of central control than by a return to nineteenth-century 'laissez-faire'. Attitudes are changing. Some of the freedoms for which our ancestors struggled have lost their reality. Freedom of religion in a country where only a minority take part in regular formal worship has lost much of its old significance. Freedom of speech and of assembly have a diminished value in a political system where Governments, secure behind the barrier a disciplined party can provide between elections, are not notably responsive to public opinion. Freedom of property is no longer sacrosanct since the central Government has used the power of compulsory purchase.

These changes are recognisable features of modern society. The danger involved in the steady erosion of individual freedoms is obvious enough. The point of greater interest is to discover whether there are any assured limitations to the authority of the State over the citizen in Britain. Is there, perhaps, some inner citadel of freedom which is certain to remain intact short of the supreme emergency of war itself?

If formal assurances were sought the prospects would be bleak indeed. So far as we have any written constitution at all it consists of a few historic statutes and in the judge-made law of the courts. It would be entirely legal and constitutional for these slender protections to be swept away altogether by new Acts of Parliament. Since Parliament can be claimed to be representative of the people this great power would seem to matter little. Any great changes in our constitutional habits would, in effect, be sanctioned by the people themselves and would be correspondingly acceptable. Yet much of this traditional view is a polite fiction. The concept of the Sovereignty of Parliament has steadily been drained of significance ever since the wide extensions of the franchise from 1867 onwards. Policy is fashioned and decisions taken not by Parliament, nor by the House of Commons, nor even by the majority party to any great extent, but by the Cabinet and Prime Minister. There is nothing new about this. It was evident during the ministries of Disraeli and of Lord Salisbury and has become increasingly obvious ever since. The situation has been worsened by the existence of a third party, resulting more often than not in the election of a Government supported by less than half the voters. As has been pointed out already (see Chapter 7) the ideal solution for this would be the union of the Labour and Liberal parties to form a Radical party, though there seems little hope at the moment that the leaders of these two parties will ever be able to agree on a common programme.

This would only be a partial answer to the problem. The question of the limitations to State action still remains unanswered. The words of historic documents give no permanent assurance of freedom; nor do the words uttered inside and outside Parliament if they are divorced from the power of influencing decisions. Nor is there any longer the balance of power between the main institutions of government which Montesquieu believed to exist when he visited Britain in 1732 to study the constitution. His findings were published in 1748 as L'Esprit des Lois and make an interesting comparison with the organisation of power in modern times. He was impressed by the judicious division which made one section of government act as restraint on another. The King and Ministers comprised the Executive. They controlled the armed forces, foreign policy, and, with Parliament's consent, levied taxation. Parliament was the Legislature, and besides controlling taxation gave annual consent for the continuance in being of the armed forces, and had some limited powers of calling Ministers to account. The Judiciary was virtually independent in its actions, subject to its duty of enforcing the statutory law passed by Parliament. It has been pointed out that Montesquieu's analysis was not completely accurate; there was greater fusion of the powers than he thought. But this is largely a quibble. In the early years of the eighteenth century a balance of power was very nearly achieved. No single branch of government could claim complete dominance. The monarchy had abandoned its claims to absolute supremacy and no institution had arrogated to itself similar powers. Since that time each century has witnessed changes in the constitutional relationship of the divisions of government and each change has brought closer the risk of destroying the balance completely. This is not an argument against change; the governmental system of the eighteenth century was notoriously imperfect and unrepresentative; but it is an argument against floating helplessly with the tide of constitutional change without realising the consequences. In the nineteenth century it was Parliament which extended its powers in the face of a decorous rearguard action by the monarchy persisting into the last years of the century, when it became the strictly limited constitutional monarchy with which all are familiar. Having won that battle Parliament now settled its internal struggle by making the House of Lords subordinate to the House of Commons by the Parliament Act of 1911, reinforced later by that of 1949. Yet, all this time, the Cabinet was extending its hold over the branches of government and over Parliament itself, until now there is no doubt of its dominance.

It might seem, therefore, that the balance of power has been completely destroyed. The extension of the franchise has removed any possibility of the House of Lords acting as a check upon a Government determined to have its own way. The monarchy, though not entirely negligible in influence potentially, could only oppose governmental action in the unlikely event of being assured of mass public support in doing so. The House of Commons for a variety of reasons, some of them unavoidable in the circumstances of modern times, cannot bring to bear on governmental policy the critical scrutiny which ought to be the essential strength of our system. Of the various institutions which at different times have struggled for supreme authority in the State, the Cabinet alone has increased its strength. Firmly guided by the Prime Minister, supported by party loyalty, buttressed by party discipline and the workings of our electoral system, aided by the administrative expertise of the Civil Service, and fed with information by the large numbers of planning and research units, the Cabinet seems to have obtained a position of unassailable power. Act of Parliament is the supreme law, and it is the Cabinet, almost exclusively, which initiates the important Acts of Parliament.

Against this formidable power all that can be set in the scales is the imponderable of public opinion. So far as there is a balance of power in Britain today it is achieved by the force of public opinion. The limits of power are the limits of public tolerance. But these limits change. The public is far more ready now to accept State control than it once was. Yet there are limits, not very clearly discerned perhaps, but still of the utmost value as restraints on the growing power of the Executive. What then are the essential features which still command respect and whose continued survival gives some reasonable guarantee of freedom for the citizen? One of the most important guarantees is undoubtedly the continued independence of judicial proceedings, and on this there is fortunately still a high degree of sensitivity in Britain. The great bulk of judicial work is divorced from political considerations, but the interest roused by the semi-political offences committed in the demonstrations for nuclear disarmament showed a keen public awareness over the crucial issues. The degree of force permissible to the police in dealing with passive disobedience, the rights of the accused in court, and the nature of the punishment imposed have all rightly received considerable publicity. Another recent matter in which public interest has been shown concerns the working of the administrative tribunals. It was a healthy sign that sufficient disquiet arose over the use of these tribunals by Government Departments to lead to the setting-up of the Franks Committee and to subsequent Government action in the Administrative Tribunals Act of 1958. Public opinion and governmental action do not always coincide in this way, but it is reassuring that both Governments and governed accept the impartiality of judicial proceedings as vital.

Local government is another sphere in which at least a degree of independence of central Government is crucial in a state with respect for freedom. Full independence is scarcely possible. The need to maintain a reasonable uniformity of standard, coupled with the fact that over half of local government revenue comes from Government grants, means that much of local government policy is controlled from the centre. This control is generally unobtrusive and local government, reinforced by the 1958 Act, by its electoral system, and by its use of unpaid councillors, shows a reasonable degree of independence. Party politics are firmly established in local government, but councillors, with their greater independence of status, are not so party-conscious as members of the House of Commons. The balance between central control and local independence is fairly maintained, and any undesirable extension of governmental influence over local affairs would be very conspicuous to the many thousands of councillors and to Opposition M.P.s. This is a good guarantee for the continuance of the limited freedom existing in local government at the moment.

Judicial and local government activities are specialised aspects of government. Important though they are, it is Government policy and legislation, with their direct impact on the citizen, which command more attention. There are restraints which Parliament can bring to bear upon governmental actions but only in extreme circumstances. Public opinion can often find more effective expression through group action than it can through the House of Commons; it is expression of public opinion in this way rather than through political representation which now constitutes the strongest barrier against unpopular Government action. It should be pointed out in fairness that this notion of barriers, and of a division between Government and people is sometimes said to be a false one; that Government and people are one. But this identification is absurd in a country where the electoral system seldom produces a majority Government, and where the intricacies of governing make it impossible for the public to play any real part in determining policy. Government is by the expert rather than by the people, not through any malicious design, but through the complexities of modern life. It might be considered, for instance, that Britain's entry into the Common Market should have been made the subject of a referendum, since this step might lead to a constitutional change. But a 'yes' or 'no' answer to a question of such difficulty would have such varying value, according to the extent of information of the voter, that it could not be a sound basis for a policy decision. There are many matters, in foreign and economic policy especially, where all the voter can do is to leave the decision to the politicians whom he has put in power. He will rarely be able to express worthwhile approval or disapproval of decisions which have been made, simply because the ramifications of policy are now so extensive that only an expert with all the information at his disposal can accurately assess the merits of foreign policy and economic measures.

This also applies, though with somewhat less force, to many matters of domestic policy. There are limits, however, which no Government has the right to infringe, and which ought to be plain to any citizen with a knowledge of the basic freedoms. Freedom of speech, of association, of assembly, and governmental respect for the judicial system, are fundamental rights still potentially of the greatest importance in any free society. Each of these freedoms is basically concerned with the right to express dissent without fear of retribution by the State; this must be backed, too, by the willingness of the State to right a legitimate grievance if the freedoms are to have any real significance. The danger in modern society is that, while there is freedom to express dissent, the means of securing a remedy for grievances may well deter all but the most persistent. It is that which has led to the appointment of a Parliamentary Commissioner. His powers are so excessively limited that the office cannot seriously be regarded as a main line of defence against abuses of individual rights by the Executive. However, it is something that the office has been created at all. It at least gives a basis for a judicious widening of his powers later, and for use of officials with similar powers at local level.

Although it is easy to be critical of Britain's cautious approach to change, there is a rational basis for this conservatism, easily overlooked by critics without the responsibility of power. Reduced to its simplest terms, the alternatives to the present system are either to give the Executive less power or more power. It is instructive, consequently, to study in some detail the American and French systems of government which represent, respectively, these two possibilities, since this gives a useful basis for comparison. At the outset it is worth remembering that there are discrepancies between constitutional theory and practice which occur in any political system. Here the intention is to concentrate primarily on the way in which the American constitution and the constitution of the Fifth French Republic are intended to work, rather than on this or that deviation from the pattern produced by particular circumstances.

The first point of difference between the American and British systems of government is that the Americans have a written constitution, the constitution of 1787. Although it is almost two hundred years old and has had over twenty amendments made to it, its fundamental features still survive. The constitution, for instance, formally states in its preamble the right of citizens to freedom of religion, speech, Press, assembly, and to equality before the law. It proclaims among other objectives its aims 'to establish justice', 'to promote the general welfare', and 'to secure the blessings of liberty'. Uneasiness over the extension of the power of the Executive in modern times in Britain has led to suggestions that Britain, too, would gain from a new Bill of Rights defining individual freedoms and making them constitutionally sacrosanct. At the moment these freedoms are secured, formally, by Acts of Parliament, but the fear is that what Parliament has given Parliament, under governmental direction, could easily take away. If there were a Bill of Rights the risk of governmental restrictions on basic individual and group freedoms could be largely reduced. The power of amendment would have to exist, but it would be easy to insert in a Bill of Rights a clause which provided that alteration in its terms must be the subject of a popular referendum. In the United States, with its strongly marked state separatism, much the same effect is secured by the requirement that any amendment to the constitution must have the support of three-fourths of the states before it can be accepted. In addition, any proposal for constitutional amendment must have the support of at least two-thirds of the members of each House of Congress; if the initiative for change comes by petition from one of the state legislatures, it must have the support of two-thirds of the members of that legislature as well as the requisite support in Congress itself. This is a much more elaborate barrier against any alteration of a fundamental kind than exists in Britain, where a Government has the constitutional power, if it can be certain of maintaining its majority in Parliament, to introduce Acts of Parliament which could make fundamental inroads upon individual freedoms.

If the freedoms were protected by a Bill of Rights it would be necessary to create a Supreme Court, on the American model, to nullify any action by any Government, group, or individual which was contrary to the terms of the Bill. In the United States, although it is true that the President appoints the judges of the Supreme Court, the appointment is for life, so that after the initial appointment the possibility of making the judges subservient to the Executive by packing the Court with political nominees is remote. The manner in which the Supreme Court can restrain Executive power is clearly evident, for instance, in the opposition by the Supreme Court between 1935 and 1937 to parts of President Roosevelt's New Deal programme on the grounds that the rights of individual states might be violated. The intentions of the Executive in this instance were benevolent; the New Deal programme was an attack on the problems of poverty created in America by the financial crisis of 1929 to 1931. Nevertheless the judges of the Supreme Court believed that the jealous safeguarding of state freedoms was of more fundamental importance even than the President's war on poverty. In an attempt to override this opposition, Roosevelt proposed that the judges of the Supreme Court should be obliged to retire within six months of attaining their seventieth birthday; this enforced retirement would, at that particular stage, have produced retirements which Roosevelt would have regarded as opportune, and have led to the appointment of other judges likely to have more sympathy with Roosevelt's intentions. Congress, however, was unconvinced of the need for change and Roosevelt's proposal was defeated in the Senate. It could be argued, of course, that in this instance the Supreme Court was carrying the doctrine of inviolable freedoms to absurd lengths; yet the episode does show that a written constitution, interpreted by an impartial Supreme Court, can be a solid barrier against Executive power. Perhaps the Court was over-sensitive about the threat to state rights posed by Roosevelt's plan, but if so it was a fault on the right side. 'Moderation in the defence of liberty is no virtue', and on other occasions the Supreme Court might exercise its powers on behalf of states or citizens more beneficially perhaps than it did on this occasion.

Finding suitable members for a Supreme Court in Britain would not be difficult in a country where the judiciary has for so long enjoyed a reputation for political impartiality; nor would it be unduly difficult to arrive at a statement of the rights and duties of citizens which would find general acceptance in a new Bill of Rights. These privileges of citizenship could then be defended with the same zeal as the American Supreme Court showed in defending state rights in the example given, and which it has shown, similarly, in safeguarding individual and group rights. In Britain itself the need to defend the rights of individual states does not arise, and is unlikely to do so unless the pressure for the creation of regional assemblies with local law-making powers grows much stronger. Britain has neither the size, resources, nor federal tradition to make likely the creation of regional units having the degree of independence of American states, though if this were to happen it would be a further insurance against undue dominance of the state by the central Executive. On the other hand the need to protect individual citizens and groups against the risk of erosion of their liberties is as relevant to Britain as it is to any other Western democracy; the argument for imitation of the American system seems correspondingly strong.

It would be a mistake, however, to believe that a written constitution and a Supreme Court to interpret it would make individual freedoms permanently secure. Ingenious legal interpretations of a written constitution can quickly undermine the intentions of its originators. In the United States, for instance, the practice of the segregation of coloured people in hotels, schools, and public transport in the southern states was upheld by the Supreme Court in 1896 on the grounds that, though separate facilities were provided for white and coloured people, these facilities were allegedly equal in acceptability. In 1954, however, the Supreme Court came to the opposite conclusion on this issue. It decided that segregation itself produced inequality. The point is that there had been a widespread change of outlook on segregation in the United States between 1896 and 1954. In Britain this change would have been expressed by an Act of Parliament, a more flexible way of reflecting public opinion than reliance on the verbal ingenuity of lawyers and judges. The instance quoted from the United States is not an isolated one. There was a similar reversal on the issue of the advocacy of Communism, which in 1940 was ruled to be illegal, in spite of the assertion in the constitution of the principle of freedom of speech. The witch-hunting of possible offenders against this ruling became so indiscriminate in the post-war years, however, that the Supreme Court changed its mind and sanctioned the non-violent advocacy of Communism. The Court's interpretations of the constitution may even run the risk of being contrary to public opinion, a paradoxical situation in a democracy. In 1962, for instance, the Supreme Court ordered the abolition of prayers in schools on the grounds that religion was the concern of the individual and not of the state. Logically the wording of the written constitution justified this interpretation; whether the decision was in accordance with public opinion, as it would have to be in Britain on an issue such as this where tradition, moral education, and strong religious feelings provide a logic of their own, is another matter. Certainly the risk of wholly arbitrary interpretation of the constitution cannot be entirely discounted in the American system. Logic is too narrow a basis for the complex art of government. The demand for a new Bill of Rights shows a misplaced faith in the power of words. It is perfectly possible to combine written guarantees of freedoms with all the practices of dictatorship, as the history of some of the South American states has shown. People are more important than paper. The conclusion remains that the real restraint on Executive power comes from the force of public opinion.

There is another important feature of the American system of government in which public opinion operates with greater certainty than it appears to over Supreme Court decisions, and that is in the thoroughgoing application there of the principle of the Separation of Powers. Supreme executive power is in the hands of a President, legislative power in the hands of Congress, consisting of the Senate and the House of Representatives, and judicial power, ultimately, in the hands of the Supreme Court. The fusion of the three powers of government with the attendant risk of authoritarian or dictatorial government is thus avoided. There is an overlapping of the Executive and Legislative powers in Britain in that the Prime Minister and his Cabinet members, who initiate the great bulk of legislation, are not only members of the Legislature but also by means of firm party discipline have control over it. In the United States the President and his Cabinet officers are not members of Congress, regional and business interests are often stronger than party loyalties, making party discipline on the British model a remote possibility, and it may well happen too that the majority in Congress may not be of the same party as the President. This latter point is the product of the American electoral system. While the President is elected for a four-year term, there are biennial 'mid-term' elections for the House of Representatives and for one-third of the Senate. Thus, while the President may have won general support for his policies at the moment of his election and will find it easy to persuade members of Congress to propose and pass the measures he favours, if he alienates popular opinion by his performance during his first two years in office it becomes more probable than not that he will then be confronted with a Congress in which at least one of the Houses, and possibly both, will be able to block his policies; this could reasonably be regarded as a salutary check on the policies of a leader whose policies in office have not lived up to the expectations of those who elected him. British Prime Ministers, virtually assured of office for four or five years, are much more strongly placed to pursue policies which the electorate dislikes. British Ministers are rarely frustrated in their legislative intentions; an American President is fortunate if half his policies emerge as completed legislation by the end of his term of office. It might be argued that the British system is more efficient and that it leads to more coherent government; it can hardly be argued that it is more democratic.

In all issues, external or internal, great or small, there are constitutional restraints on Presidential power. Congress as a whole has to give assent to a declaration of war. Treaties have to be ratified by the approval of the Senate; that this is more than a formal power was conspicuously evident at the end of the Versailles peace settlement of 1919, when the American Senate refused to give its approval to President Wilson's signatures to the peace treaties and to the Covenant of the League of Nations. In current American politics the influence of the President in foreign affairs is subject to modification by the powerfully composed Senatorial Committee on Foreign Affairs. The Senate also has the power to refuse to confirm Presidential appointments. Furthermore, unlike the House of Lords, it has no special restrictions imposed on it over bills dealing with money. In short the United States has a real bicameral legislature, not a sham one as in Britain. Composed of two members from each state, popularly elected, the Senate suffers from none of the social and constitutional inhibitions which have reduced the powers of the House of Lords to derisory significance.

With the exception of the additional powers of the Senate already mentioned, the powers of the two Houses of Congress are equally balanced, and a bill has to pass through both Houses as a necessary preliminary to becoming a law. In Britain the final stage which makes a bill into an Act is the giving of the Royal Assent. The occurrence of some extraordinary constitutional situation might warrant the use of a royal veto, but so far this has always been of more interest to theorists than to those who study the actual working of the constitution. In the United States, on the other hand, the Presidential veto is frequently exercised. When exercised it effectively blocks the law proposed, since it can only be overcome if each House passes the bill again with two-thirds of the respective members supporting the measure, and agreement to this extent is normally difficult to secure. While Congress can restrain the power of the President it is equally apparent therefore that the President can restrain the power of Congress. The principle of checks and balances, sometimes cited as a distinguishing and favourable characteristic of the British system of government, is more strongly marked in the American system. Their system recognises that unbridled authority is a menace whether exercised by one man, a President, even though popularly elected, or by an assembly, Congress, also popularly elected. The federal nature of the American Government obviously has some influence in creating fear of an over-strong central executive, but the American system is founded on a positive respect for democracy as well as on the more negative characteristic of state separatism.

The American voter plays a greater part in the choice of his leaders and representatives than does his British counterpart. In the primary elections to choose party candidates, for instance, the American voter often has a better opportunity than exists in the British system of choosing a candidate from the wing of the party which corresponds most closely with his own views. The primary laws vary from state to state, but the general intention is to secure that the voters rather than party headquarters choose the candidate. Admittedly, the local constituency association in Britain is usually the most powerful influence in the choice of a candidate, and these associations reflect such organised political feeling as there is in constituencies; admittedly, too, party bosses are influential in

American electioneering; nevertheless, whatever the human imperfections of the system the machinery of the American system for
the choice of candidates gives the voter more chance for directly
participating in the choice of a candidate. The American voter,
moreover, participates more frequently in the electoral process than
does the British voter. He votes for the House of Representatives
and for one-third of the Senate every two years; he votes for State
Governors and for local officials annually, and he votes for the
Presidential candidate every four years. In Britain the elector votes
for members of the House of Commons every four or five years in
normal circumstances; he has no say in the composition of the
House of Lords; he elects councillors in local government.

It could also be claimed that the British voter has less influence
on the choice of a Prime Minister than the American voter has on
the choice of a President. The American method of choosing a
President works in this way. The two major parties, the Repub-
licans and the Democrats, hold party conventions and choose their
respective candidates. When the Presidential election takes place
the American voters do not vote directly for the men they want but
for the state electoral college. The number of members of this
college is determined by the number of members the state has in
the House of Representatives and in the Senate. Each state has two
members in the latter, but its membership of the House of Representatives is determined by its population. New York, for
instance, has over forty members, but Alaska, Vermont, Wyoming,
Nevada, and Delaware have so small a population that they only
have one member each. By convention the electors of the electoral
college in each state cast their votes *en bloc* for the candidate whose
party had the majority of popular support in the election. In effect
therefore the President is chosen by popular vote. In fundamentals
it might be argued that the British method of choosing a Prime
Minister is very similar. The British voter knows at the General
Election who the leaders of the parties are and the qualities of those
leaders may often be the decisive factor in the way he casts his vote:
to that extent the choice of leaders in the two countries may seem
virtually identical. But in Britain there is nothing comparable to the
party conventions for the choice of Presidential candidates. In the
main British parties the leader is chosen by the Parliamentary party
organisations. Furthermore, changes of leadership within a
Government's tenure of office are no rarity in Britain. Sir Anthony

Eden (1957) and Mr. Macmillan (1963) both resigned office when Prime Ministers, as did Sir Alec Douglas-Home (1965) when Leader of the Opposition, and their places were filled either by consultation between leading Conservatives or, since the adoption of an elective system within the Conservative Party in 1965, by the votes of Conservative M.P.s. Admittedly constituency feeling is not overlooked, nor would it be wise to do so, but the party leaders in Britain are less obviously the choice of the people than they are in the United States. This is not to be equated with the idea that the Americans live in some kind of democratic Utopia. Manipulation of public opinion reaches extremes there which are not known in the more dignified electioneering campaigns in Britain. Nor is it possible to feel satisfied with a system which gives elected representatives in the United States so much patronage over administrative appointments—the 'spoils' system. Nevertheless the right to choose the chief official of the State—President or Prime Minister—by popular vote is a crucial one in a democracy, and at least it can be said that the electoral mechanism for doing so in the United States comes nearer to this ideal than the British system, whatever view one forms about the way in which the respective systems work in practice.

If the powers of the President are thus crimped and confined, it might well be asked why he is considered in general estimation to be so powerful. Part of the answer lies in what he represents. He is the spokesman of the most powerful nation in the world, and his leading role is emphasised by the relative insignificance of the Vice-President and of the Cabinet Officers, who correspond approximately to Cabinet Ministers in Britain. A Presidential visit to Europe or the Far East to visit Heads of State, or to inspect areas of American interest, naturally makes him a focus of attention, since the visit itself may signalise a modification of American policy, with repercussions for her allies and enemies. But in internal affairs, too, the President's position is stronger than an examination of the constitutional mechanism alone would lead one to think. His role as commander-in-chief of the armed forces of the United States, for instance, has greatly increased in significance with the development of the nuclear deterrent and the strategy of military containment of Communism. He has wide powers of appointment of ambassadors, ministers, consuls and federal judges, though these appointments have to be approved by the Senate. His

Cabinet, consisting of the twelve departmental heads, is rarely called together, nor need the President take any notice of the advice of the Cabinet when he does summon it. Britain has taken some steps towards Prime Ministerial rather than Cabinet Government, but the process falls well short of the state of affairs in the United States. Cabinet unity and collective responsibility still have some relevance in the British governmental system. In the United States, on the other hand, the situation, as Professor Finer describes it, is that 'Instead of decision by Cabinet, we have decision by tête-a-tête'. This is a consequence of the reliance by Presidents on what have been variously called 'brains trusts', or under President Kennedy a 'courtier system', both consisting of personal advisers often drawn from outside orthodox political circles altogether. There have, of course, been echoes of the same system in Britain where Mr. Wilson used Mr. Kaldor and Dr. Balogh as economic advisers during the early years of his Government. In Britain. however, it seems increasingly clear that the role of these non-political advisers is very much subordinate to that of the Cabinet Ministers, especially the leading ones, and that their influence is ephemeral. In the United States the non-political advisers appear to have a stronger influence, though the necessary reservation needs to be made that the influences at work on current policy-making both in Britain and the United States cannot be realistically analysed by constitutional commentators. Even the most distinguished of them can do little more than hazard guesses about possibilities. What is clear, however, is that the President of the United States carries a greater burden of solitary Executive power than does a British Prime Minister, and the key role of the United States in world affairs accentuates the President's responsibility; this would account for the reliance of the President on personal advisers; the responsibility of supreme Executive power is too great for any one man in modern international affairs especially. This is evident in the European countries, including Russia, and is certainly no less true in the United States. The constitutional restraints on the President still give him frightening power, as the Cuban missile crisis showed in 1962. Roosevelt's comment on the Presidency was that its power came only partly from its influence on administration. 'It is', he said, 'pre-eminently a place of moral leadership'. World developments since Roosevelt's time have emphasised this aspect of Presidential power.

Recognition of the democratic virtues which underpin the American constitution ought not to obscure the weaknesses which can be a consequence of the Separation of the Powers doctrine. The separation of Legislature and Executive in membership as well as powers creates practical difficulties. The President and his departmental heads have to bring influence to bear to persuade Congressmen to support legislation conceived by the Executive, a problem which does not trouble British Governments in quite the same way. Furthermore, administratively, it is far from ideal for the Executive to have to pilot a bill through Congress from the outside, since modification of bills to make them more effective in administrative terms is less easy when the Executive has to work through an intermediary. This Separation of Powers may also produce a separation of policies. It can easily happen in the American system that President and Congress are pulling in opposite directions, and this situation is worsened by the aptitude of Congressional committees for developing policy views of their own unrelated to majority Congress opinion; there may even be the further complication that the slight importance attached to Cabinet unity in the United States can lead to the promulgation of a policy by an American Secretary of State which is at variance with the policy of the President. The potential divisions present in the American system of government are not merely remote academic possibilities. The clash between President Truman's wages policy in 1945 and that put forward by Henry Wallace, his Secretary of Commerce, and the bizarre situation which occurred in 1948 when the Appropriations Committee amended the aid scheme for Europe which had just been approved by the President and Congress, illustrate what may well seem to be disadvantages in the American principle of divided authority. Although the President is assisted by the various subdivisions of the Executive Office in co-ordinating governmental activity, his task in this respect is much harder than that of the British Prime Minister and Cabinet who do not have to work under the disadvantage of being excluded from the Legislature. The separation principle is prejudicial in another respect too. The President's right to serve for a fixed four-year term means that he is irremovable except by death. A President who, through illness or idleness, neglected his duties is not vulnerable, as a British Prime Minister is, to an enforced resignation following a hostile vote in the Legislature.

Both the American and the British systems of government have their weaknesses. The latter is based on a compromise, increasingly uneasy perhaps in modern times, between authoritarianism and democracy. In the United States, on the other hand, the constitutional mechanism is more conspicuously favourable to democracy in the Federal Government, though not necessarily in the state governments. The compromise which the Americans seek is between separatism and democracy. The British system can be likened to a car with faulty brakes, the American system to a car with a surplus of back-seat drivers; neither is ideal.

The United States exemplifies a country where the constitutional restraints upon Executive power are greater than they are in Britain. The opposite is true of France, where strong Executive control under General de Gaulle was the reaction against the instability of French politics in the post-war years.

Between 1945 and 1958 there were twenty French Governments. France seemed ripe for the remedy of authoritarian rule, and in de Gaulle had a leader well fitted for the role. The General, however, while wishing to end the governmental instability with which France had been plagued for too long, still preferred to keep a representative form of government. A new constitution, that of the Fifth Republic, was given final approval in 1958 by means of a popular referendum. Its terms tilted the balance of power firmly, though not necessarily decisively, in favour of the Executive rather than of the Legislature. One of the major conditioning factors in British and American history has been the need to guard individual and group freedoms jealously. The French share this feeling, too, in some ways; regionalism, separatism, individualism, anarchism even, are powerful influences on French thought. Yet possibly the very ferocity of their individualism makes many of them appreciative in cooler moments of the value of firm centralised control exercised in a unitary state. Their history influences them in another way too. The dominant admired figures in British history since the mid-seventeenth century have been Parliamentarians; in America the corresponding figures are the Presidents, subject to popular vote at four-yearly intervals, and in modern times restricted to not more than two terms of office. In France the men who have most caught the people's attention are the autocrats, Louis XIV, Napoleon, and it is not too fanciful to regard General de Gaulle as being a member of the same constitutional lineage.

France, the United States, and Britain are all democracies, but are not democratic to the same degree. In the United States, Britain can see a constitution which is more fundamentally democratic than her own; in France, Britain can see a constitution less democratic than her own. The American constitution shows Britain the kind of democracy she might once have created herself; the French system shows her the kind of democracy she might become.

In 1958 General de Gaulle was elected President by an electoral college of Parliamentarians and mayors and delegates of local councils in France and her overseas territories. In the 1962 elections, the General, to the dismay of constitutionalists, went over the heads of the electoral college, and proposed a bill to be submitted to popular referendum by which the President should be directly elected by all the people. This referendum approved the President's proposal, though only tepidly, 46·4% disapproving. The General's strategy in this issue could be looked upon as enlarging the democratic basis of electoral procedure; the voice of the people was to be heard from the people themselves and not through their spokesmen in the electoral college. What was disturbing, however, was the frailty of the checks on the power of the President to amend the constitution. The intention in the 1958 constitution had seemed quite clearly to be that, when a proposal for constitutional amendment was made by the President, the first step should be the submission of the proposal to both Chambers of Parliament where approval would depend on the proposal receiving a three-fifths majority of the votes cast. The obvious danger in by-passing Parliament, as the General did in 1962, was that the importance of Parliament in the constitution would be diminished. Without the brake of Parliamentary control the potential limits to Presidential power cannot now so easily be discerned. Nor is there in France any judicial organisation with the authority of the American Supreme Court to challenge constitutional amendments. The nearest equivalent is the *Conseil Constitutionnel*. This has nine members, three being appointed by the President of the Republic, and three each by the Presidents of the two Parliamentary Chambers. The *Conseil* in 1962 offered no opposition of any consequence to the change in the procedure for choosing a President, in spite of the fact that they would have had strong support from constitutional lawyers, and in spite of the fact that the *Conseil d'État*, the administrative court, condemned the Government's action. By one decisive step, therefore, de Gaulle was able to create in France a plebiscitary Presidency with all which that implies in the diminution of Parliamentary control. The United States, too, has a plebiscitary Presidency, but the office is subject to more controls than the Presidency in France. By the 1958 constitution the French President has the power to appoint the Prime Minister, who then suggests to the President the names of other members of the Government, an arrangement also likely to strengthen the dominance of the Executive.

The separation of Executive and Legislature is far less strongly marked in France than it is in the United States. The President, for instance, has the right to dissolve Parliament and call for a new election. He is also vested with emergency powers which are sometimes very freely used against any internal or external threat to the Republic. De Gaulle's handling of the disturbances which broke out in Paris in May, 1968, gave some indication of the great extent of his powers in practice. In a broadcast to the nation he announced that neither he nor his Prime Minister, M. Pompidou, would resign. He declared the Assembly to be dissolved and ordered a General Election. Prefects, the Government officials who supervised local administration, were given full police powers and Gaullist party members were to assist them in maintaining order. The powers of an American President or of a British Prime Minister pale by comparison. The French President has at least as much legislative initiative as a British Prime Minister. In addition he has much greater powers of control over local government than his American or British counterparts, and much greater power to effect fundamental constitutional change. It could be argued that this great dominance is desirable for France and that, furthermore, the growing authoritarianism of modern Governments is a reasoned reaction against some of the deficiencies of democracy. The days when Macaulay could look on parliamentary government as the apex of political achievement, and as a nostrum for the ills of Britain's less fortunate neighbours, have gone. At the same time liberalism, in its widest sense, has been an expanding creed ever since the eighteenth century, in spite of set-backs. Even the icy authoritarianism of Russia has experienced a slight thaw. It still seems premature to believe that liberalism has exhausted its impetus; a reversion to authoritarianism would be an attempt to reverse the flow of a main current of history, and likely in the long run to fail.

The two Chambers which make up the French Legislature consist of the National Assembly and the Senate. The dominance of the President reduces their importance. The Senate is indirectly elected on a territorial basis representing the *départements* of France and her territories overseas. In this respect it resembles the American Senate, but its powers are less great. Although it has equal legislative powers with the National Assembly, except that money bills cannot be initiated in the Senate, it has none of the checking powers which the American Senate has over Presidential actions in treaty-making and appointments, for instance. In policy debates and criticism of the Government the French Senate is more akin to the House of Lords and takes second place to the National Assembly. The members of the latter are elected in single-member constituencies, using the second-ballot system where the candidate fails to obtain an overall majority in the first ballot. One of the consequences of this system is to reduce to a disturbingly low percentage that section of the electorate who voted for the majority party in the first ballot. Inevitably the winning majority includes many who would not have been selected had there been no second ballot; voters have a chance to secure that their second choices may sometimes win seats; but the system is less decisive than the British one tends to be. French party allegiances, as one would expect historically, are more influenced by concepts of Left and Right than by regional or business interests as they are in the United States. The ferocity of group separatism in France, aided to some extent by an electoral system encouraging to the smaller parties, leads to a less narrowly based two-party system than that found in Britain or the United States. There are sizable groups of Communists, Socialists, Radicals, M.R.P. (Catholic party) and Conservatives, and the possibility of a coalition Government is always more of a likelihood in France than in the other two countries. The exceptional powers of the President, however, make a coalition Government less a source of weakness than it would be in Britain, for instance.

France, like the United States, attempts to safeguard the rights of the individual citizen by means of a written constitution. The preamble to the French constitution of 1958 proclaims the attachment of the French people to the Rights of Man and to the principles of national sovereignty as defined by the Declaration of 1789. The constitution shows a regard for individual rights. The freedoms of religion, speech, Press, assembly, and equality before the law are formally secured. The French, however, cautiously add the reservation that political parties and groups in exercising their freedoms must respect the principles of national sovereignty and of democracy. The constitution also includes some contemporary additions to the traditional freedoms. These, borrowed from the constitution of the preceding Fourth Republic, include the right to strike, the right to racial equality, and the right to enjoy the benefits of social welfare.

In spite of, or perhaps because of, its greater age, the American Constitution has more built-in protections against arbitrary power than the French constitution. The Separation of Powers is more of a reality in the American system, not only between the Executive, Legislature, and Judiciary, but also between the agencies of central and local government. The American President, correspondingly, has less constitutional authority than the French President, so much so that some modern American students of their constitution believe that the United States would benefit, politically and socially, by a strengthening of the powers of the central Executive. Nevertheless, a comparison of the two constitutions leaves the impression that the American emphasis on the limitation of Executive power is wiser than the French system which hovers precariously between instability and authoritarianism. There is a stability about the American system of government since 1789 which has been blatantly missing in France during the same period. It is difficult to escape the feeling that French constitutions are apt to be ephemeral, however firmly based on particular principles they appear to be at a given moment.

Comparison of the American and French systems of government with each other, and with that prevailing in Britain, can be instructive. Constitutional habits change just as social habits do. International trends, such as the extension of the power of the State over the individual, leave their mark, not simply through mutual imitation but because the problems of government are very much the same for all. This is understandable and acceptable so long as the essential framework of a free society is kept. Study of the American and French systems shows the possible natural directions of development for Britain. It has sometimes been argued that the idea of organic development of the constitution is false, that the constitution does not grow as a tree puts out branches. It does not so much grow as explode, like an unpredictable firework, first in one direction, then in another. This is true of some countries but not, since the seventeenth century, of Britain. Development is still slow and still largely predictable. If the British approach to government changes during the last part of the twentieth century, it is probable that the type of government which emerges will have more kinship with the systems found in the fellow democracies of America or France than with the version of democracy which exists behind the Iron Curtain. Which of the two approaches is preferable, the American or French, may be evident from the preceding analysis.

Ultimately, the key to the matter, as this book has emphasised, lies in the power of public opinion, and this applies as much to those who hold public office as to those who do not. So far there is little reason to believe that public opinion is a feeble barrier to extensions of Executive power. The bitter opposition of sections of the Trade Union movement to a statutory wages policy, and the strength of the public outcry over the Government's Stansted Airport proposal, are merely two instances which demonstrate this to be so. In spite of the now familiar background of emergencies, which itself justifies a greater degree of State control than was once necessary, the essential freedoms in Britain appear to have survived. They are not so firmly established as they were, but are still sufficiently vigorous to give reality to the description of our society as a 'free' one. It should be clear, however, that these freedoms cannot retain their full significance unless they are actively maintained. It is not sufficient to believe that tradition alone is the only safeguard required for the citizen's rights. A study of the changing attitudes towards the freedoms since Stuart times would show how unwise it is to pin overmuch hope on precedent in the direct relationship between Government and citizen. The best protection of all comes not from the past, but from the present, in the existence of vigilant, well-informed public opinion. The dangers are apathy and cynicism. The steady increase in the number of non-voters at general elections since 1950 is particularly disquieting. Over eleven million voters, 28% of the electorate, did not vote in the 1970 election; the need for more lively political awareness could scarcely be more obvious.

FURTHER READING

Sir Ivor Jennings, *The British Constitution* (C.U.P., 1958).

J. P. Mackintosh, *The British Cabinet* (Stevens, 1962).

R. Butt, *The Power of Parliament* (Constable, 1967).

F. Stacey, *The Government of Modern Britain* (Clarendon Press, Oxford, 1968).

C. F. Strong, *Modern Political Constitutions* (Sidgwick & Jackson, 6th Edition, 1963).

H. Finer, *The Theory and Practice of Modern Government* (Methuen, 4th Edition, 1961).

E. S. Griffith, *The American System of Government* (Methuen, 1961).

J. Blondel and E. D. Godfrey, *The Government of France* (Methuen, 1968).

J. Blondel, *Introduction to Comparative Government* (Weidenfeld and Nicolson, 1970).

J. H. Price, *Comparative Government* (Hutchinson, 1970).

See also Comments on Further Reading, p. 211.

# Comments on Further Reading

SOME readers, particularly in schools, may be grateful for advice on textbooks where concise statements on the factual background of the institutions described may be found. Two short books of value in this respect are *Government in Great Britain, the Empire, and the Commonwealth* (Cambridge University Press, 4th Edition, 1965) by L. W. White and W. D. Hussey, and *Whitehall—Town Hall* (George Harrap and Co. Ltd., 6th Edition, 1967) by F. W. G. Benemy. *The British Constitution* (Macmillan and Co. Ltd., 2nd Edition, 1968) by J. Harvey and L. Bather is a very painstaking and useful analysis of their subject.

There are several books which range widely over the different aspects of the working of the British constitution, and which serve as a good preparation for the detailed study of special topics. The two books by Sir W. Ivor Jennings, *The British Constitution* (Cambridge University Press, 1958), and *The Queen's Government* (Pelican Books, 1960), are a sound introduction to the subject. The collected essays edited by Lord Campion in *Parliament—a Survey* (Allen and Unwin Ltd., 1963) make a stimulating study; narrower in scope, but still useful is *British Government since 1918* (Allen and Unwin Ltd., 1950), another group of essays edited by Lord Campion. As a complement to these mainly academic studies Lord Morrison's *Government and Parliament* (O.U.P., 3rd Edition, 1964) gives an interesting insight into some of the practical problems of government. Another book springing from practical experience is *Thoughts on the Constitution* (Oxford University Press, 1953) by the Right Honourable L. S. Amery. His suggestion for a smaller Cabinet remains of current interest. *Some Problems of the Constitution* (Hutchinson and Co. Ltd., Revised Edition, 1961) by G. Marshall and G. C. Moodie provides useful supplementary material to basic study of constitutional topics. *The Government of Modern Britain* by F. Stacey (Clarendon Press, Oxford, 1968), and *British Government and Politics* by R. M. Punnett (Heinemann, 1968) are very useful. Up-to-date in references, they admirably preserve the balance between traditional constitutional analysis and the behavioural approach to politics favoured in some quarters.

The books mentioned so far might well be consulted on the specialist topics too, but there are of course many books on particular aspects of government. On the monarchy (Chapter 1) there are, in particular, Sir Charles Petrie's *The Modern British Monarchy* (Eyre and Spottiswoode Ltd., 1961), and D. Morrah's *The Work of the Queen* (Kimber and Co. Ltd., 1958). For a detailed study of the recent influence of the monarch in constitutional matters the biography of King George VI (Macmillan and Co. Ltd., 1958) by Sir John Wheeler-Bennett is most useful. From the wealth of material on the historical development of the monarchy it would be invidious to single out one specialist book rather than another. For a wide view of a long and formative period, however, E. N. Williams' *The 18th Century Constitution 1688–1815* (Cambridge University Press, 1960) is valuable. For background knowledge of a much longer period, Sir David Keir's *Constitutional History of Modern Britain 1485–1959* (A. & C. Black Ltd., 6th Edition, 1960) is most informative.

The subject-matter of Chapters 2–5 (The Cabinet, Prime Minister, Ministers of the Crown, Civil Servants, and the relationship of Government to the citizen) is closely interrelated. Several of the books mentioned earlier, such as Lord Morrison's *Government and Parliament*, L. S. Amery's *Thoughts on the Constitution*, and *Parliament—a Survey*, edited by Lord Campion, all have relevance to this section. In addition J. P. Mackintosh's *The British Cabinet* (Stevens and Sons Ltd., 1962) is a most illuminating description of the way in which the British Cabinet works, and the influences to which it is subject. For the specialist, *Cabinet Government* (Cambridge University Press, 3rd Edition, 1959) by Sir W. Ivor Jennings is useful. The interesting and indeed crucial problem of the extent to which Cabinet action can be influenced by opinion outside its own ranks is considered, directly or indirectly, in many other books. R. T. Mackenzie's *British Political Parties* (Heinemann, 2nd Edition, 1963), G. A. Campbell's *The Civil Service in Britain* (Pelican Books, 1955), J. D. Stewart's *British Pressure Groups* (O.U.P., 1958), S. A. Walkland's *The Legislative Process in Great Britain* (Allen & Unwin, 1968), J. Blondel's *Voters, Parties, and Leaders* (Pelican Books, 1966),

R. Rose's *Politics in England* (Faber, 1965), and S. H. Beer's *Modern British Politics* (Faber, 1965) provide a particularly valuable nucleus of information. The detailed study by D. N. Chester and N. Bowring, *Questions in Parliament* (Oxford—Clarendon Press, 1962), should be consulted for a full assessment of the influence of that form of Parliamentary procedure. For an examination of the functions and importance of the Prime Minister there is Byrum E. Carter's *The Office of Prime Minister* (Faber and Faber Ltd., 1956) and, more recently, *The Cabinet* (Cape, 1970) by Patrick Gordon Walker. If detailed studies of the working of Government Departments are required then the books in the New Whitehall series, published by Allen and Unwin, are very helpful. Amongst these are Sir Frank Newsam's *The Home Office* (1954), Lord Strang's *The Foreign Office* (1955), and Lord Bridges' *The Treasury* (1964). T. E. Utley's *Occasion for Ombudsman* (Johnson, 1961) gives several interesting examples of the risk of infringement of traditional rights of citizens by the action of Goverrment authorities. On this subject the Whyatt Report, *The Citizen and the Administration—the Redress of Grievances* (Stevens and Sons Ltd., 1961) is concise and instructive.

For Chapter 6 on the House of Commons, there is a wide choice of older books on Parliamentary procedure. They are mostly still of some value, since procedure does not change radically. Lord Campion's *An Introduction to the Procedure of the House of Commons* (Macmillan and Co. Ltd., 3rd Edition, 1958) is one of the best known and authoritative. Among recent books Eric Taylor in *The House of Commons at Work* (Pelican Books, 5th Edition, 1963) and Peter Richards in *Honourable Members* (Faber and Faber Ltd., 1959) contrive to deal with intricate subject-matter without crushing interest with a weight of knowledge. On Parliamentary control of finance B. Chubb's *The Control of National Expenditure* (Oxford University Press, 1952), and P. Einzig's *The Control of the Purse* (Secker and Warburg, 1959) are excellent. K. C. Wheare's *Government by Committee* (Oxford—Clarendon Press, 2nd Edition, 1955) is most instructive on the work of Committees inside and outside Parliament. *Parliament at Work* (Stevens and Sons Ltd., 1962) by A. H. Hanson and H. V. Wiseman describes Parliamentary procedure by a series of ably chosen excerpts from proceedings of the House of Commons. Modern reforming trends are admirably surveyed in *The Power of Parliament* (Constable,

1967), by R. Butt, and in *The Reform of Parliament* (Weidenfeld & Nicolson, 1964) by B. Crick.

Voting systems (Chapter 7) are the special interest of the Electoral Reform Society (Albany Institute, Creek Road, London, S.E.8) which supplies pamphlets on application. Books on the subject are not common but there is *Voting in Democracies* (Faber and Faber Ltd., 2nd Edition, 1959) by Miss Enid Lakeman, who is director and secretary of the Electoral Reform Society, and J. D. Lambert. D. E. Butler's *The Electoral System in Britain since 1918* (Oxford University Press, 1963) is a useful description of the existing system.

The House of Lords (Chapter 8) has received scant attention as a specialist topic. References to its value will be found in the general books mentioned at the beginning of the book-list. In particular, the account of the House of Lords by F. W. Lascelles in *Parliament—a Survey* (Allen and Unwin Ltd., 1955) should be consulted. There is also *Shall we reform the Lords?* (Falcon Press Ltd., 1948) by Martin Lindsay, and the Fabian pamphlet No. 305 *The Privy Council as a Second Chamber* by Anthony Wedgwood Benn. The fullest study, however, is that by P. A. Bromhead, *The House of Lords and Contemporary Politics, 1911–1957* (Routledge and Kegan Paul Ltd., 1958).

There are several excellent books on the working of the Judiciary. *The Criminal Law* (Pelican Books, 3rd Edition, 1963) and *The Magistrates' Courts* (Pelican Books, 1955), both by F. T. Giles, give useful accounts of procedure. The role of the Justice of the Peace in the system is considered in more detail in L. Page's *Justice of the Peace* (Faber and Faber Ltd., 2nd Edition, 1947) and in F. Milton's *In Some Authority* (Pall Mall Press Ltd., 1959). The work of the other laymen in the system, the jurors, is described and discussed in Lord Devlin's *Trial by Jury* (Stevens and Sons Ltd., 1956). The difficult but important matter of disentangling the principles underlying the judicial system was attempted in Professor A. V. Dicey's famous analysis of the Rule of Law in *The Law of the Constitution* (Macmillan and Co. Ltd., 10th Edition, 1959). These views have since been strongly challenged by Sir Ivor Jennings in *The Law and the Constitution* (University of London Press, 5th Edition, 1959). A study of the latter, in particular, will show how difficult it is to be both accurate and enlightening in defining the principles on which the English judicial system is based. R. M. Jackson's

*The Machinery of Justice* (Cambridge University Press, 4th Edition, 1964) makes interesting reading on the matter of the relationship of the Executive to the Judiciary, particularly in the section which considers the idea of a Ministry of Justice. Other recent assessments of the relationship between the Executive and the Judiciary are to be found in *Protection from Power under English Law* (Stevens and Sons Ltd., 1957) by Lord MacDermott and in the publications of *Justice* (Stevens and Sons Ltd.).

The new developments in the structure and finance of local government were discussed in Chapter 10. The details of the proposed changes are contained in the publications of Her Majesty's Stationery Office. The White Paper (Cmnd. 1562, 1961) gives the Government's views on the proposals of the Royal Commission on Greater London. The report of the Commission is contained in Cmnd. 1164, 1960. *The Redcliffe-Maud Report* of 1969 (Cmnd. 4040) and Mr. Senior's *Memorandum of Dissent* (Cmnd. 4040-1) are important sources. So, too, in the sphere of finance, is the Allen Report of 1965 *The Impact of Rates on Households* (Cmnd. 2582). For those wishing to study why these proposed changes have become necessary there are several books which give reliable descriptions of the structure and functions of local government authorities. J. H. Warren's *Municipal Administration* (Sir Isaac Pitman and Sons Ltd., 2nd Edition, 1954), L. Golding's *Local Government* (English Universities Press, 1959), W. E. Jackson's *Local Government in England and Wales* (Pelican Books, 2nd Edition, 1959), and *Local Government in England and Wales* (Home University Library, 2nd Edition, 1953) by Sir J. Maud and S. E. Finer, all give ample material on these matters. *Servant of the County* (Dennis Dobson, 1956) by M. Cole is an informative account of the work of a London county councillor, of especial interest in view of the subsequent changes in the London area. *The Devolution of Power* (Penguin Books, 1968) by J. P. Mackintosh is an excellent brief analysis of regionalism and nationalism.

Authors have been understandably reluctant to commit themselves to print on the subject of the rapid movement of so many former British dependencies towards self-government (Chapter 11). The success of the transition is less certain than its speed. Many problems remained unresolved and balanced assessment is peculiarly difficult. J. Strachey's *The End of Empire* (Victor Gollancz Ltd., 1959) is possibly the best attempt to fill this gap.

There are, too, a few books which are helpful in showing the general pattern followed in granting self-government. Amongst these are J. Coatman's *The British Family of Nations* (George Harrap and Co. Ltd., 1950), Sir Ivor Jennings' *The Approach to Self-Government* (Cambridge University Press, 1956), M. Wight's *The Development of the Legislative Council 1606–1945* (Faber and Faber Ltd., 1947), and Sir C. Jeffries' *The Colonial Office* (Allen and Unwin Ltd., 1956). *West Africa and the Commonwealth* (Pelican Books, 1957) by D. Austin is an attempt to describe the constitutional developments in that area with a sense of immediacy which is apt to be lacking in the purely academic approach. For those with a special interest in the legal background of the Commonwealth relationship two books by K. C. Wheare, *The Statute of Westminster and Dominion Status* (Oxford University Press, 5th Edition, 1953), and *The Constitutional Structure of the Commonwealth* (Oxford—Clarendon Press, 1960) are useful. *Britain and the Commonwealth* (Allen & Unwin, 1965) by H. V. Wiseman is a valuable recent assessment of the extent to which the Commonwealth idea remains significant. *Colonies into Commonwealth* (Blandford, 1966) by W. D. McIntyre also gives some attention to the same issue, but devotes considerable space to the historical background of the Commonwealth countries.

Chapter 12, on the strengths and weaknesses of the British constitution, was based in part on the general surveys already mentioned. Among the more recent books, R. Butt's *The Power of Parliament*, J. P. Mackintosh's *The British Cabinet*, and F. Stacey's *The Government of Modern Britain* were particularly helpful. In addition, *The British Constitution* (Cambridge University Press, 1958) by Sir Ivor Jennings was useful as an example of the traditionalist approach to the subject. The comparative study of constitutions is not yet strongly developed in this country. Books on the subject are beginning to be more numerous, however. *Modern Political Constitutions* (Sidgwick & Jackson, 6th Edition, 1963) by C. F. Strong, and *Introduction to Comparative Government* (Weidenfeld & Nicolson, 1970) by Jean Blondel provide a very strong basis for advanced students. For the sixth-former, *Comparative Government* (Hutchinson, 1970) by J. H. Price provides a very useful assessment of the governmental systems of Britain, France, the United States of America and the U.S.S.R. Two instructive books, from American sources, are *The Theory and Practice of Modern Government* (Methuen, 4th Edition, 1961) by H. Finer and *The American System of Government* (Methuen, 1961) by E. S. Griffith. *The Government of France* (Methuen, 1968) by J. Blondel and E. D. Godfrey is correspondingly valuable on that country's system of government.

It may not be out of place to remind students new to the subject of Government of the many excellent radio programmes which deal with past and present developments in political studies. The talks given by Norman Hunt, Lecturer in Politics at Exeter College, Oxford, in the mid-1960s on features of the British and American governmental systems were an outstanding example of the value of this source of information. Journals, too, are valuable in a subject characterised by the rapidity of change. It is well known that books can only attempt to describe the constitution as it was, not as it is. The specialised studies which appear in periodicals such as *Parliamentary Affairs* (published by the Hansard Society) and *Political Studies* are particularly useful for their authoritative treatment of developments almost as they occur. Occasionally, too, *Public Law* (published by Stevens and Sons Ltd.) has articles of relevance to general constitutional development though the main interest is concentrated on specifically legal matters. No bibliography would be complete without mention of the abundant source material to be found in the publications of Her Majesty's Stationery Office. Apart from official reports and similar material the Stationery Office also publishes in pamphlet or book form concise statements of factual information on governmental matters. The annual edition of *Britain: an Official Handbook* compiled by the Central Office is particularly useful for reference for students new to the subject. A wisely chosen selection of documents as an accompaniment to constitutional studies is to be found in G. H. L. Le May's *British Government 1914–1953*; *Select Documents* (Methuen and Co. Ltd., 1955). Finally, it may be worth reminding school readers of the many excellent articles on the subject of government to be found in sections of the national Press. They are an invaluable means of becoming well-informed on a subject where alertness to new developments in governmental practice is essential for the student at any level.

# Index